ICONS OF STYLE

Chappell Roan

First published in 2026 by Welbeck
An Imprint of HEADLINE PUBLISHING GROUP LIMITED

Cataloguing in Publication Data is available from the British Library

ISBN 978 1 80279 810 4

Printed and bound in Dubai

FSC www.fsc.org MIX Paper | Supporting responsible forestry FSC® C104740

Headline's policy is to use papers that are neutral, renewable and recyclable products and made from wood grown in well-managed forests and other controlled sources. The logging and manufacturing processes are expected to conform to the environmental regulations of the country of origin.

HEADLINE PUBLISHING GROUP LIMITED
An Hachette UK Company
Carmelite House
50 Victoria Embankment
London EC4Y 0DZ

The authorised representative in the EEA is Hachette Ireland,
8 Castlecourt Centre, Dublin 15, D15 XTP3, Ireland (email: info@hbgi.ie)

www.headline.co.uk
www.hachette.co.uk

ICONS OF STYLE

Chappell Roan

The story of a fashion legend

Glenys Johnson

WELBECK

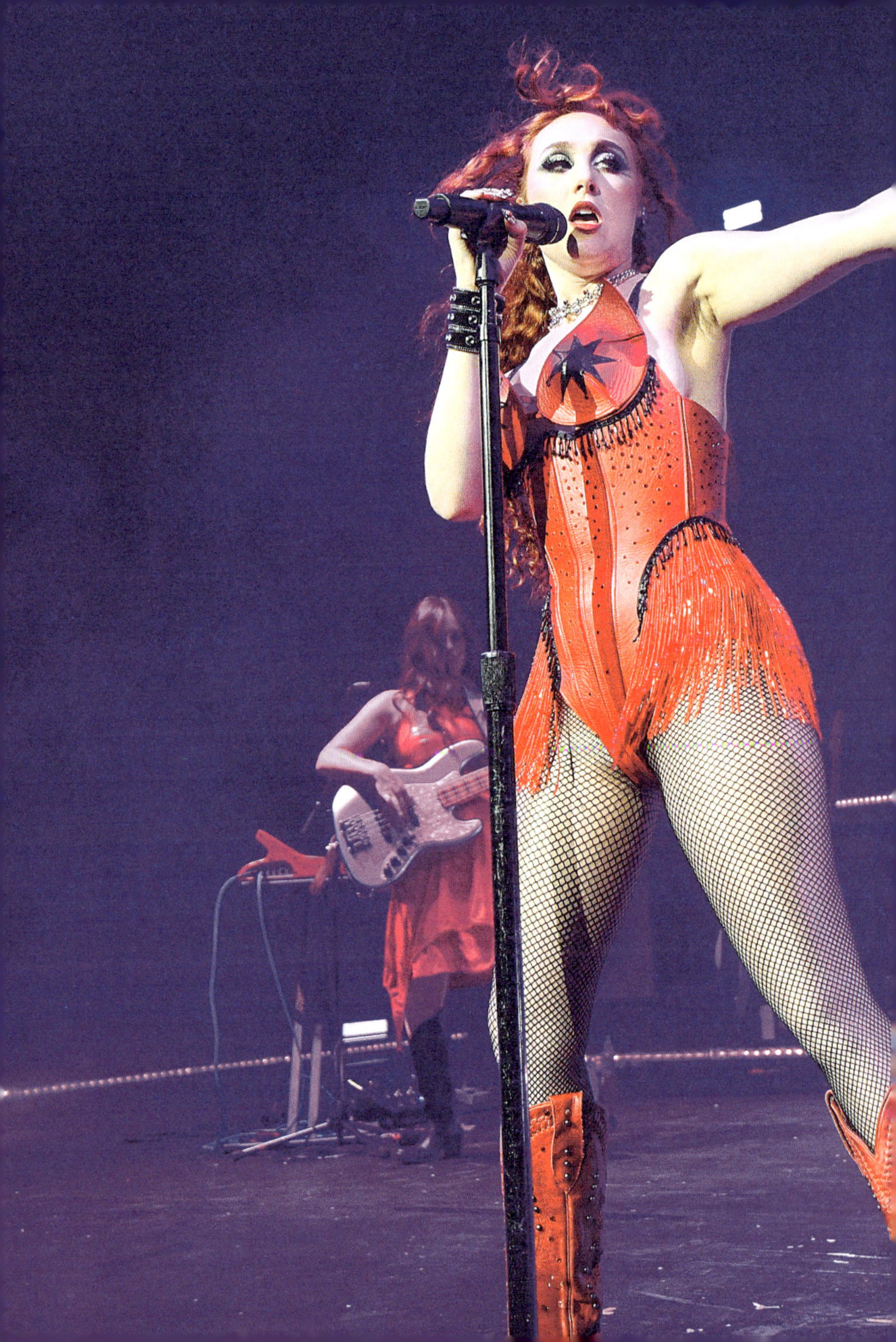

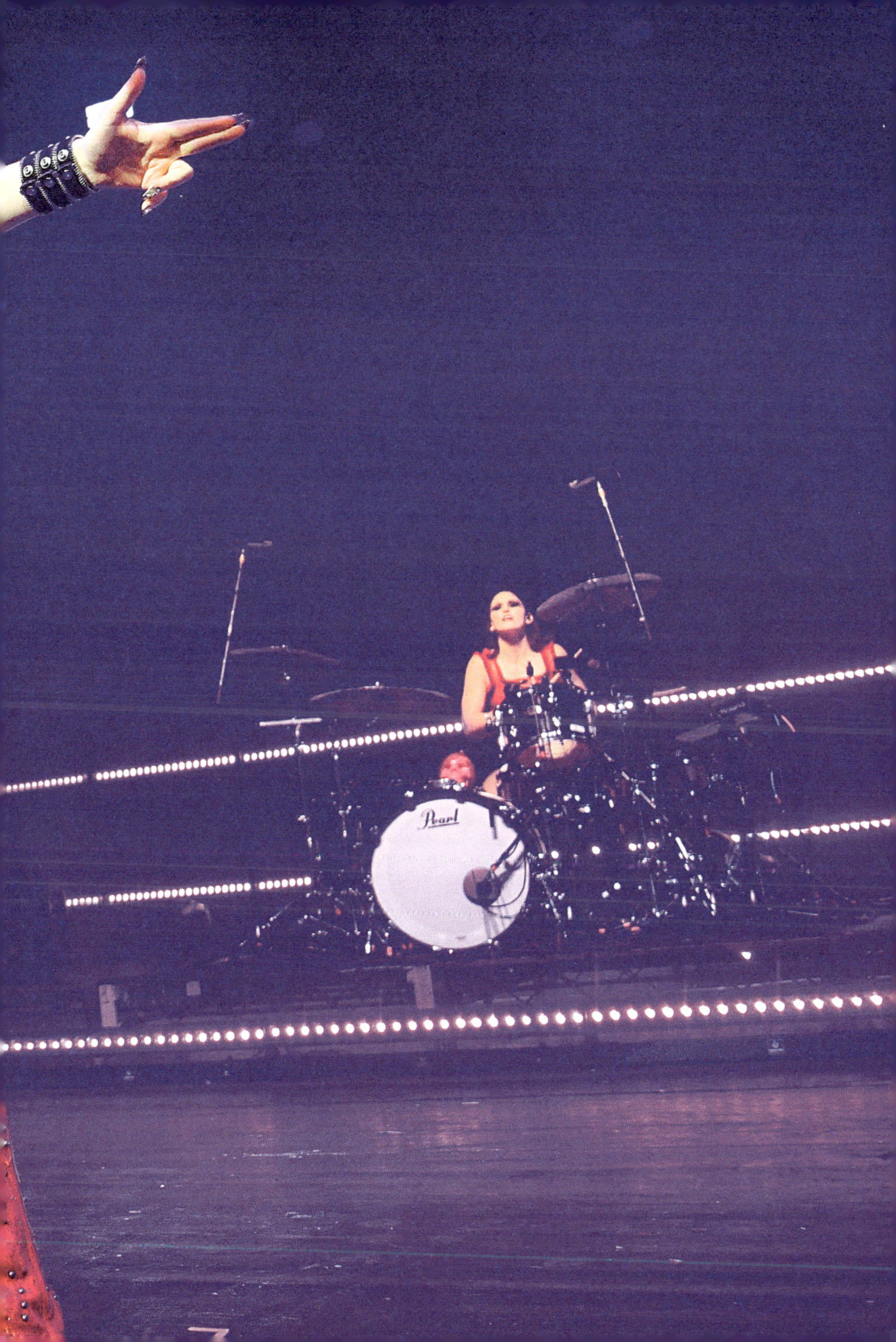

"I pretty much base my aesthetic off what a

pop star would have worn when I was eight.”

CHAPPELL ROAN

Introduction

To many, it may feel as though Chappell Roan came out of nowhere. But what could seem like an overnight success to many was actually the result of around a decade of trial, error and plenty of hard work from the Missouri native. Throughout this book we'll dissect the rich tapestry of influences that have come to shape the alter ego of Kayleigh Rose Amstutz. From her younger years spent in the widely conservative area of the American Midwest, we'll travel through some of the formative experiences that led her to become the performer we know and love today.

PREVIOUS Roan wears a custom leather design by Zana Bayne onstage at Brixton Academy in London, on 19 September 2024.

OPPOSITE *The Late Show with Stephen Colbert* in February 2024. Roan and her stylist Genesis Webb are known to tap into strong historical themes for her looks, demonstrated here with this one that's comprised of vintage pieces dating back to 1910.

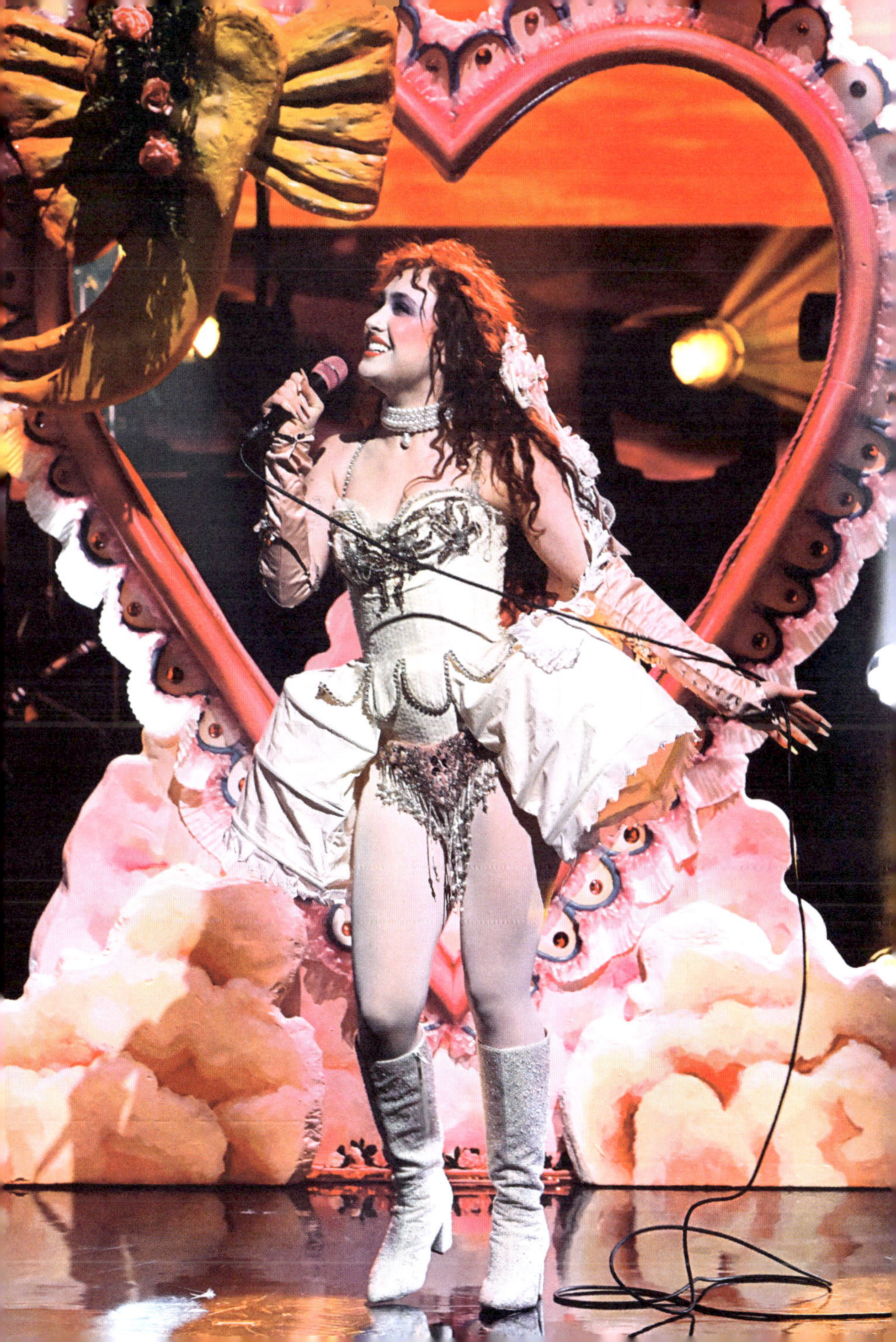

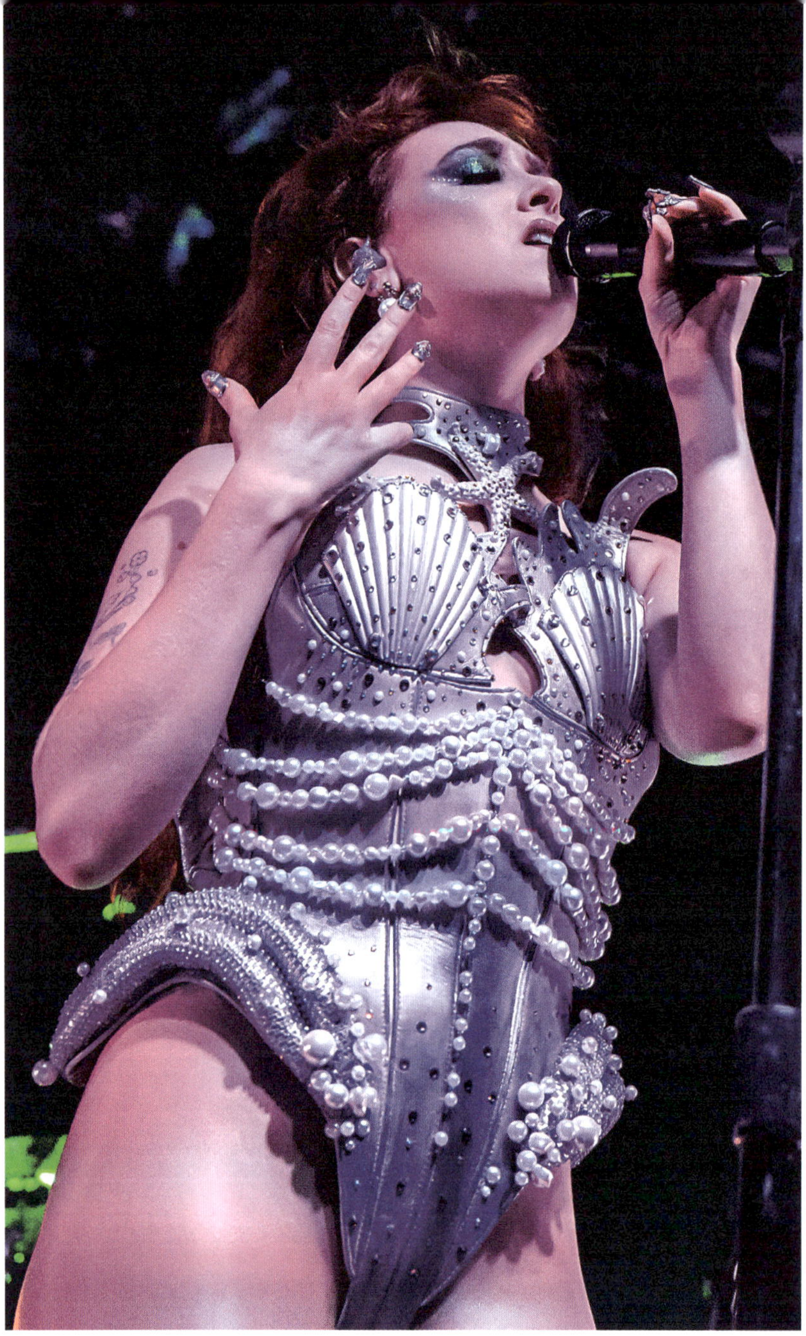

To honour what she often refers to as her "project" (alluding to the fact that Chappell Roan is more than just a character but also leans into the idea of the world her and her team have created around her), we'll refer to Amstutz by her stage name of Chappell Roan throughout. Catherine Zimmer, associate professor of film and screen studies at Pace University in New York City, is just one of the many academic minds to quickly analyse Roan and her success, highlighting the collective aspect of Roan in her August 2024 piece, stating, "Although Chappell Roan has quickly achieved 'icon status', it feels significant that interviews and articles so frequently highlight her creative partnerships, her influences, her opening acts, and her audiences. 'Chappell Roan' exists as a shared phenomenon that exceeds the individual that is Kayleigh Rose." Throughout this book we'll look at the role that Roan's team has played in creating her often otherworldly looks.

Performing in Manchester, England, in 2024, Roan wears a bodysuit designed by Zana Bayne for her Midwest Princess tour.

Roan's connection to her fans through style and her growing connections with fashion designers will also be explored, following her front-row appearances at fashion weeks and her first attendance at the Met Gala in 2025. We'll unpack some of her key looks and concepts used to create them, from the overarching theme of camp that Roan and her team practise through nearly every look they produce and the various subcultures that act as fountains of inspiration. Roan and her team have gone far beyond what's expected from the wardrobe of a pop star, proving what is possible with clothing. We'll look at how Roan's queerness comes into play with her looks, reinterpreting how themes such as Americana and high femme glamour can be used to shift existing narratives for a new generation.

As Roan's career continues to grow, so does her confidence in experimenting with her outfit choices. And we're here for all the wardrobe changes that the future brings.

Onstage during the Midwest Princess tour, at the Brixton Academy, London, on 19 September 2024.

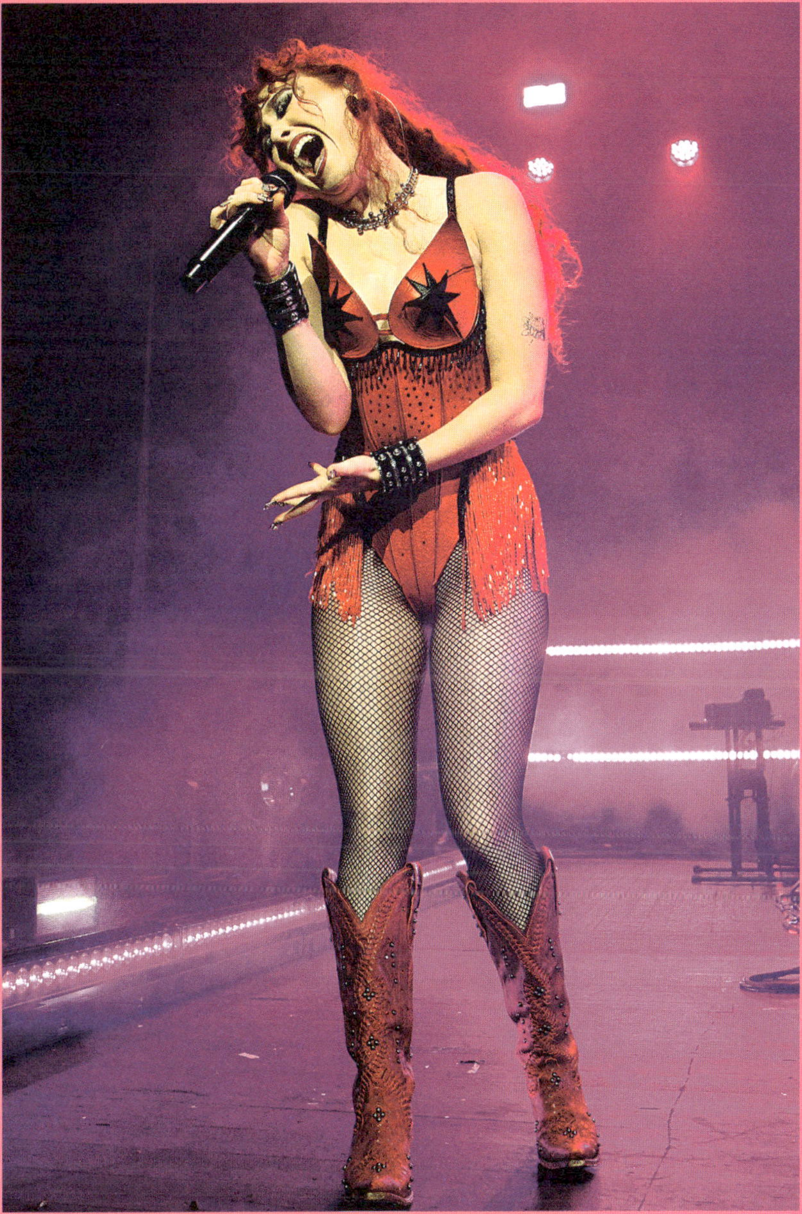

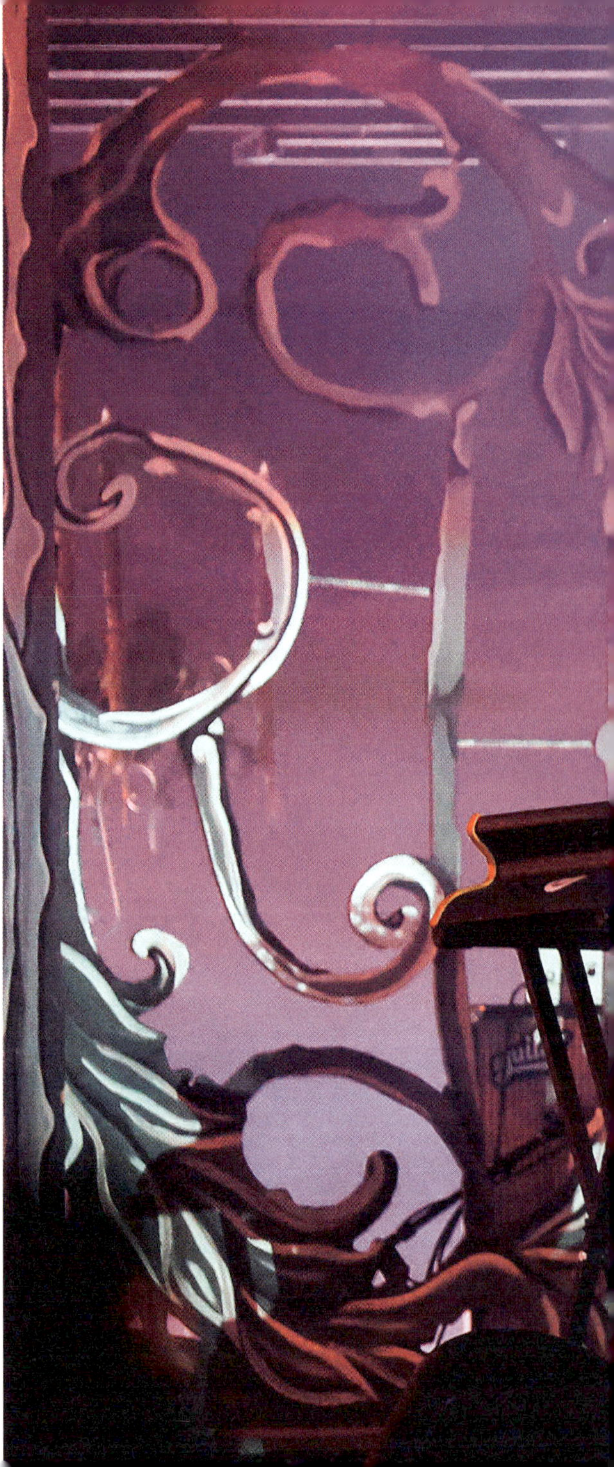

For many of her captivating summer 2025 looks, Roan brought in the talents of Gunnar Deatherage to create larger-than-life ensembles including this one worn in Budapest, Hungary, on 11 August 2025.

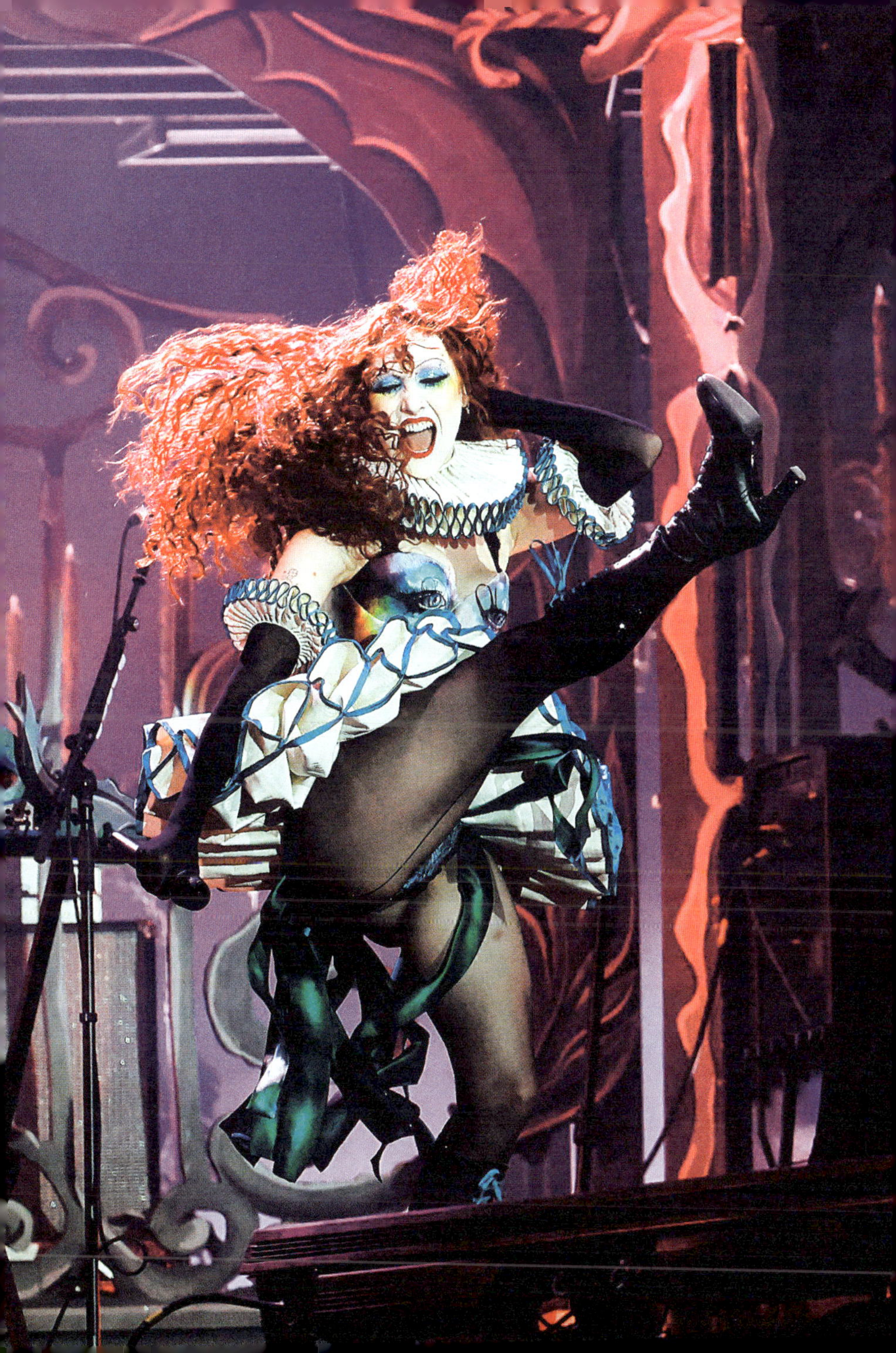

"I wanted to wear weird, fun clothes."

CHAPPELL ROAN

At the Hollywood Palladium in November 2022, opening for artist Fletcher. This would mark one of her first performances with her now trademark fire-engine red hair, after dyeing it just days earlier.

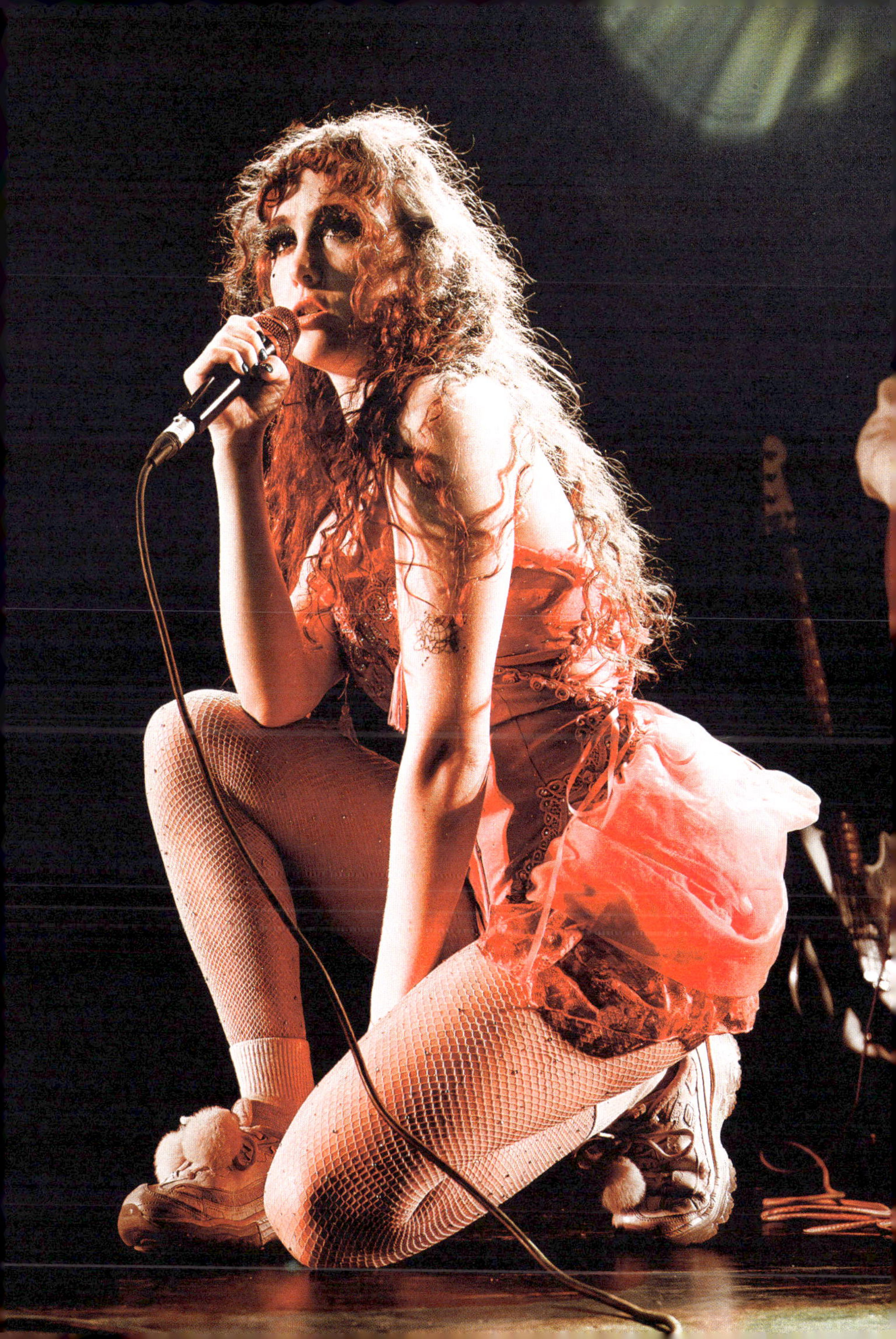

Early

CHAPTER 1

Years

Starting life in the small town of Willard, Missouri, Kayleigh Rose Amstutz noted her early life in the conservative American Midwest environment as being one rife with struggles. "I think my parents thought I was being a brat, so I had a difficult time" she told *Variety* magazine in a 2023 interview. She went on to share, "I just wanted to feel like a good person, but I had this part of me that wanted to escape so bad. I just wanted to scream." She added, "I snuck out a lot, but I still went to church three times a week, you know what I mean? So it was just this dichotomy of trying to be a good girl, but also wanting to freaking light things on fire." By the age of 15, Roan had discovered her love for singing and began uploading videos to YouTube, covering songs from artists such as Fleetwood Mac, Elton John and 4 Non Blondes.

Despite her feeling often disconnected to the mentality of many of her peers in her hometown, Amstutz now notes the Midwest as being a key source of inspiration for her work. In a September 2023 interview with *Polyester*, she remarked, "It's where I grew up and I do love certain parts of it – the peace and growing up in a trailer park; four wheeling, the farm and bonfires." And like many young American girls of the period, Roan told *NME* in 2022, she grew up idolizing the fashion of figures such as Kesha, Lady Gaga and Nicki Minaj for their bold yet playful fashion choices and energetic approach to performing. She has also famously referenced the Disney Channel programme starring a teenage Miley Cyrus and Hannah Montana as a key influence for her Chappell Roan alter ego. And another defining element she brought into her fashion evolution? "I love Bratz dolls. I love the fashion of the Bratz" she reported in a 2024 *Glamour* interview.

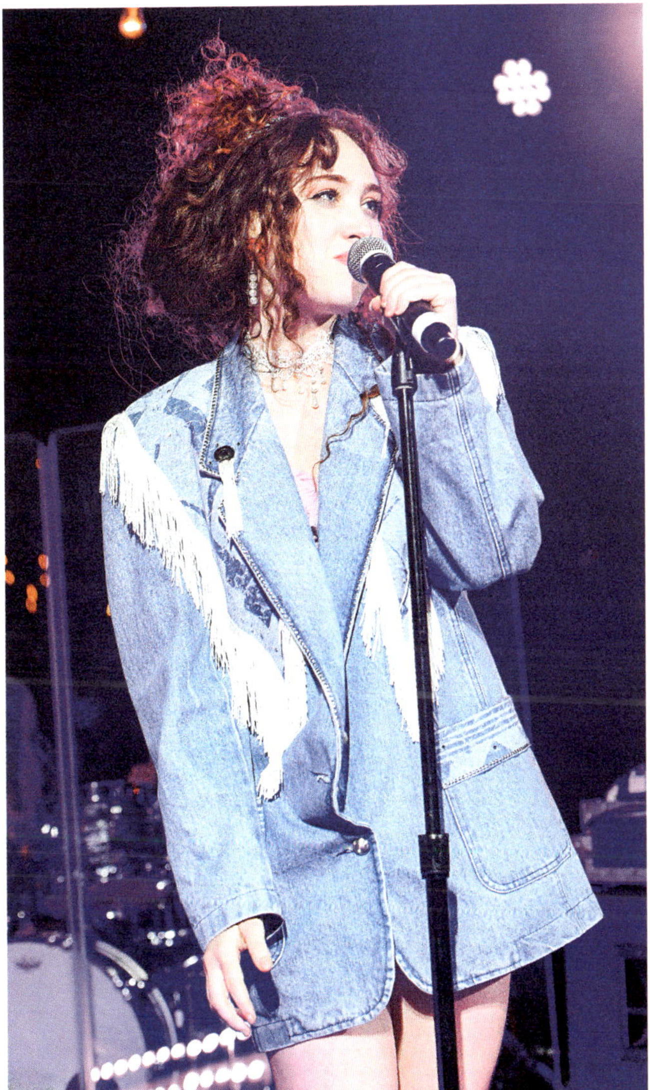

Roan performs at a GLAAD (Gay & Lesbian Alliance Against Defamation) event on 19 October, 2022, in Los Angeles, California.

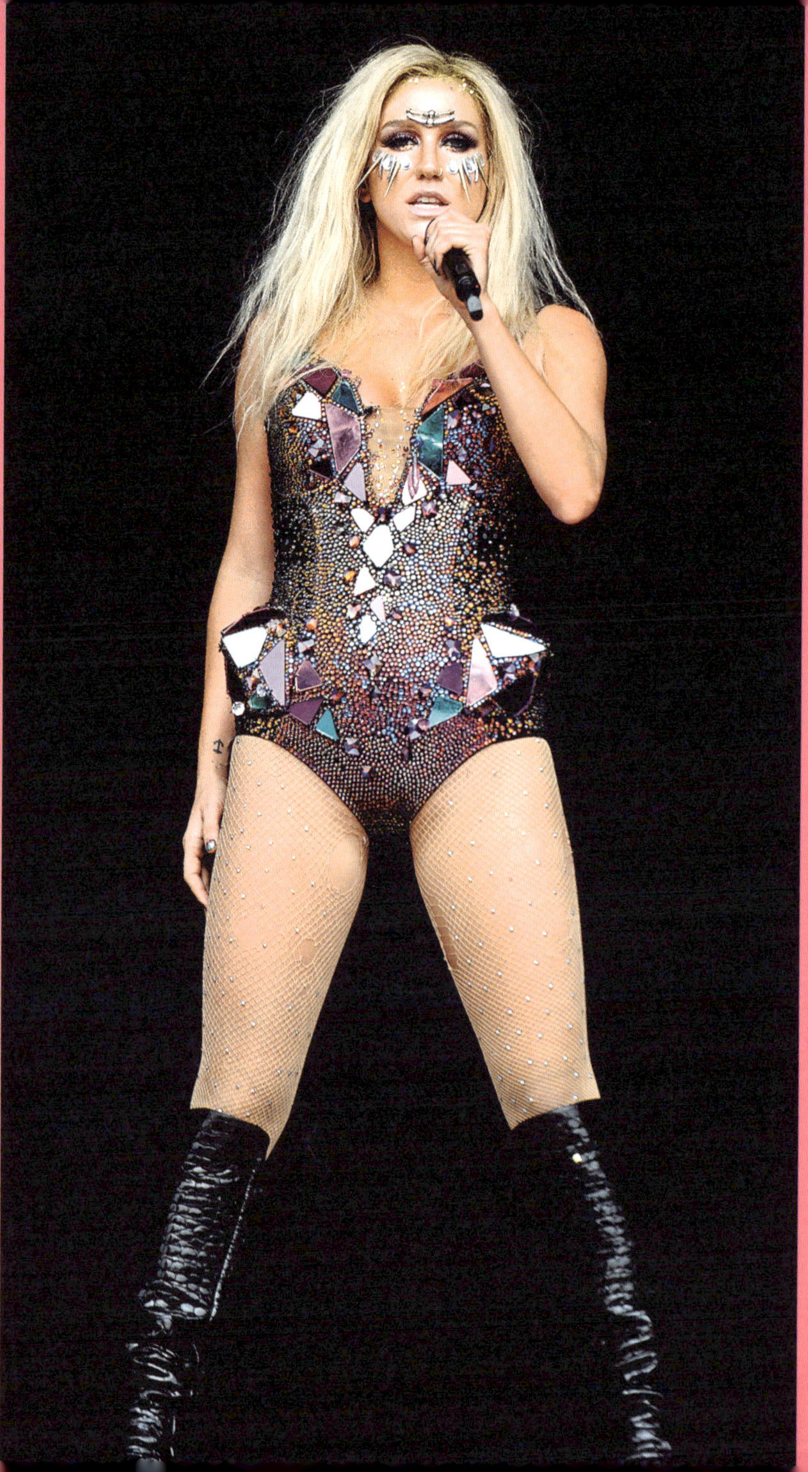

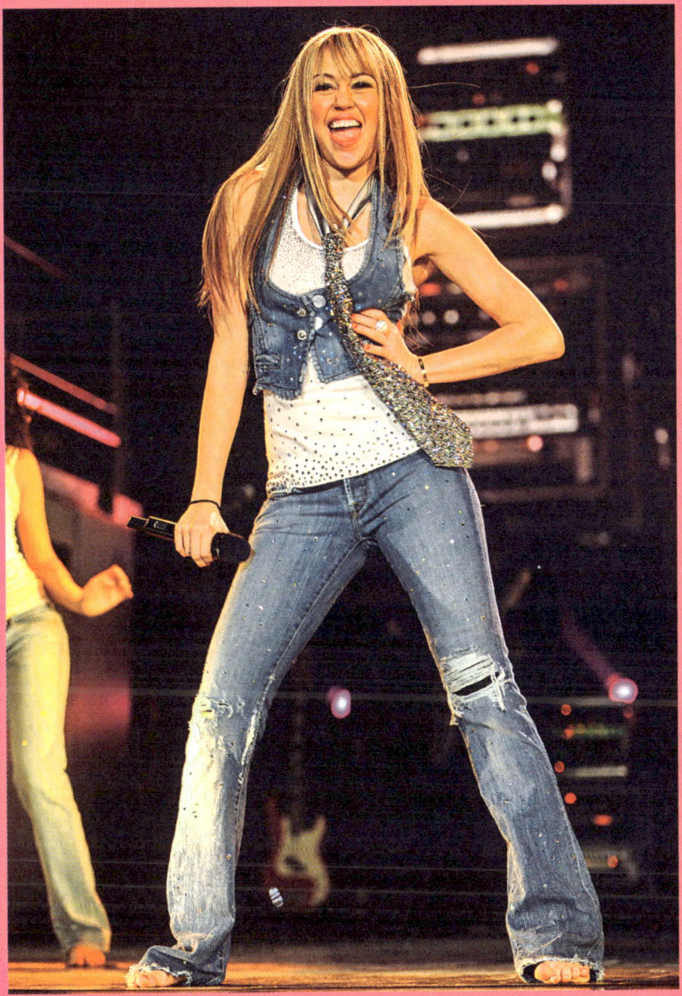

OPPOSITE Kesha, one of Roan's key influences for her bold looks and performance style, performs at London's Queen Elizabeth Olympic Park on 12 July 2013.

ABOVE Roan told *Rolling Stone* in 2024, "I want to be like Hannah Montana" (Miley Cyrus's famous Disney character, depicted here in an image from 2007).

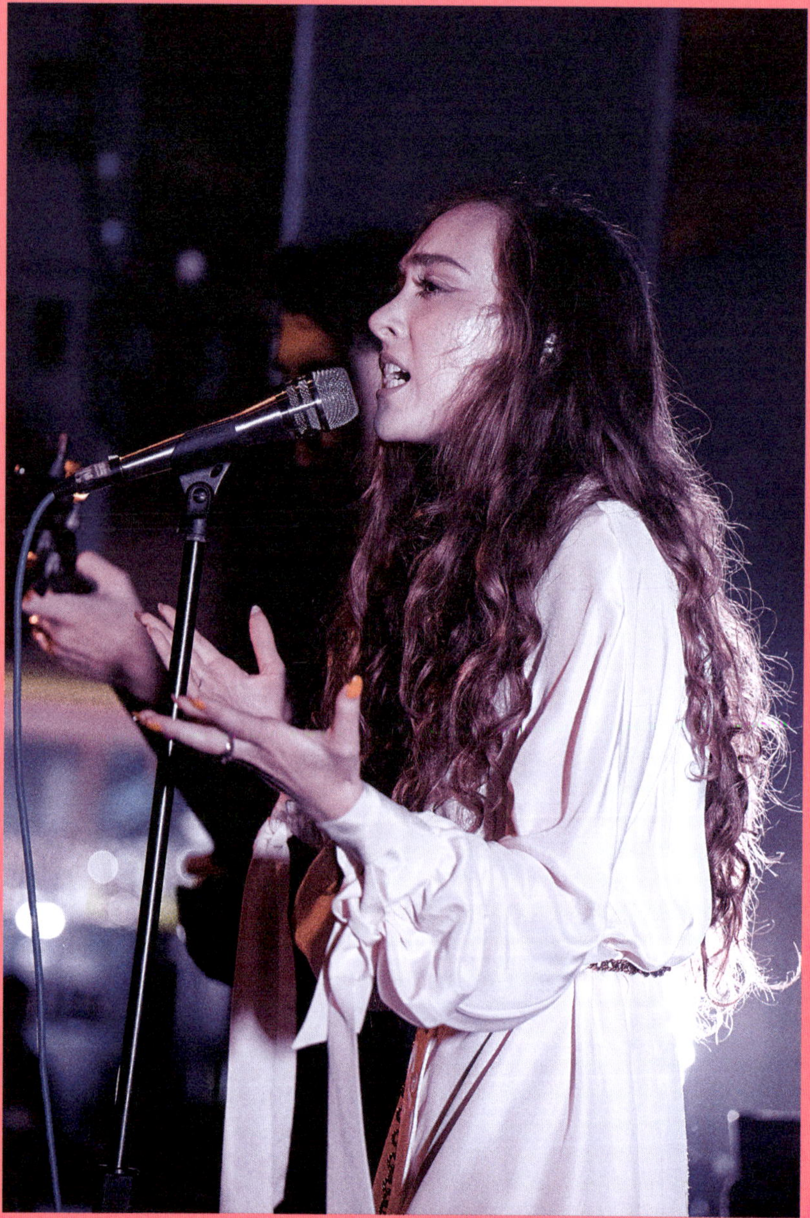

At just 17, Roan was offered a contract with Atlantic Records, with whom she signed and released her debut album *School Nights* in 2017. In many images of Roan's early career, the tone was more moody and natural, leaning towards a "girl next door" look, with humble Americana references such as denim jackets, boho-style dresses and often donning a pair of cowboy boots. Her now-signature fire engine red curls were her natural mousy brown shade and her make-up understated. When discussing the looks she presented in her earlier videos, including for her first single "Die Young", Roan told *Headliner* in 2024, "I wanted to wear weird, fun clothes, and I felt like I couldn't do that with 'Die Young'. It just felt too dark, so I purposely was like, 'I have to change, because this is not sustainable'." Roan again spoke publicly about the styles she sported in the very early days of her career, this time with drag performer Mo Heart on her series entitled *The Walk In* on Amazon Music. Roan shared, "This style wasn't always my style, I used to be witchy, dark, serious."

A teenage Chappell Roan performs in Seattle, Washington, in September 2017.

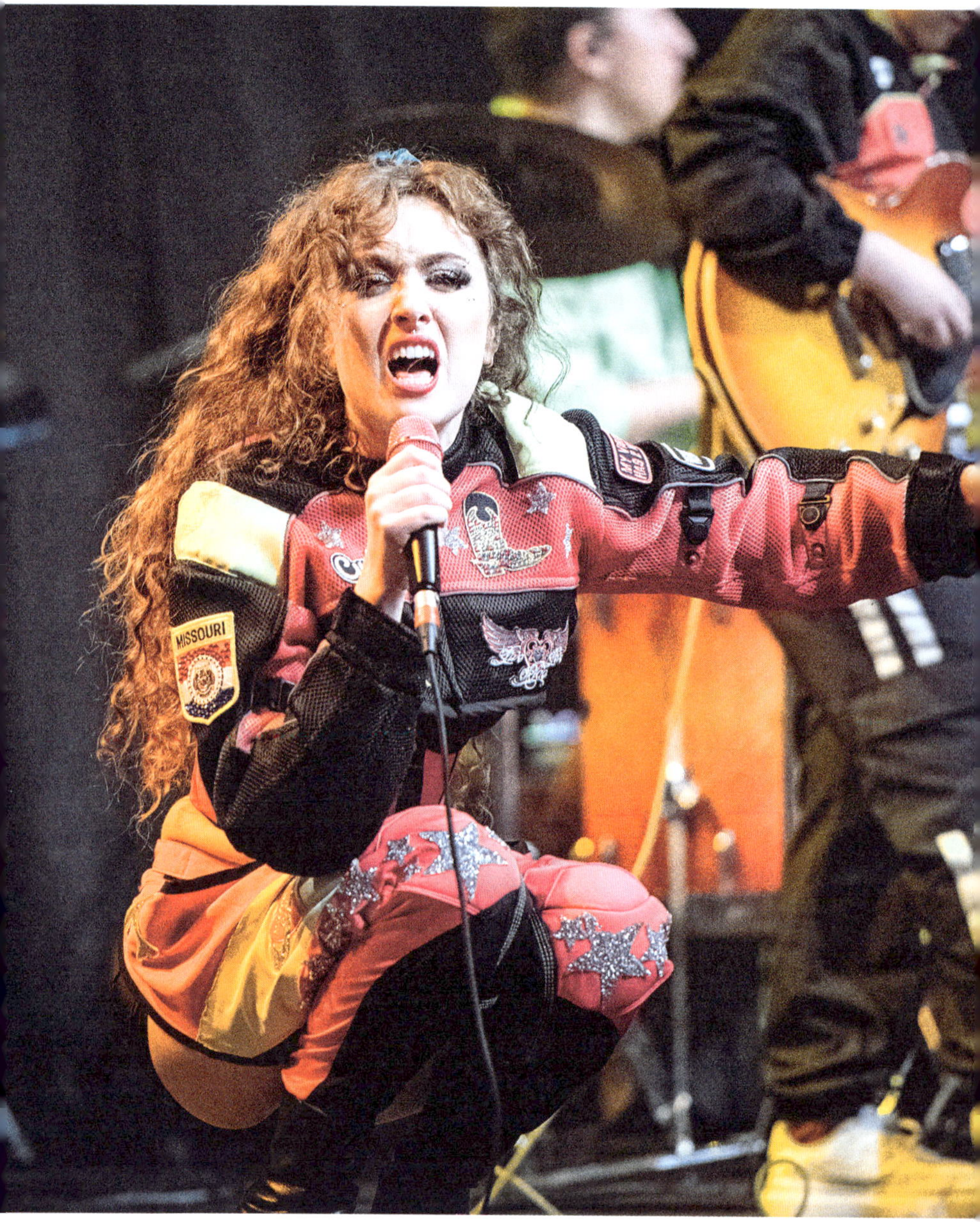
MISSOURI

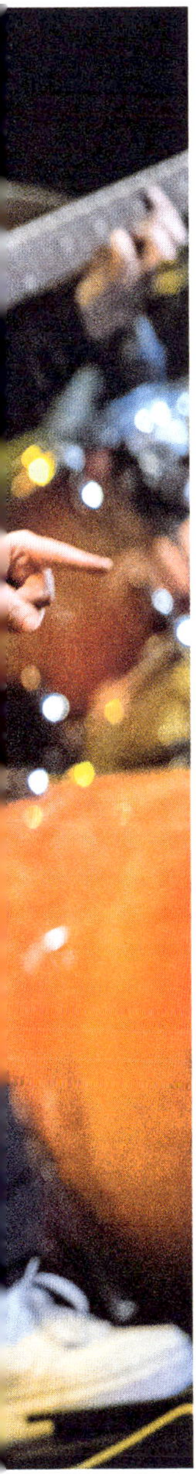

In 2018, Roan went through what many referred to as her "queer awakening" when the then 21-year-old moved to Los Angeles and found herself visiting queer spaces including The Abbey in West Hollywood. It was one particular visit that inspired her first breakout single, "Pink Pony Club". In 2024, she remarked on this time in an interview with *The Guardian*, saying, "I grew up thinking being gay was bad and a sin ... I went to the gay club once and it was so impactful, like magic. It was the opposite of everything I was taught." This shift also played a big role in her personal style and the formation of her Chappell Roan alter ego. The video featured Roan in a bugle-beaded bodysuit and Western-inspired jacket with fringe sleeves and covered in shimmering gemstones. The look, styled by LA-based Orchid Satellite, used vintage pieces courtesy of The Last Follies Closet. This marked shift progressed through her subsequent videos for "California" and "Naked in Manhattan", where she'd continued dipping her toe into brighter 1980s- and 1990s-inspired looks. Reflecting on this time, she shared with *Variety* magazine in 2023, "We had no plan and ran around New York shooting me in a bunch of different outfits that I thrifted. It was just so fun and so freeing, and it was the first time that I was like, 'Oh, I think this is what it should feel like,'" Roan said, continuing, "I learned how to do drag make-up and how to bedazzle and sew a little bit. There were so many things I had to learn out of necessity, and that's what built this project."

Roan opens for Fletcher in Vancouver, Canada, on 10 November 2022. This look was one of the many DIY styles Roan wore across the tour. It also featured across the promo images for her single, "Femininomenon", released a few months earlier.

It was around this time that Roan also found herself blowing up on social media, sharing frequent videos on TikTok that offered insight into her developing style. She began posting videos of herself applying neon eyeshadow and dancing in brightly coloured outfits (one notable look featuring a tinsel jacket with horizontal stripes that many compared to the colours of the lesbian pride flag, naturally exciting many queer fans). "I got on TikTok, and I also got to show my personality and how I love to thrift and have style and do make-up and stuff" Roan told *Dork* magazine in December 2023. She continued, "I saw that people were not only connecting to the music but this aesthetic I was building of this DIY pop girl. I was like oh, I have more to play with here than just music. I have a whole world that I can build. I just filled that out and used drag and burlesque as stakeholders." Roan often posted the pieces she gathered from her trips to local flea markets (Los Feliz Flea in LA being a noted favourite) and second-hand shops, twirling for the camera and walking us through what she loved about the looks.

Billboard's Stephen Drew spoke to Roan in December 2022, where she weighed in on this transition, sharing, "Once I let go of trying to be this very well-managed, put-together pop girl, it felt like everything just fell into place ... I leaned into the fact that my looks were tacky, and very obviously using fake diamonds and Gucci knock-offs. I leaned into my queerness for the first time. When I did that, the songs got easier to write, the shows got easier to design, and my aesthetic was finally there."

Chappell Roan onstage during the Corona Capital music festival at the Autódromo Hermanos Rodríguez in Mexico City, on 15 November 2025.

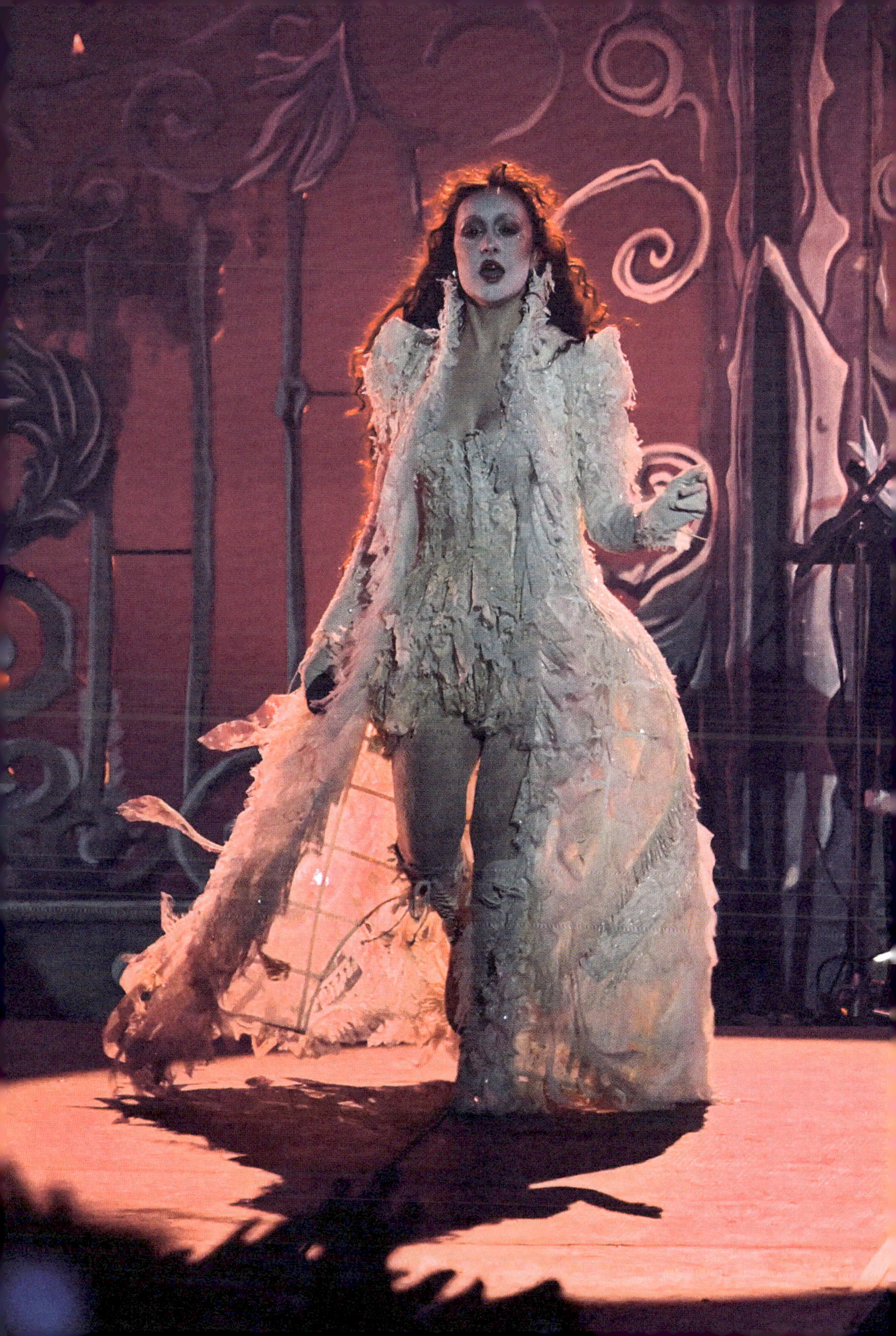

CHAPTER 2

Camp

Defining camp is no easy feat. Though the term, in this context, first appeared in the *Oxford English Dictionary* in 1909 (with the definition of "ostentatious, exaggerated, affected, theatrical; effeminate or homosexual; pertaining to, characteristic of, homosexuals …"), it dates back much further. In his 2019 essay "The Spectacles of Camp", Fabio Cleto notes that many speculate its origins as coming from the French verb *se camper* (to posture boldly) or the Italian *campeggiare* (to stand out). He goes on to share that the term camp "has proved a vital resource for theories of eccentricity, social stigma, leisure, unorthodox sexuality, and the subversion of gendered identity. And yet, camp has not given up its relentless power to frustrate any effort to pinpoint it."

The term "camp" has undoubtedly seen a surge in usage with Gen Z, becoming a term to communicate many of the themes that Roan's looks and persona conveys: bright and bold aesthetics, humour and theatrics with a DIY approach. "I was the thrift store pop girl – it was so drag; I learned how to embellish my own costumes," she said. "I was like, 'I'm gonna give it one more year – and if it doesn't work, I'll rethink.' But do you know what, it fucking worked." Roan told *NME* in 2024.

Chappell Roan wearing a custom look by London-based designer Milla Giulia Badin onstage at Montreal's Oshega Festival in August 2024.

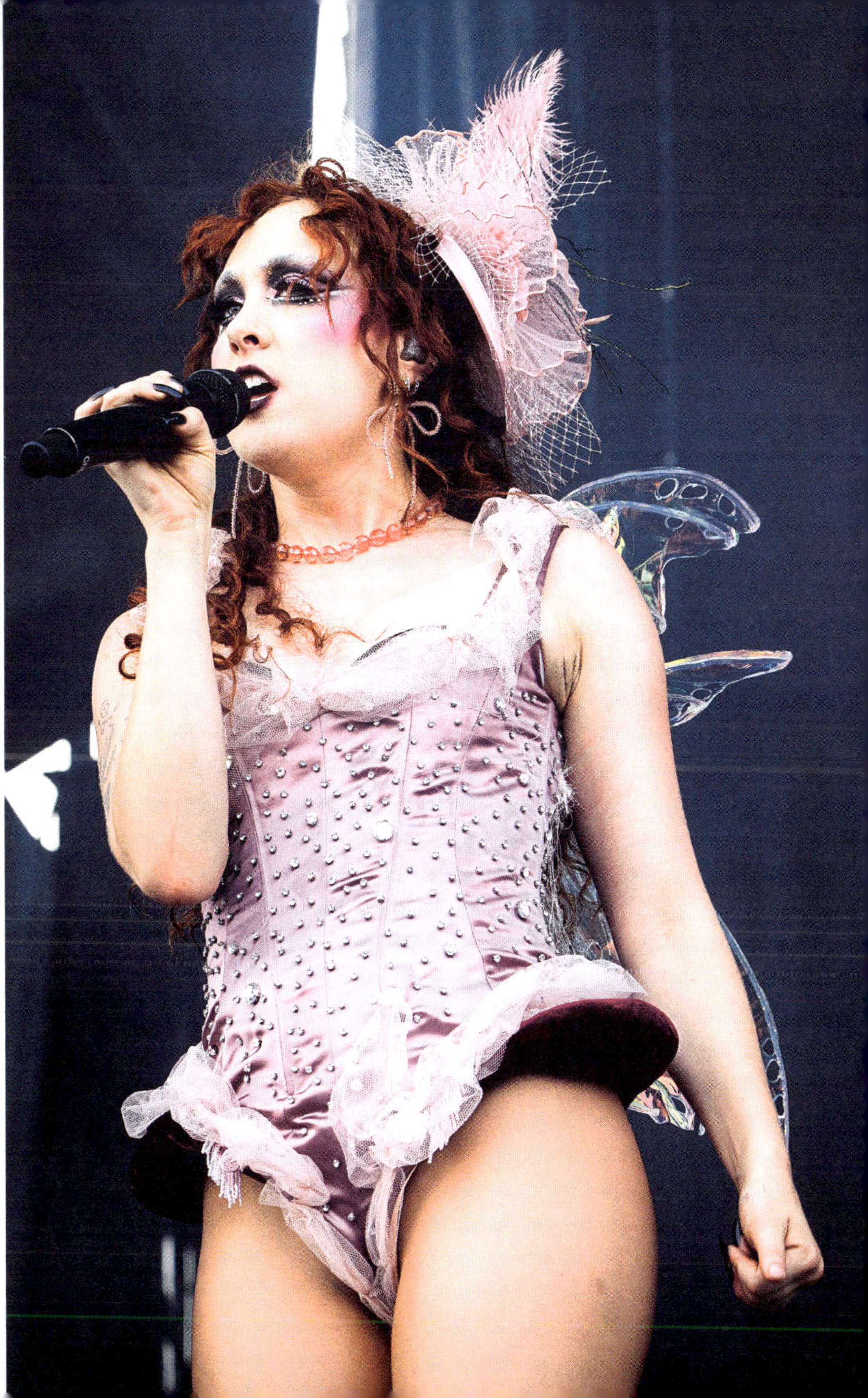

"I'm the pop star
of Good *Will.*
I'm a thrift
store *pop star.*
I'm a DIY *queen,*
know what I mean?"

CHAPPELL ROAN,
***ROLLING STONE*, 2022**

Roan partially credits her affinity for her camp image to her Missouri upbringing, sharing with Oxford's *Cherwell* newspaper in 2022, "There isn't really a place for showmanship in Missouri in the way that I would like. I want to purposely look 'trashy', not modest, very loud and provocative. To me that is a reflection of and an homage to burlesque. It's consciously camp. Because I was not allowed to express that kind of showmanship in Missouri where I'm from, the pendulum has swung so far the other way." She goes on to reflect on the image she presented in her younger years, saying, "Because when I was Kayleigh Rose, I was performing all over town in coffee shops in Springfield, Missouri and I was very modest. I always wore knee-length dresses and very high necks. Nothing like what I would wear now."

Growing up in the 2000s, Roan, like many of her American peers, was also influenced by the pop culture of the times. "I grew up with and always wanted to dress like – big dresses, big hairstyles, lots of jewelry. So I'm very inspired by my inner child – but also by drag, burlesque and Vegas showgirls. Basically, anything loud and glittery." Roan told Swiss magazine *Annabelle* in a 2024 interview. The theme of her "inner child" comes up again when discussing her influences in another piece with *Cherwell* newspaper that year, saying, "I pretty much base my aesthetic off what a pop star would have worn when I was eight. When I was little, I loved Bratz, the classic Barbie movies, Britney Spears, I was really into fairies and Spy Kids."

Throughout this chapter, we will dissect the various elements that come together to create Roan's unique approach to camp style and the wide breadth of inspirations behind them.

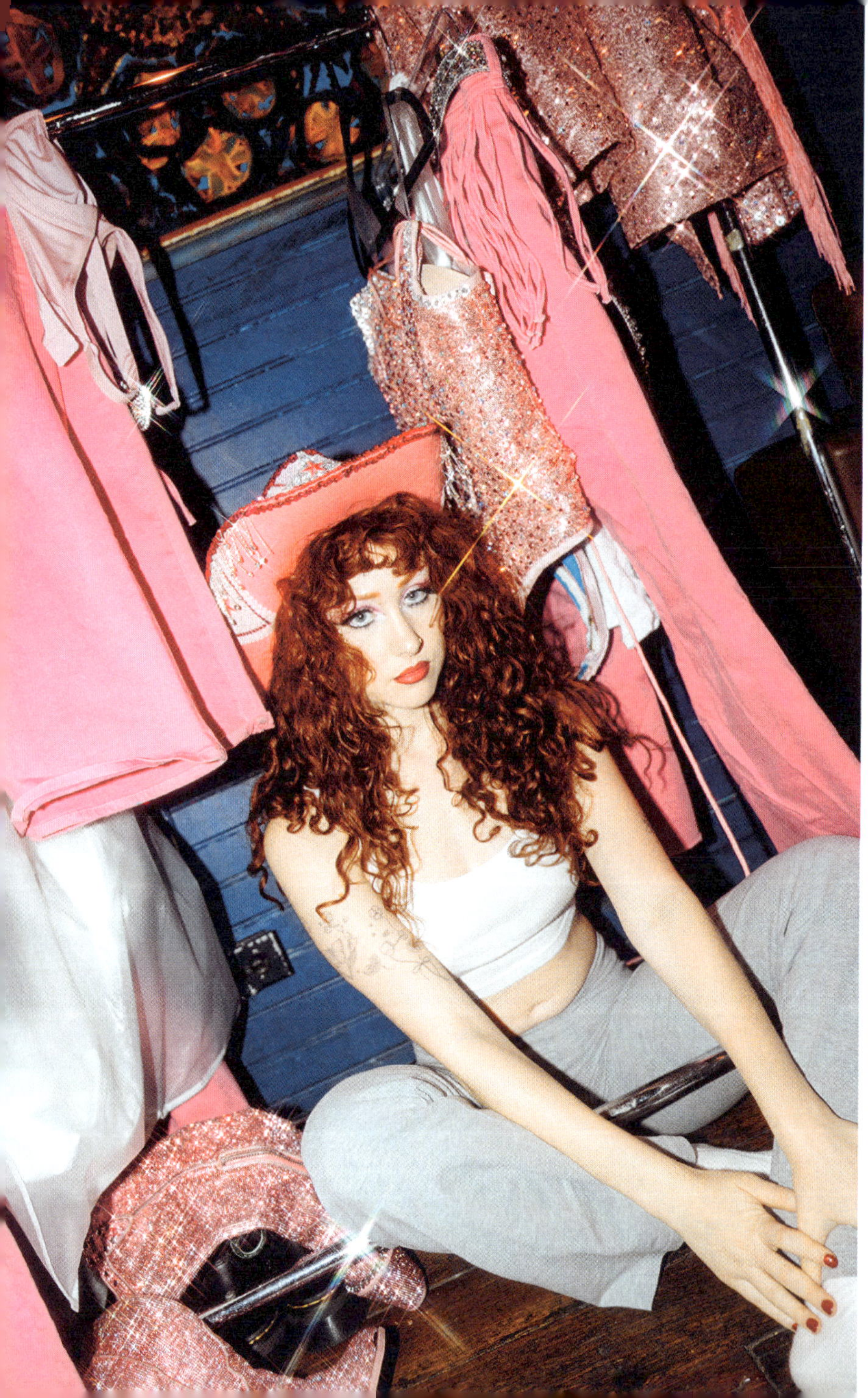

The United States of Chappell

Though Roan has highlighted how contrasting many of her looks are from those that appear on the streets of the Midwestern towns where she came of age, it is also important to understand how Midwestern elements come into play and how she has interpreted them both through her music and her fashion looks. Roan summarized this when talking to *Variety*'s Ellise Shafer: "It influences the music, my fashion, my lyrics, the energy around it. It's important for me to capture the Midwestern aspect. I don't want to lose that part of me. I thought I really did when I was younger, but now I don't anymore." Her dedication to this aspect of her identity is seen most obviously in the title of her 2023 album *The Rise and Fall of a Midwest Princess*, which skyrocketed her success as a leading pop artist and cultural icon. Roan's middle-America upbringing also plays a key role in creating one of her foundational aesthetics, the "Midwest Princess" look.

Roan poses in a pink cowboy hat in her dressing room at the House of Blues in Chicago in October 2023. Rhinestone-covered cowboy hats have since become a calling card among Roan's fans across the world.

One of the most stark examples of this can be seen in her 2024 Governors Ball performance outfit, one of the first that won her headlines from leading fashion publications around the world. Recalling the look, Roan's stylist Genesis Webb shared with *Harper's Bazaar*, "I sent Chappell a reference of a *Playboy* Bunny coming out of a cake, and she was like, 'Let's do an apple. We should have it be a bong, a smoking apple.'"

Lady Liberty has long been an inspiration for performers, including one of the kings of camp himself, Elton John, who was known to sport the famous crown-and-torch look multiple times throughout his career. The latex ensemble chosen for Roan by Webb was designed by Monique Fei, reportedly winning its way into Webb's heart due to its rear-revealing design. The Statue of Liberty look also gained respect from fans due to its timing, *Autostraddle*'s Kayla Kumari Upadhyaya shared: "I love just the sheer idea of transforming a symbol of American patriotism into a slutty queer camp persona. She was wearing this look when she announced she would not perform at the White House Pride parade as a political statement, and that also sends this one up in the power rankings."

Chappell Roan and her team have taken inspiration from the iconic American figure of the *Playboy* Bunny for a number of looks, including her Governers Ball performance and, perhaps more famously, one of the main looks in her "My Kink is Karma" music video, released in May 2022.

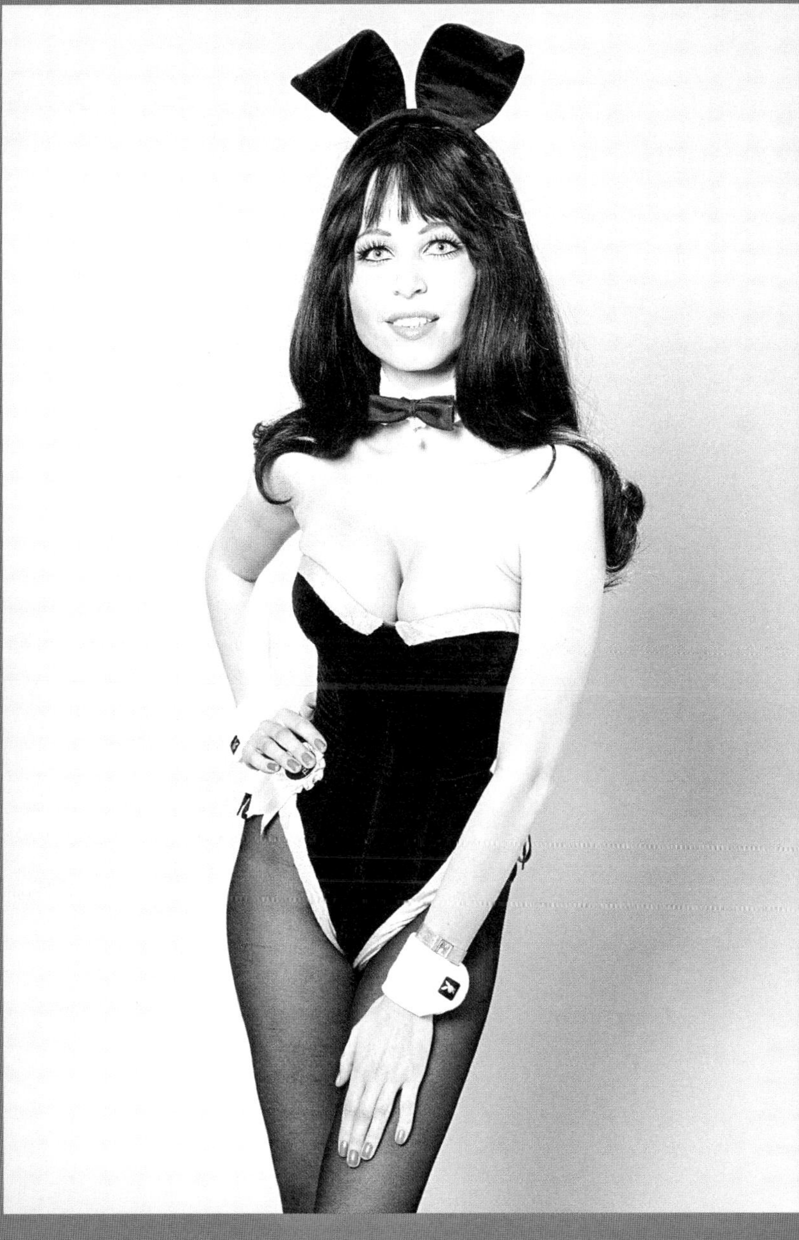

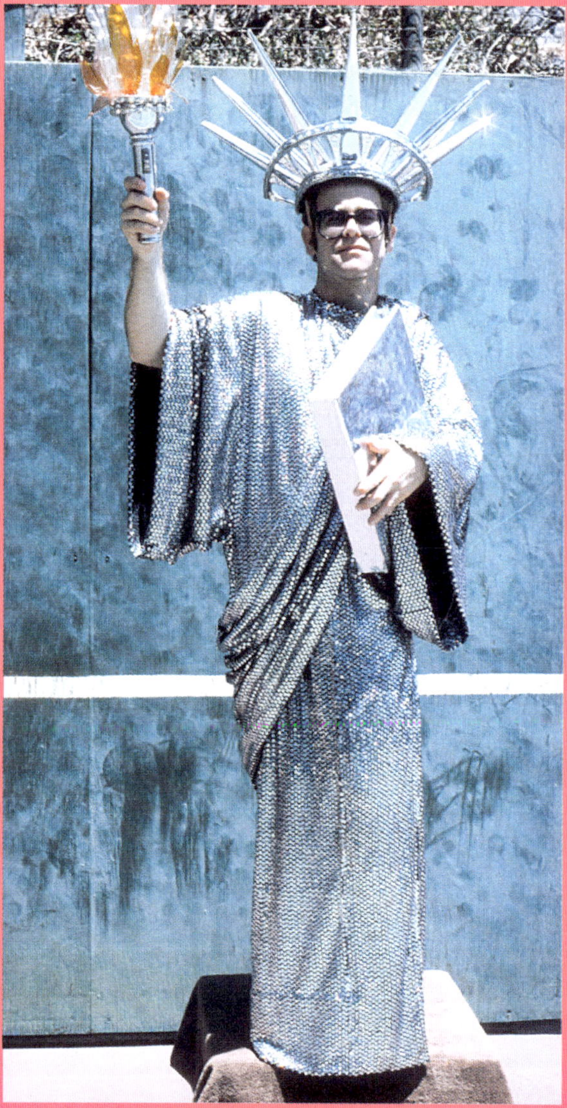

Elton John poses for a portrait session in New York City in 1980, wearing a full Statue of Liberty look.

"My outfit choices, song choices, writing style, hair/ make-up, etc. are all nods to the queens I look up to. I try to honor my queer elders; those who came before me. I am always referencing someone or something; it's all very intentional. Camp is camp. Pop is pop. I'm not taking myself or aesthetic seriously, because that's no fun. I want to have fun."

CHAPPELL ROAN VIA INSTAGRAM, MAY 2024

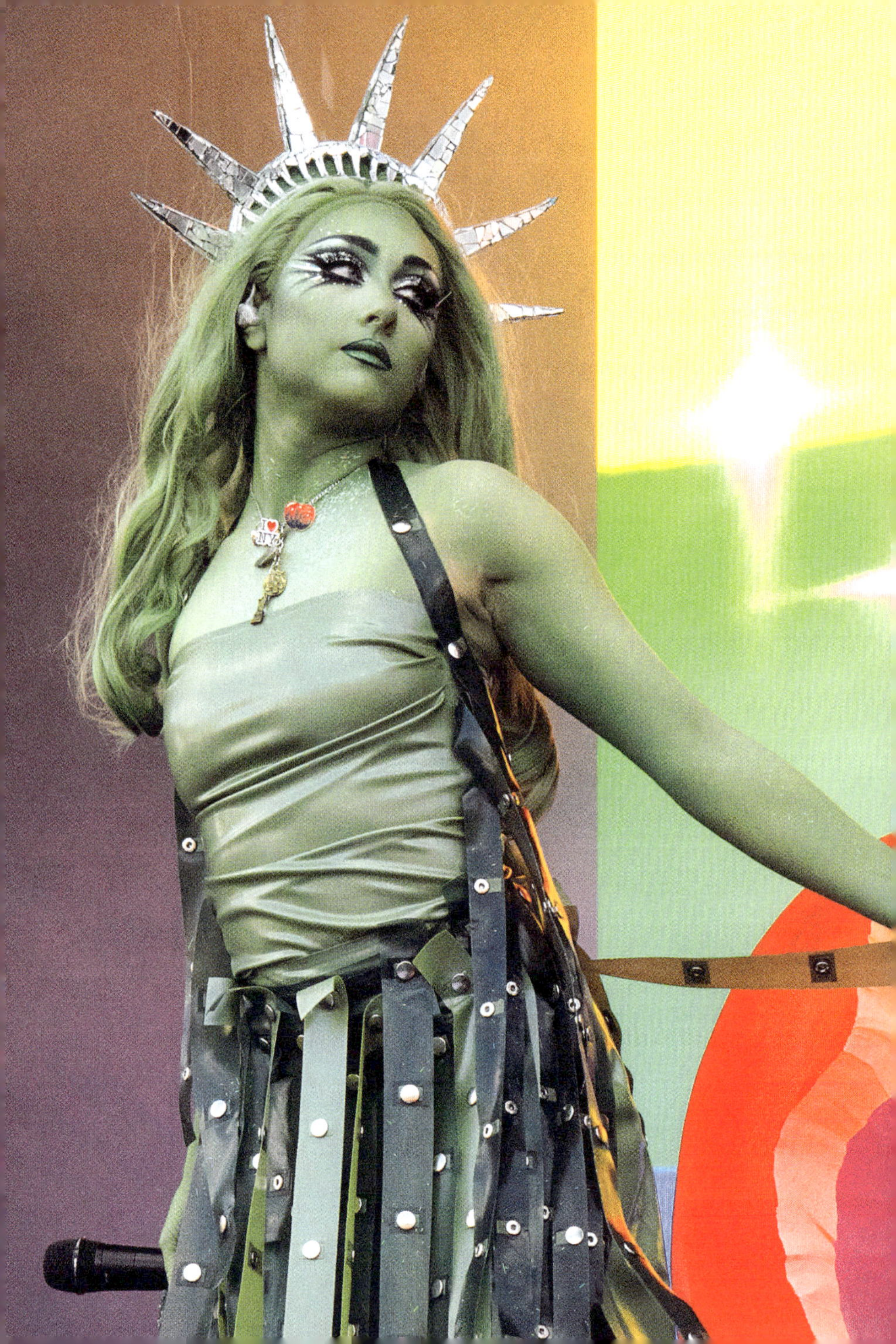

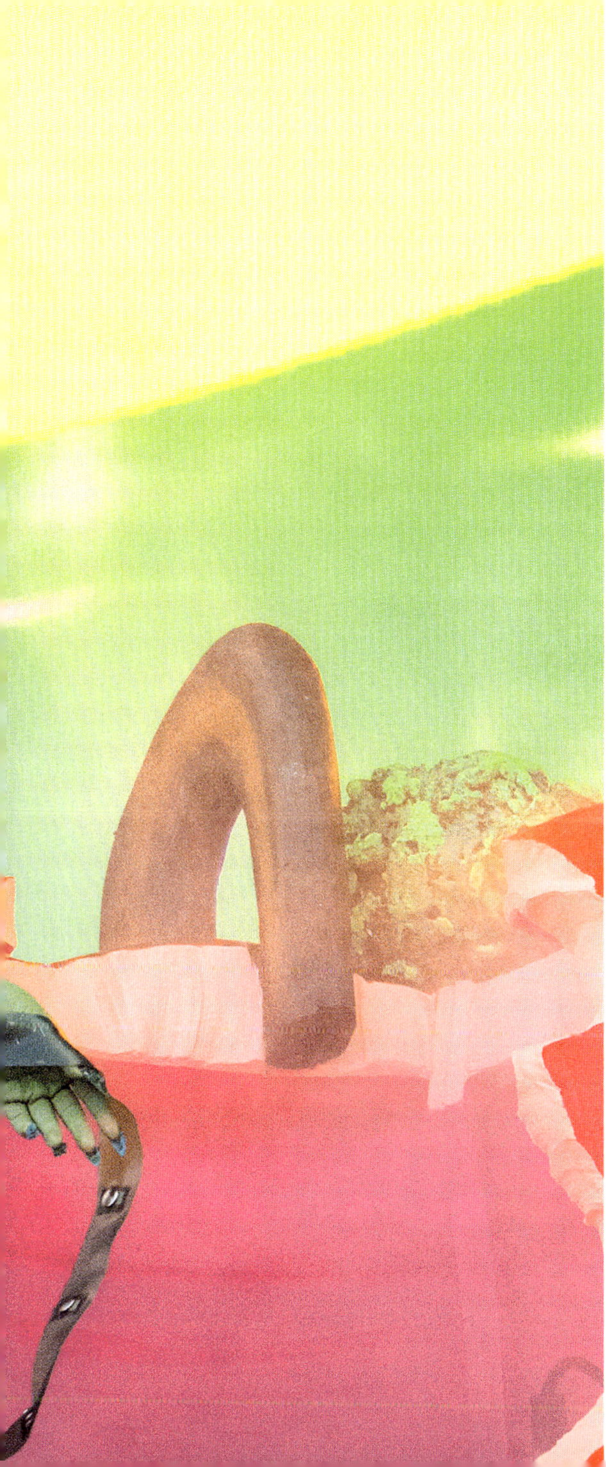

Roan used the 2024 Governors Ball in New York City to shout: “Give me your tired, your poor, your huddled masses, yearning to breathe free. That means freedom in trans rights, that means freedom in women’s rights ... and it especially means freedom for all oppressed people in occupied territories.”

Roan looked to more quintessentially American figures for one of her key looks in her "Hot to Go!" music video, released on 11 August 2023. "I wanted to be a cheerleader so bad", Roan told Audrey Fromson from *Vanity Fair*. "I never had the confidence to try out because I just thought I wouldn't, I didn't belong. And so it's another dream-come-true vibes." The video depicts Roan living out her fantasy alongside a crew of Springfield, Missouri locals, drag queens and even her own grandparents. But the look that has gone on to inspire plenty of recreations from fans around the world was the marching band-inspired blue unitard. The vintage sequin piece was sourced by stylist Genesis Webb and styled alongside a pair of white Jeffrey Campbell knee-high boots that featured seven straps that climb the star's shins. The famous fit made another appearance on stage at the Outside Lands Festival the year after the video's official release, where she reportedly performed to over 80,000 attendees. The outfit would make headlines again when, in February 2025, the unitard sold for an impressive $88,900 (£65,000) in the Give A Frock fundraiser for the LA Wildfire Relief Fund.

This sequin bodysuit was first donned by Roan in her "Hot to Go!" music video, released in August 2023. The look reappeared across multiple tour dates following, including here at the Outside Lands Festival in San Francisco, in August 2024.

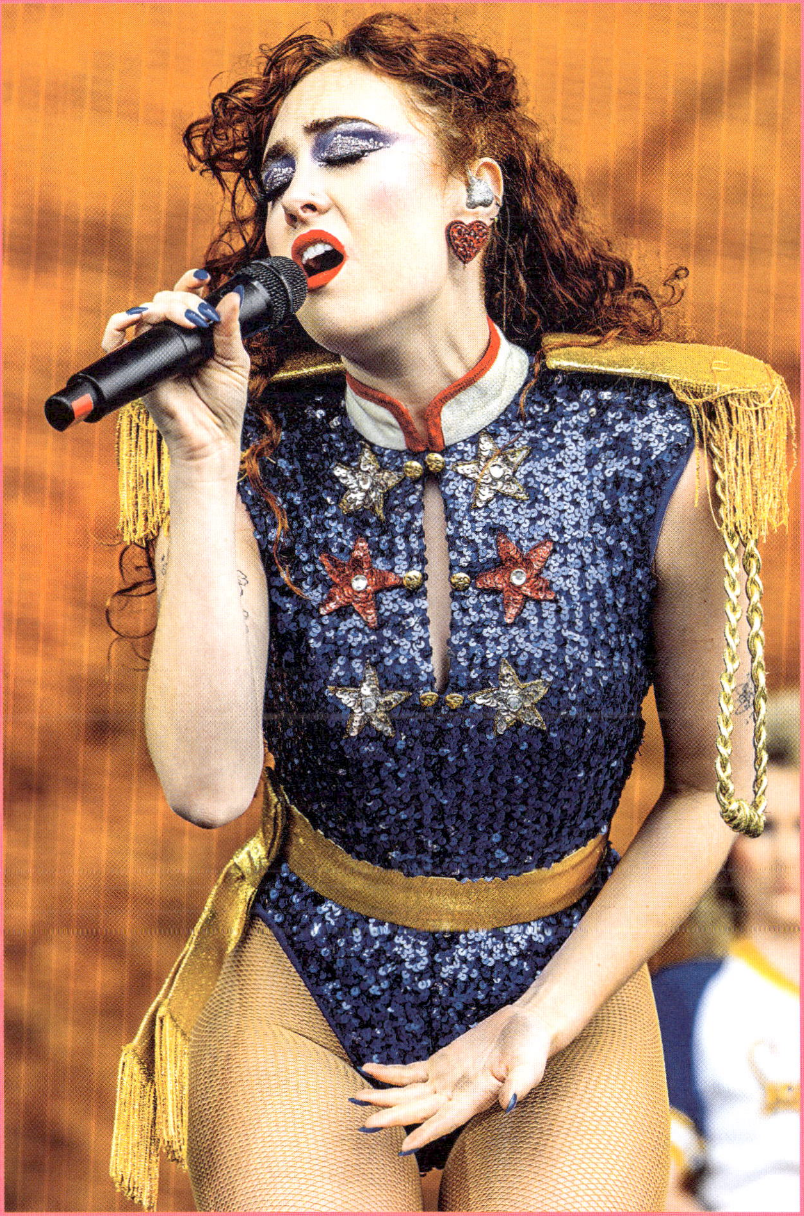

“I love the chic bitches, but I am not trying to be like that. I’m a Midwest bitch.”

CHAPPELL ROAN

Roan performs at London's Brixton Academy in September 2024 wearing a custom design by Zana Bayne.

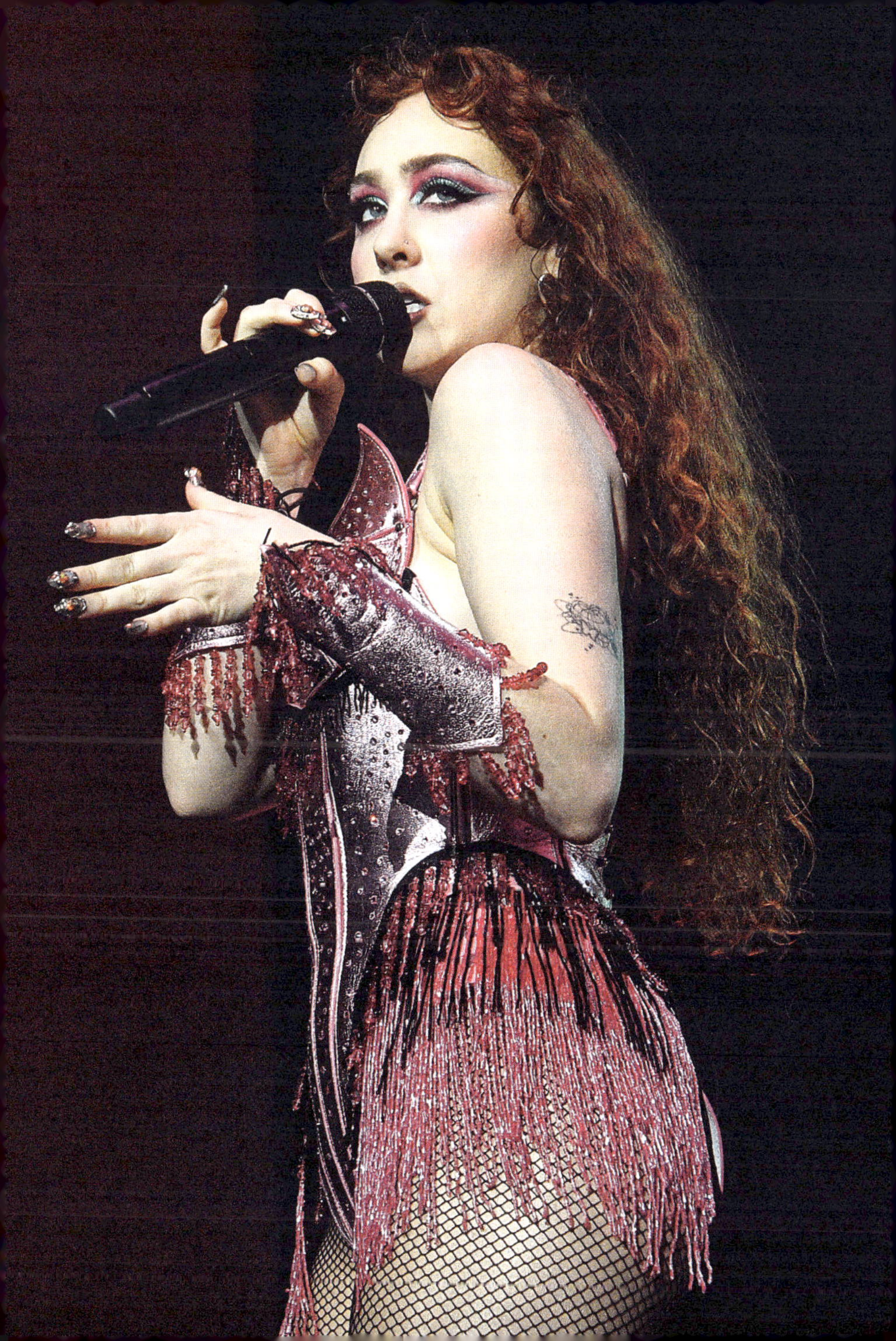

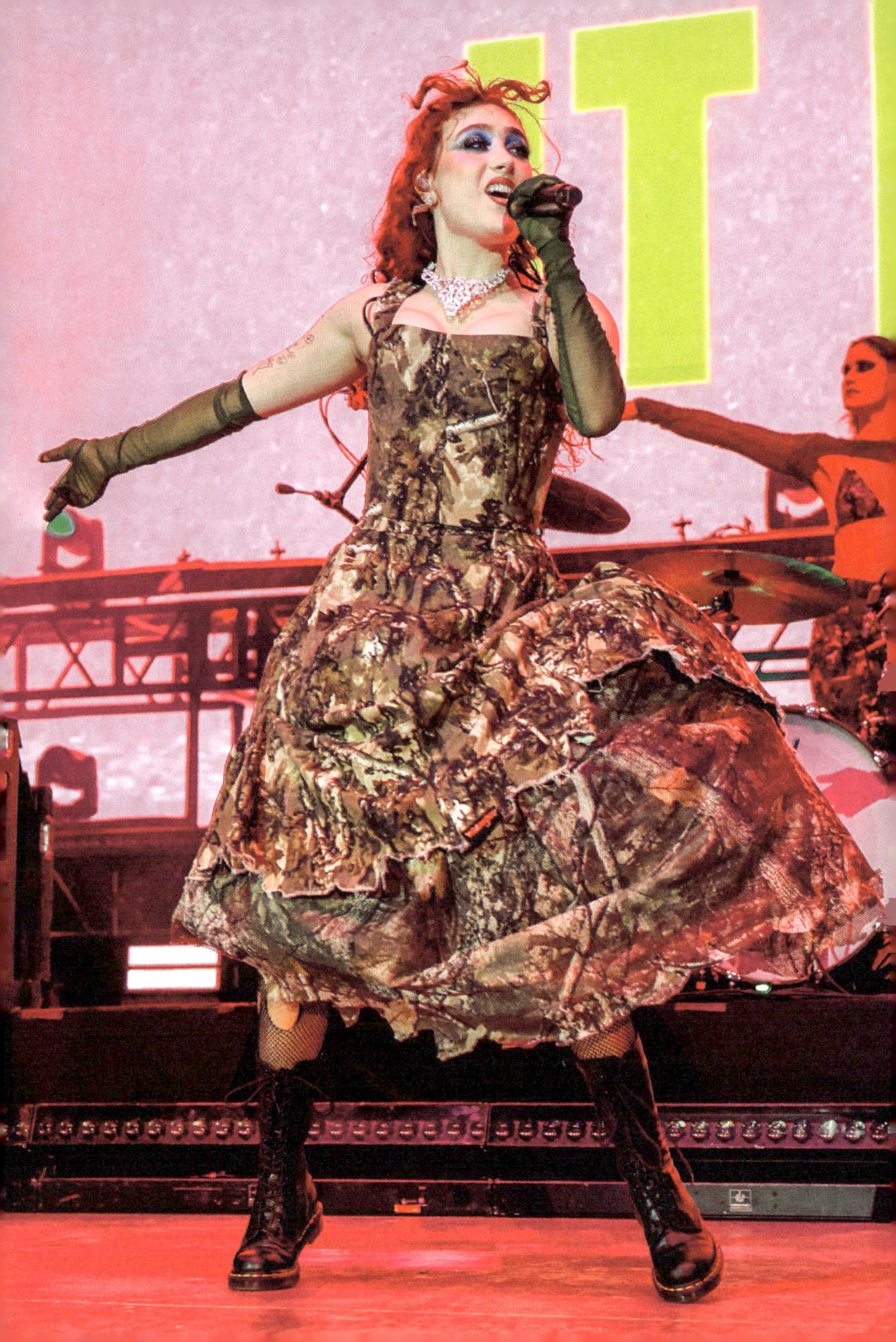

But perhaps the most Midwest Princess look of all appeared on stage during Roan's 2024 summer tour. Roan fused her penchant for ultrafeminine style with Americana sensibilities via a gown that would go on to become a firm fan favourite: the camo corset gown. Created by indie designer Sophia Hayes (better known as The CoolGirl NYC), the dress was crafted from deadstock Wrangler trousers. It resulted in a look that embodied Roan's love for fusing inspirations from her roots with her glam fantasies.

The Midwest princess theme was also one of the briefs set by Roan for some of her spring 2024 tour dates, sharing inspiration photos on her Instagram, which included Von Dutch trucker hats and plenty of rhinestone camo styles. Roan's distinctly American sentiments also reached to the off-duty looks featured on her social media accounts, where she can be seen sporting garments from labels such as Mossy Oak, a Missouri-based brand known for producing hunting equipment and function-first apparel.

The Midwest Princess theme came to life on stage in Franklin, Tennessee with Roan's camo corset gown, seen here at the sold-out October 2024 show.

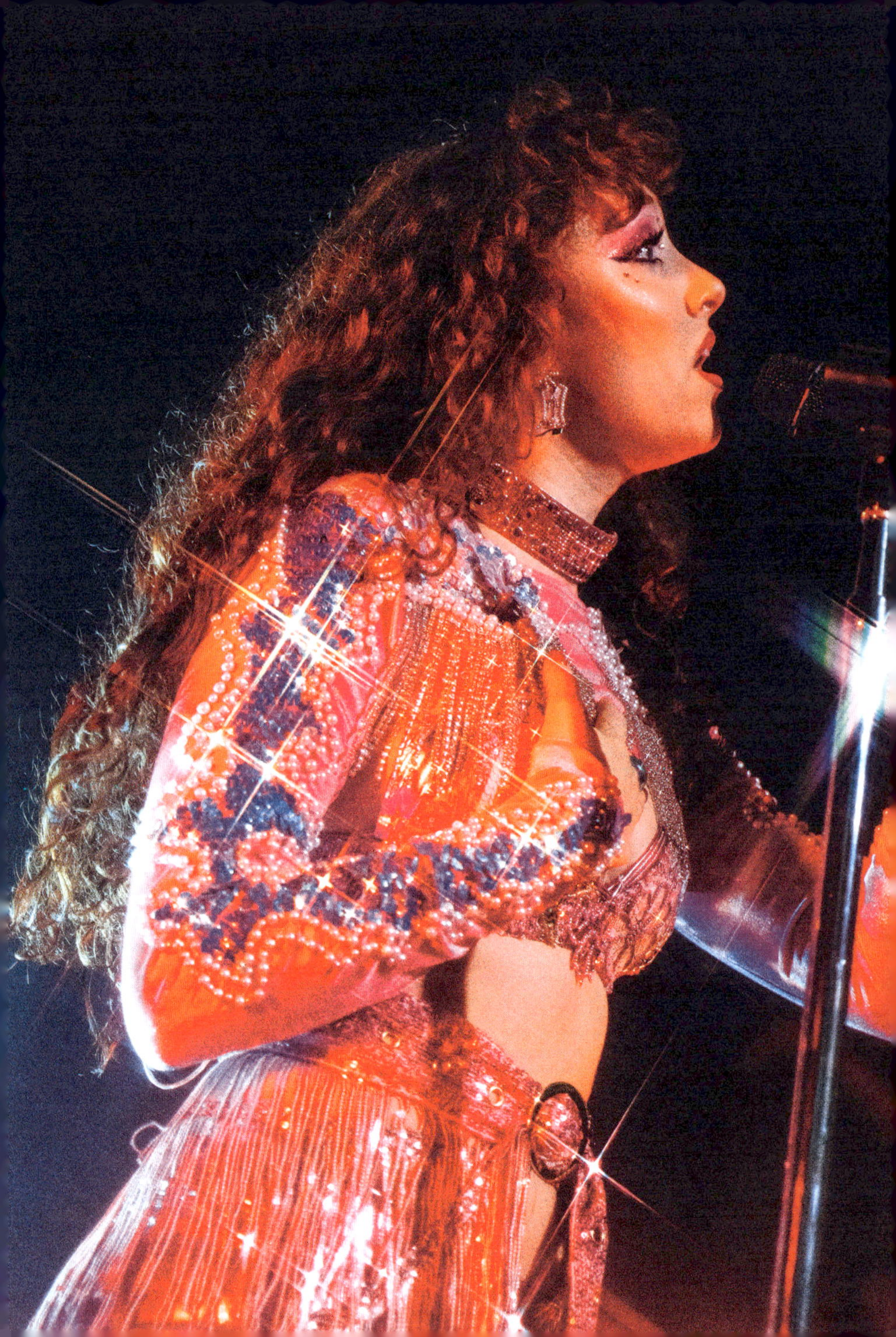

Westernwear and the world of cowboys and cowgirls have also played a key role in many of Roan's looks over the past few years. While opening for Olivia Rodrigo on her Sour Tour in spring 2022, and for Fletcher later that year, Roan often sported sequin bodysuits on stage with fringe details and matching cowboy hats and boots covered in shimmering sequins and gemstones. One of her favourite places to source cowboy hats appears to be from an Etsy seller by the name of RichMahoganyLife, whose clothes she has been seen wearing various times over the years. She featured on Roan's personal Instagram in August 2024 and onstage during her Midwest Princess Tour in 2023.

The 2024 Midwest Princess tour saw plenty of Western-inspired looks, including this one featuring pieces by costume label Jackalope Land and LA-based EastnWest label.

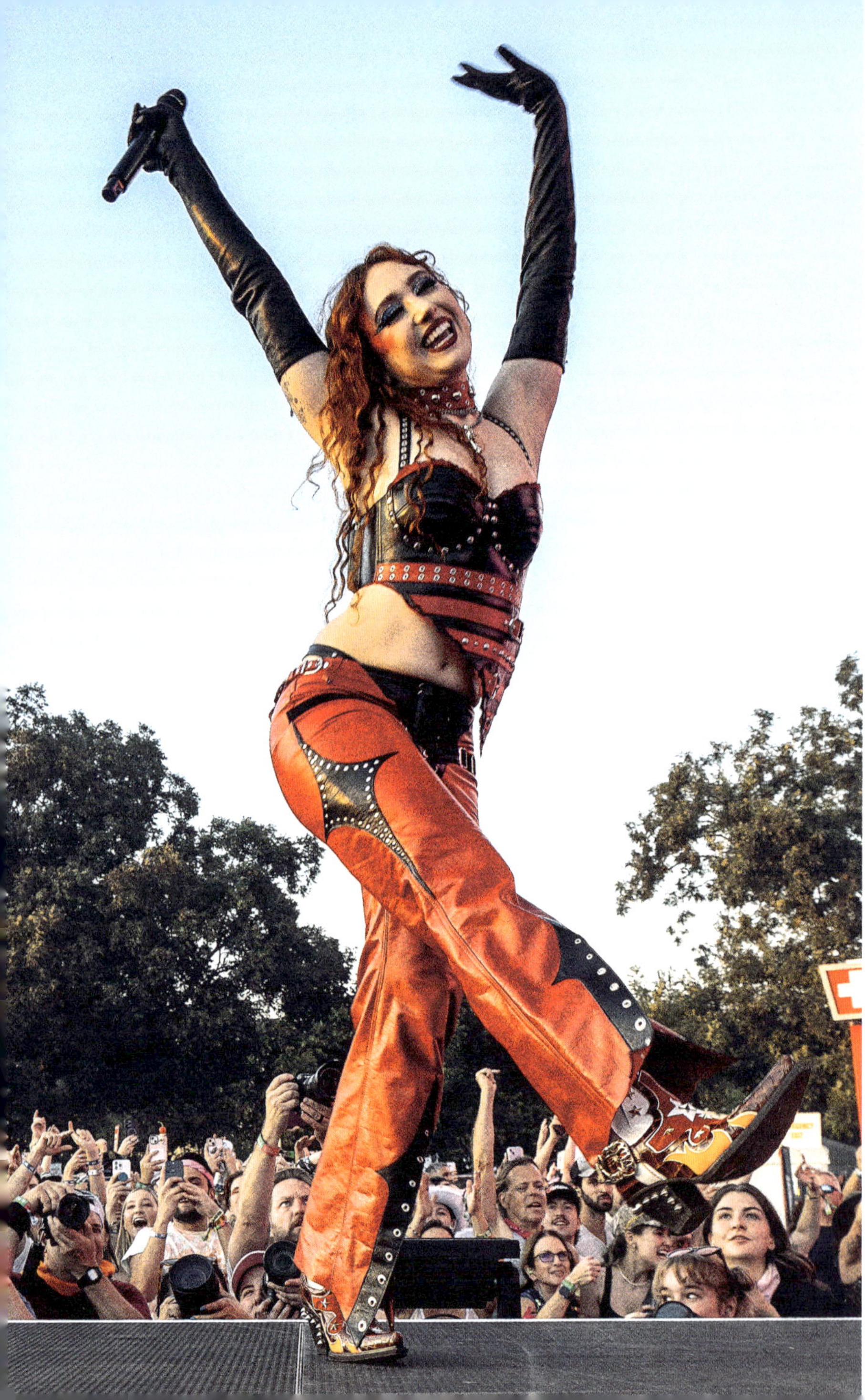

She has also been known to sport custom leather designs that nod to both fetishwear and Western staples, including her get-up for the Austin City Limits Festival in October 2024. The red bra and hot pants combo was lovingly crafted by Zana Bayne, reportedly with only three days' notice. The LA-based label used panels of red leather and white snakeskin-embossed leather with metal belt buckle features on the shoulder straps. The top-and-bottoms set was also styled with arm band sleeves and a matching choker. Leatheracci, the label founded by NYC legend Calvin Durham in the late 1960s, created the white leather chaps, while the wrist cuffs were provided by the Pennsylvania-based, independent accessories designer Sexman. The look also featured earrings from UK label g1000 and boots courtesy of Steve Madden. The make-up look was executed by the talented Ali Scarf, the make-up artist responsible for a number of Roan's hit looks including her 2024 *NME* magazine spread and her Elton John AIDS Foundation Academy Awards party performance in 2025.

For her second performance at the Austin City Limits Music Festival in October 2024, Roan sported a custom Zana Bayne ensemble with cowboy boots that appear to be from Christian Louboutin.

The Western theme continued through a number of further performances in late 2024 and into 2025, including Roan's *SNL* live show in November and her Grammy Awards performance in February 2025. The *SNL* performance look was another Zana Bayne design, this time with a pink and white gingham-style leather approach. Both the top and hot pants included blue ribbons in the side-tie feature and matching scalloped trim, adorned with gemstones courtesy of A-Morir, the gemstone experts behind plenty of famous looks from fellow style icons such as Beyoncé, Lady Gaga and Grace Jones. (The NYC-based studio also helped Roan's Met Gala 2025 look – quite literally – shine.) And, of course, the look was worn with matching cowboy boots. This pair were from the Texan label Lane, with customization to fit with the two-piece outfit. The look also won a place in many fans' favourite outfit lists due to the giant wig, and many were quick to highlight its vintage pin-up aesthetic. The creation, by Ghastly Wigs, featured hand-tied streaks and highlights, while celebrity nail artist Juan Alvear provided the matching nails.

In February 2025, Roan attended music's biggest night of the year, the Grammys. The event saw plenty of wardrobe changes from the pop star and it was her "Pink Pony Club" performance style that gave a firm nod to cowgirl fashion. Roan started the song sat upon a giant pink pony (of course), wearing another custom Zana Bayne number alongside a rhinestone cowboy hat and shimmering Steve Madden cowboy boots. Stylist Genesis Webb shared with *Vogue*, "Chappell established rodeo clown as the thematic foundation for the performance, which provided a conceptual starting point. She shared a Pinterest board of reference images, primarily featuring Galliano and Guo Pei." Bayne also spoke to *Vogue* about the evening's look, sharing, "I combined aspects of all the silhouettes we've done on her in the last year and make a 'super Chappell' look." Bayne continued, "Throughout the costume are special details to bring the rodeo clown princess fantasy into reality, with everything crafted in my downtown Los Angeles studio."

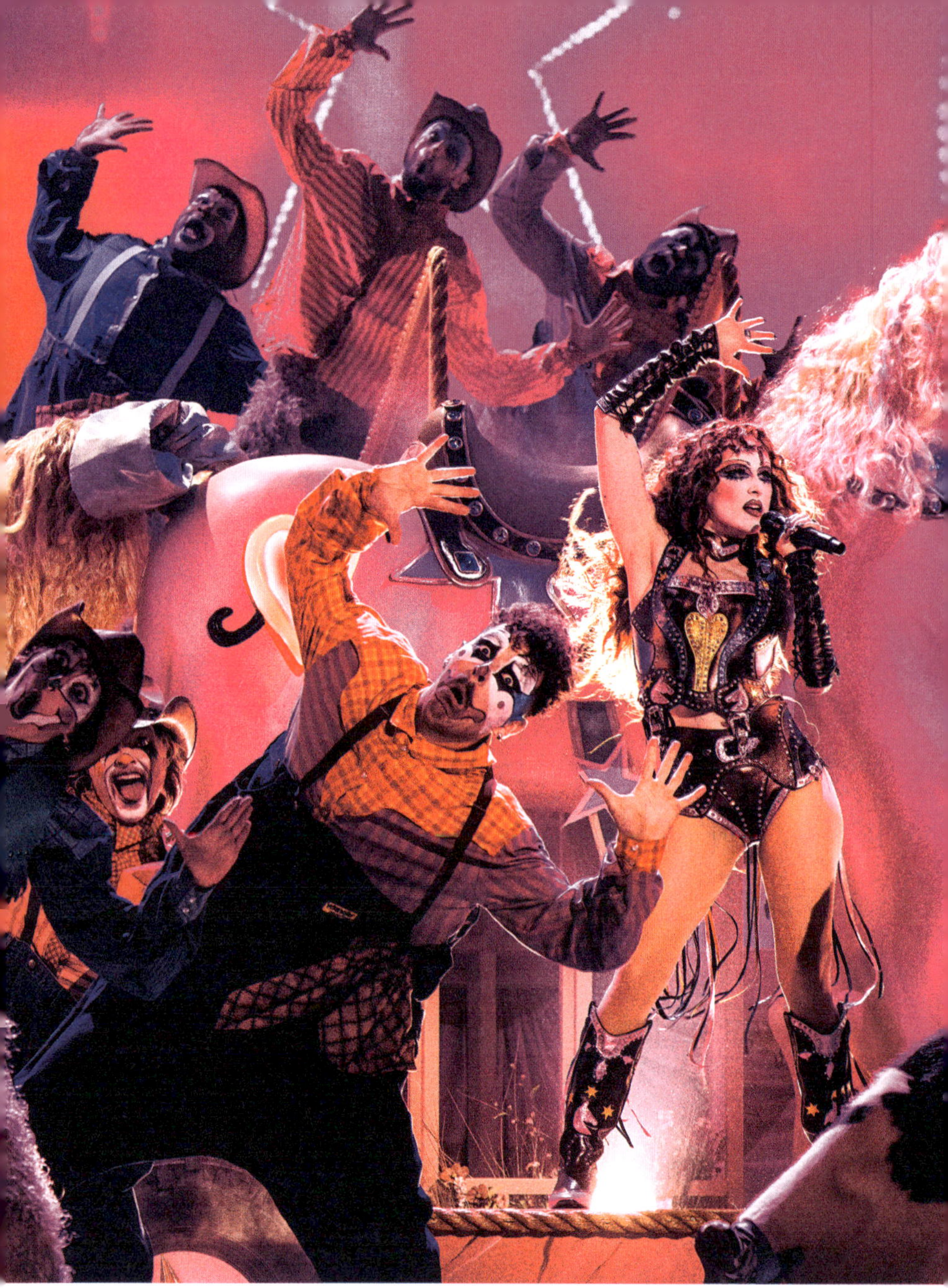

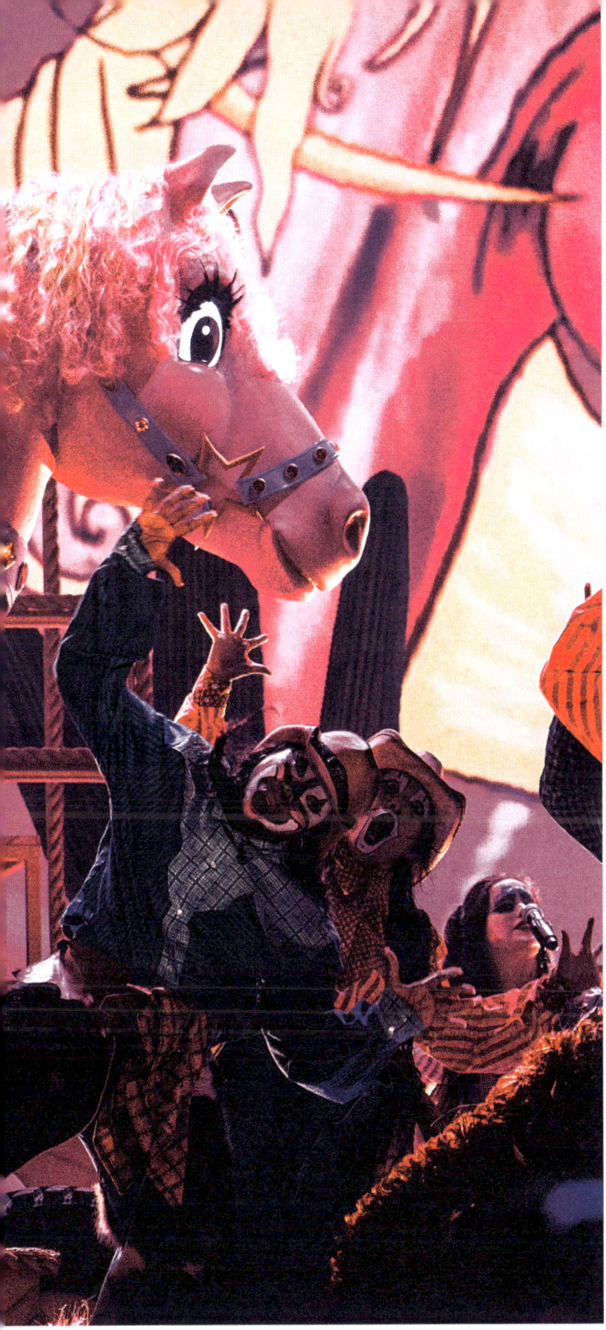

Stylist Genesis Webb brought the rodeo clown theme to life with a custom Zana Bayne design worn by Roan, while Chloë Royer styled Roan's band in custom pieces by Age of Aquarius.

Burlesque / theatre

Roan has publicly noted the 1995 film *Showgirls* – a camp classic which focuses on the life of a young woman trying to make it in Las Vegas as a dancer – as being one of the biggest inspirations behind her public persona. "I'm very inspired by that movie, the costumes and make-up", Roan told the *Daily Californian* in a 2023 interview.

Roan's burlesque influences can be seen in a number of her most iconic looks, notably that of her *The Tonight Show Starring Jimmy Fallon* appearance in October 2024. Roan appeared wearing what fans have dubbed the "swan" look, featuring dramatic feathers and a snow-kissed make-up style. Callie Holtermann of *The New York Times* reported that Genesis Webb initially presented Roan with inspirations for the look after watching the 2020 Uldus Bakhtiozina film *The Fisherman's Daughter*. The Russian director comes from an arts background and is known for creating stunning visuals through photography and costume design. This resulted in her first feature film becoming known for its dramatic wardrobe and strong aesthetic elements. Roan and Webb worked together to infuse a number of other influences into the look, including the 2003 animated Barbie version of *Swan Lake* as well as Alexander McQueen's 2009 The Horn of Plenty collection and its accompanying runway show. Webb then looked to designer Gunnar Deatherage to create the white outfit and sourced the contrasting black look from design duo The Blonds.

Roan in sequin bodysuit from partywear label Easy Tiger during her performance on Olivia Rodrigo's GUTS tour in February 2023.

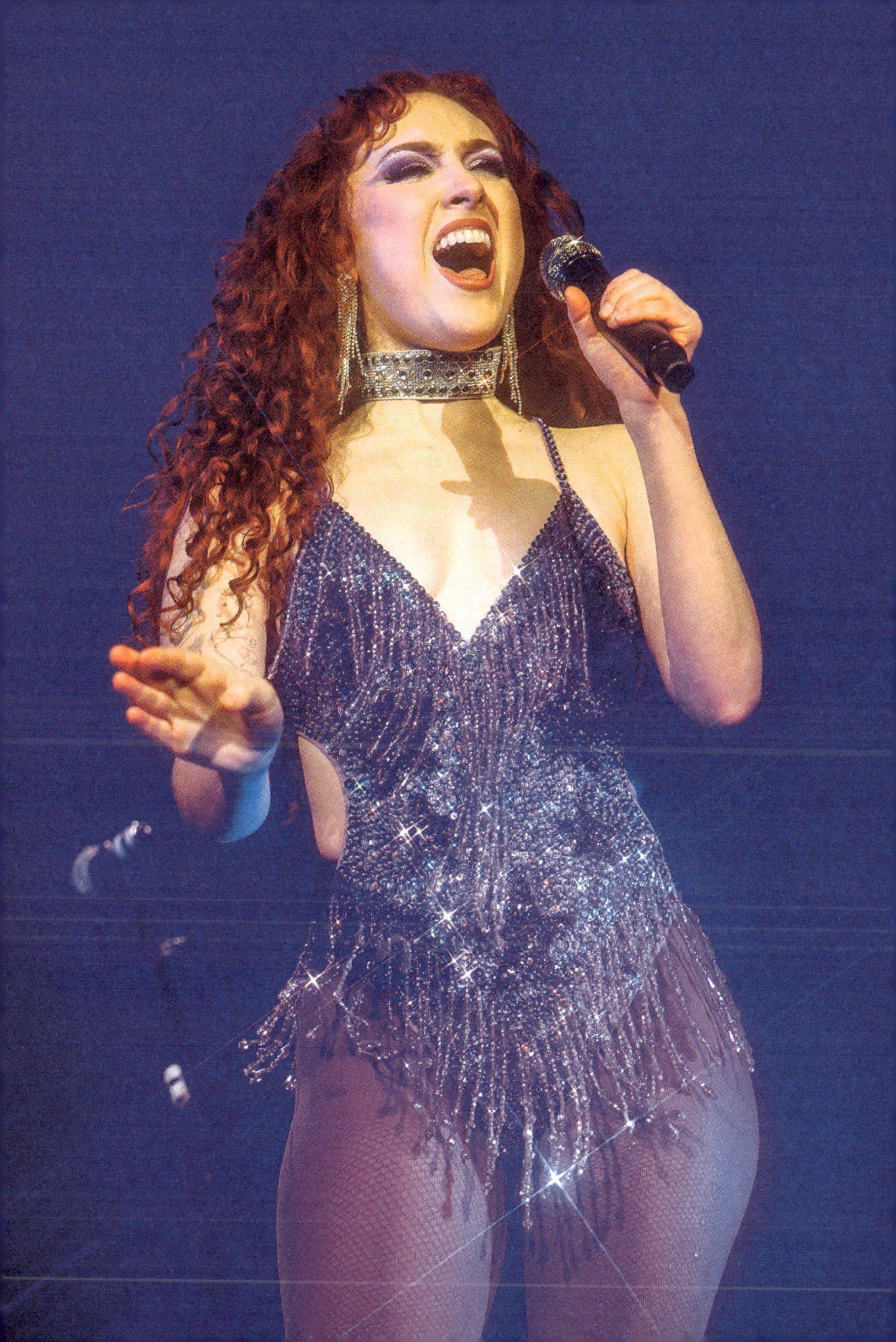

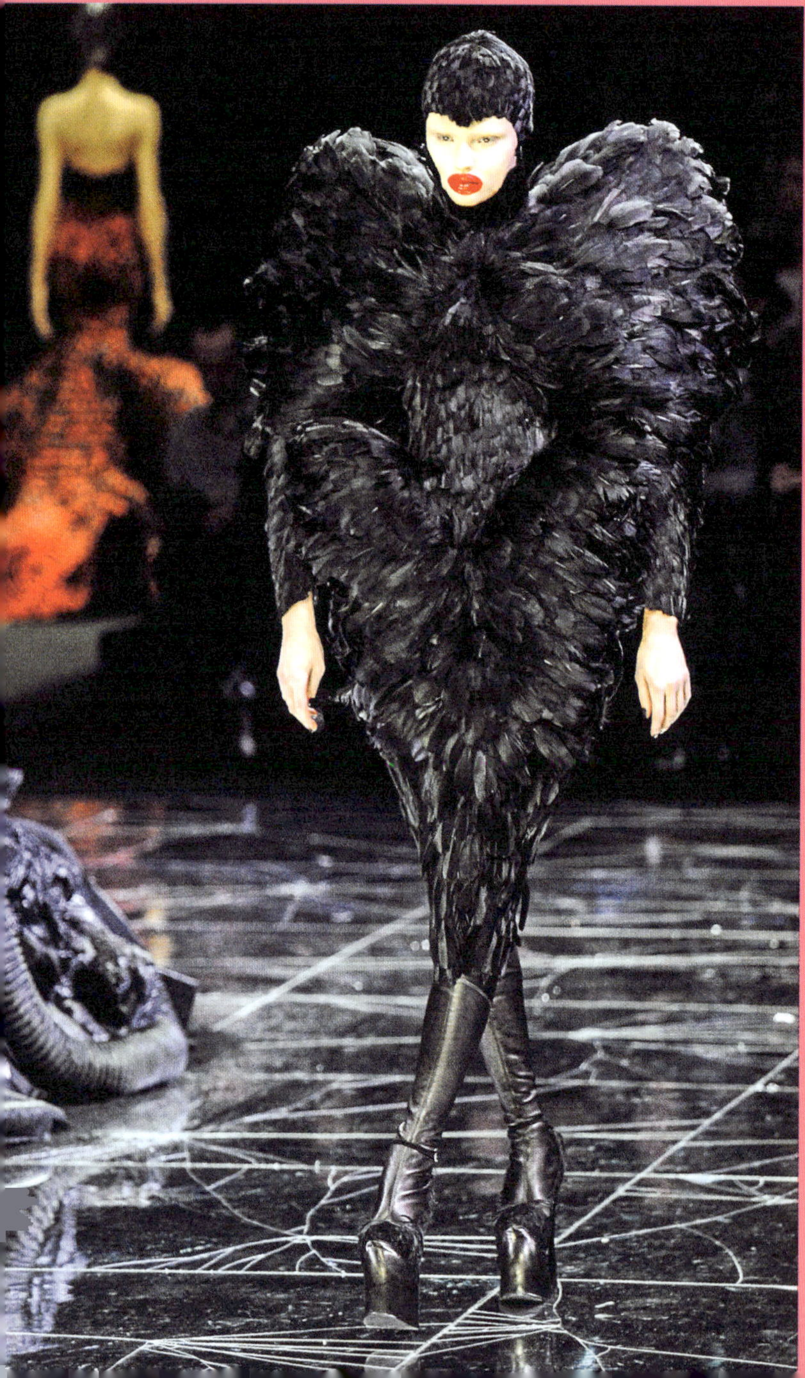

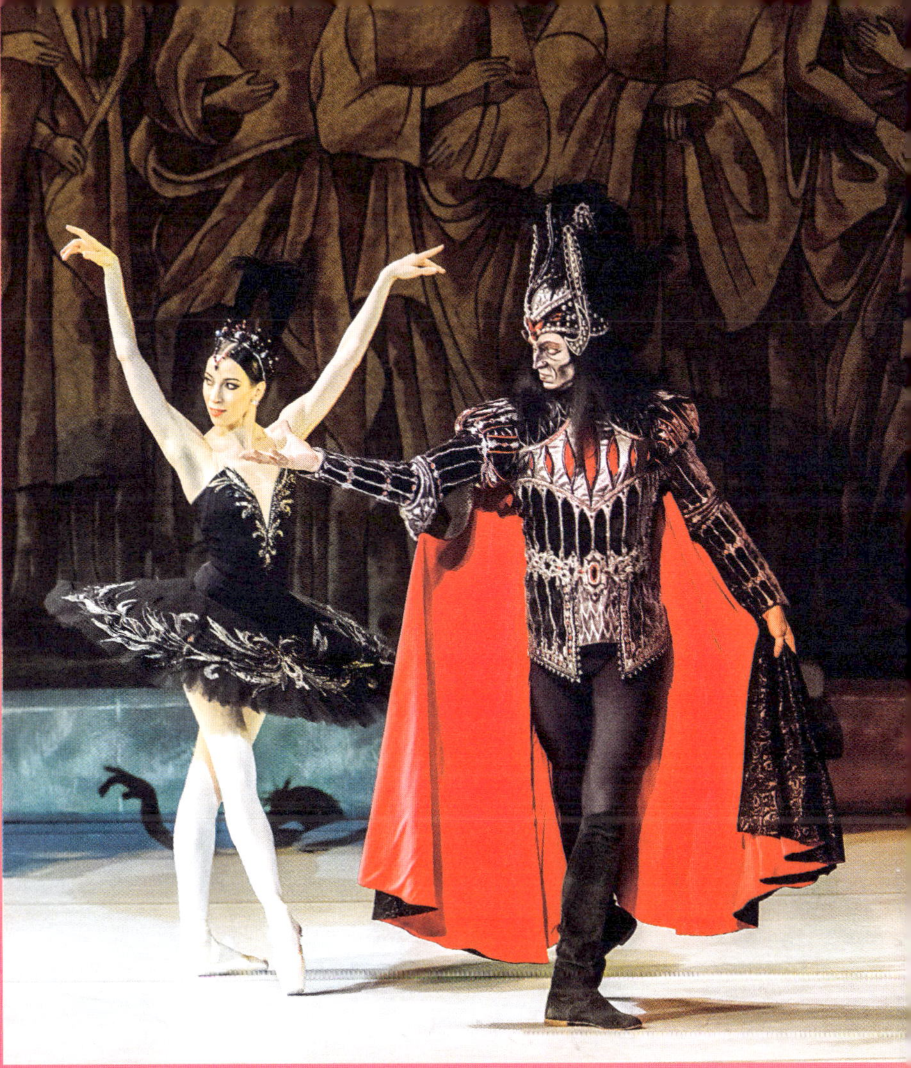

OPPOSITE A model walks the runway of Alexander McQueen's Autumn/Winter 2009 collection in Paris, on 9 March 2009.

ABOVE Viktoria Tereshkina and Andrei Yermakov perform in the Mariinsky Ballet production of *Swan Lake* at the BAM Howard Gilman Opera House in Brooklyn, New York, on 15 January 2015.

The final look of the evening took a step away from the more traditional theatre of ballet and entered the burlesque realm with an ensemble that was heavily influenced by dancers from the legendary Casino De Paris, resulting in a look that Webb noted as her favourite of 2024. Webb again employed the talents of Gunnar Deatherage to create the pieces, including the larger-than-life Napoleon-esque headpiece.

"There were these gorgeous photos of dancers from the Casino De Paris from 1915 that almost felt like paintings ... the shapes were unique and imaginative, and it was all very flashy in an old-world kind of way, so we decided to combine elements from a few of those photos, and then I added in some of my own ideas that felt complementary to the concept", Deatherage told *InStyle*. He went on to share, "The hat saw many iterations before landing on the final look, but we love it in all of its lampshade/Napoleon glory!" Deatherage revealed that the look took over 500 hours to create, making it the most labour-intensive project of his entire career. The bodysuit offered cut-out panels crafted from soft velvet and adorned with plenty of fringe trims. Attached at the waist were dragonfly wings which Deatherage sculpted from layers of foam before sewing them together and mounting them onto a leather belt. The finishing touches came from 1,000 chartreuse crystals.

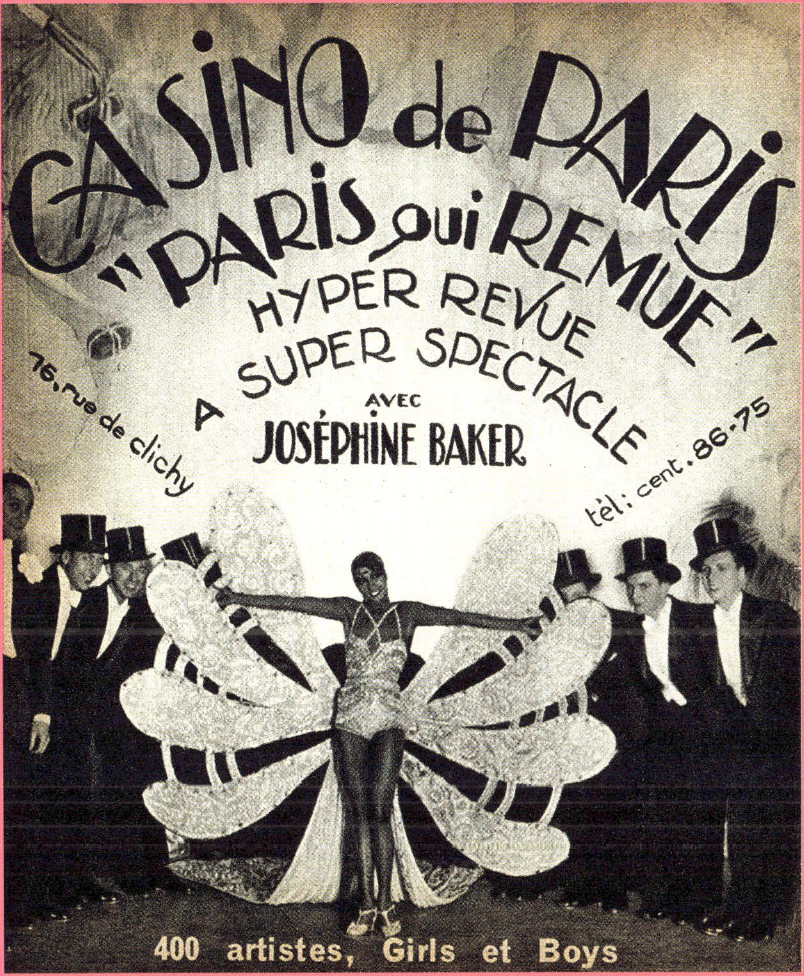

Josephine Baker featured on the cover of a presentation booklet for the Casino de Paris in 1931.

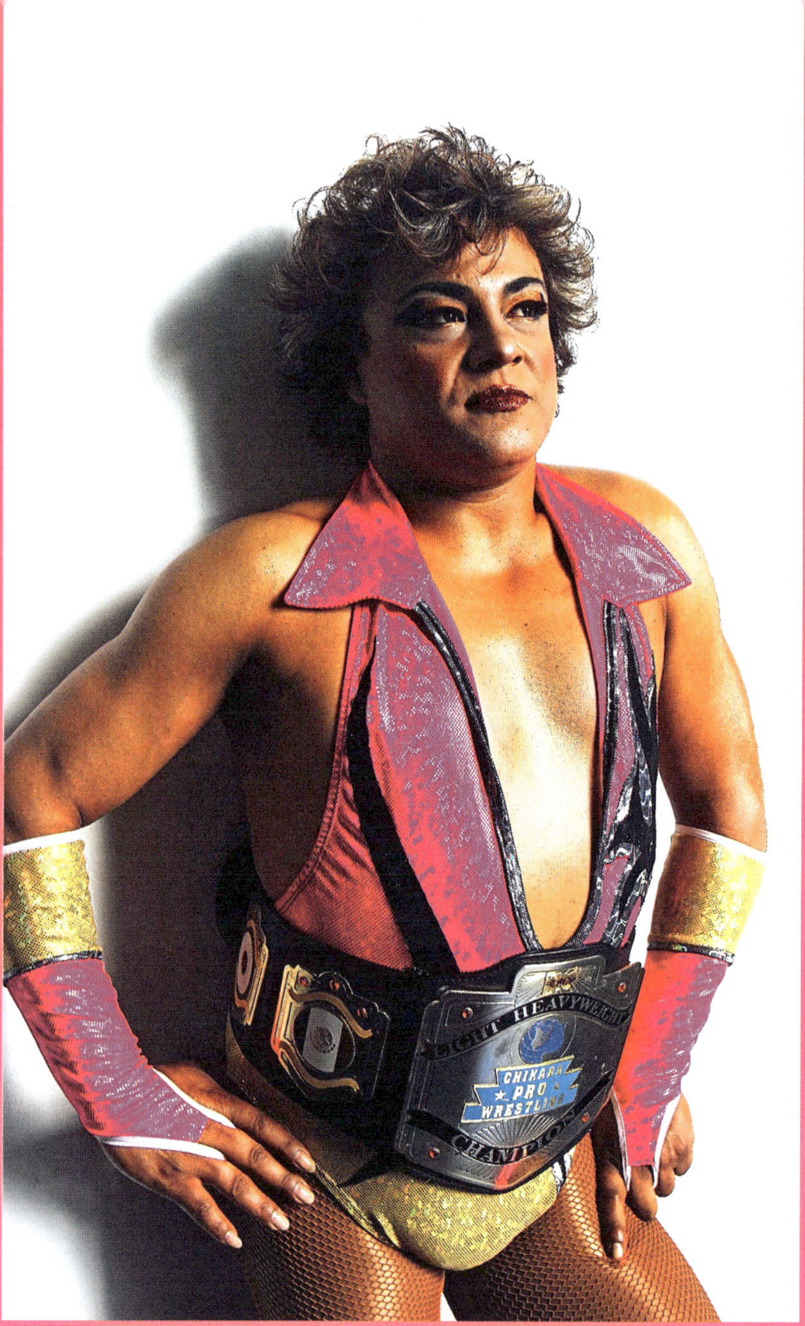
CHIKARA
PRO

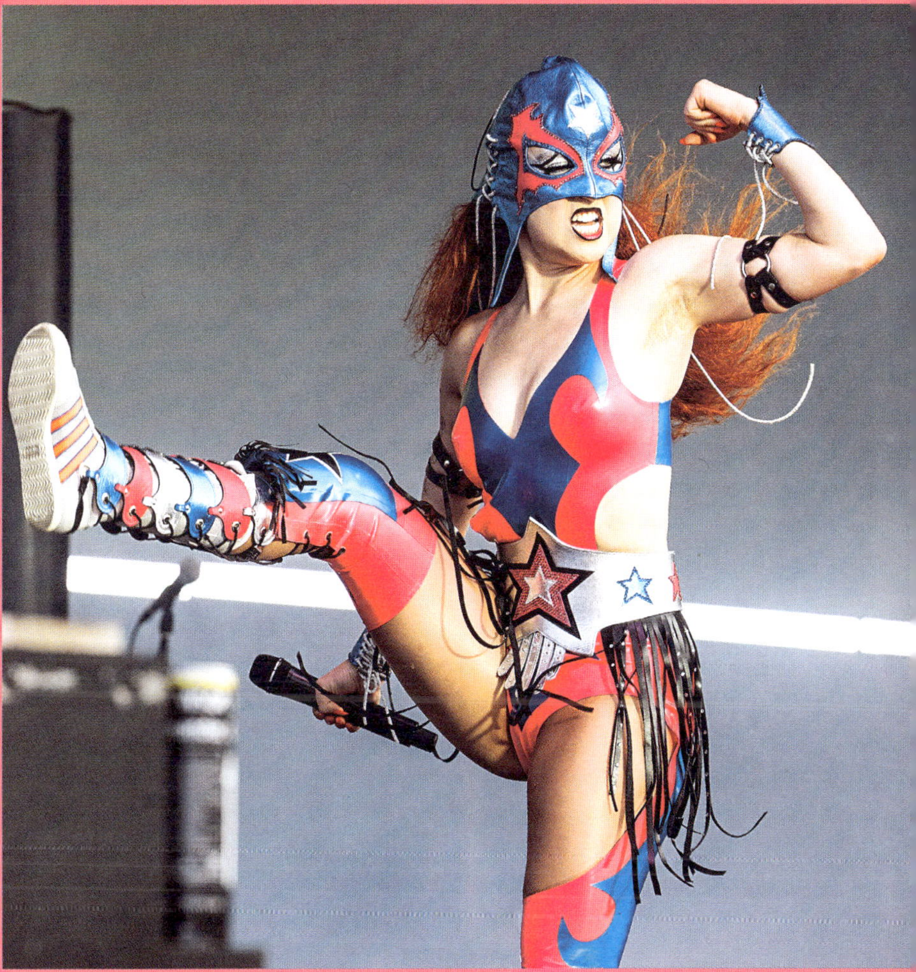

OPPOSITE Lucha Libre wrestler Cassandro in London on 5 June 2008.

ABOVE Roan's knee-high Adidas Japan VH-style trainers, mask and belt complete an authentic wrestler look.

Another type of performer that Roan has referenced in her looks is that of Lucha Libre Mexican wrestlers, which she sported during her record-breaking Lollapalooza performance in August 2024. The set brought in a whopping 100,000 spectators – more than the festival had ever gathered before. Webb brought in the talents of Zana Bayne to create the latex bodysuit and matching face mask combo. Roan has spoken fondly of this look, notably in her *Call Her Daddy* podcast interview when she remarked playfully, "The Lollapalooza one was so fucking awesome because I got to wear tennis shoes." The tennis shoes referenced were the knee-high Adidas Japan VH-style trainers, adorned with custom leather panels to match the bodysuit and knee pads. Even style icons appreciate some practical footwear from time to time it seems. Some have pointed out that aside from the fact that Chicago is often seen as the home of American wrestling, the look may also be a nod to a particular area of Mexican wrestling (referred to in Spanish as *exóticos*) known for its drag-like sensibilities, which brings traditionally feminine elements into male performers' costumes. *Exóticos* can also be said to be key players in driving forward acceptance and inclusion for Mexico's LGBTQI+ population.

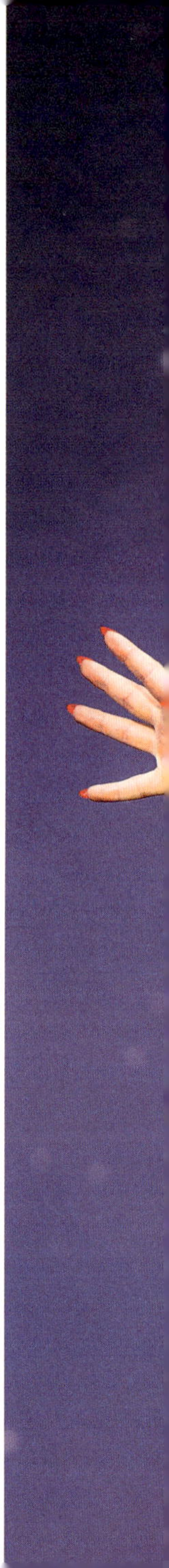

Roan performs at Chicago's Lollapalooza in August 2024 wearing a latex bodysuit by Zana Bayne.

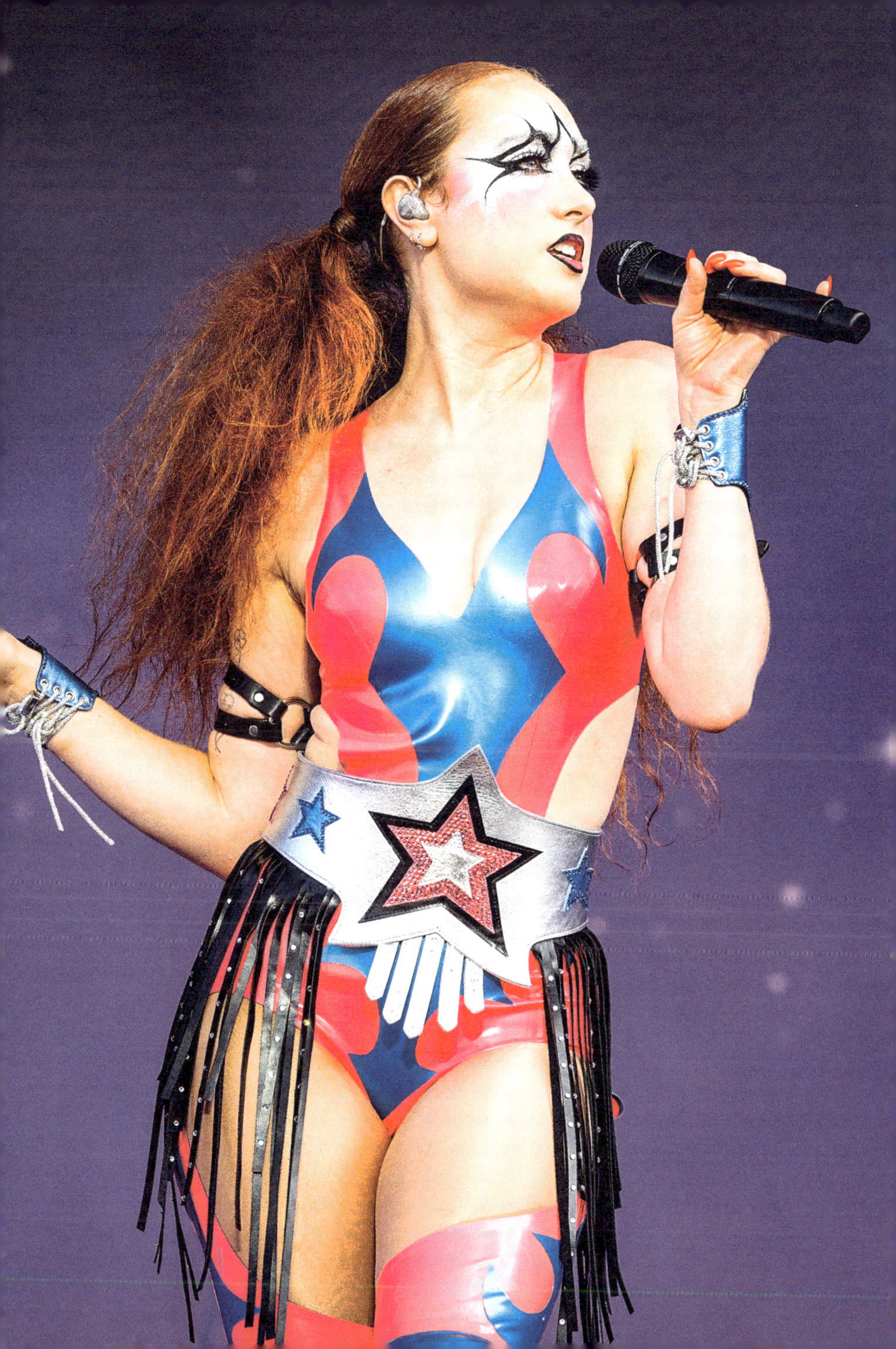

Drag performers

Not unlike the definition of camp, the definition of drag can be a contentious topic. The definition of drag, as in a drag queen or king, is usually defined as a type of performance which revolves around someone dressing up in an exaggerated manner to mimic a gender expression, usually in the name of entertainment. In his article in *The Conversation* that addresses the question of whether women can be drag queens, theatre-maker and PhD candidate Jonathan Graffam-O'Meara stated, "Drag can be a performance of the opposite gender, but it can also hold space for diverse performances of gender to be explored. Where all those living within, in-between and beyond the gender binary can engage in playful and powerful imaginative acts that offer a momentary escape into the utopic and euphoric."

One of Roan's favourite drag artists, Sasha Colby, attends the *RuPaul's Drag Race* season 15 finale in Los Angeles, California, on 1 April 2023.

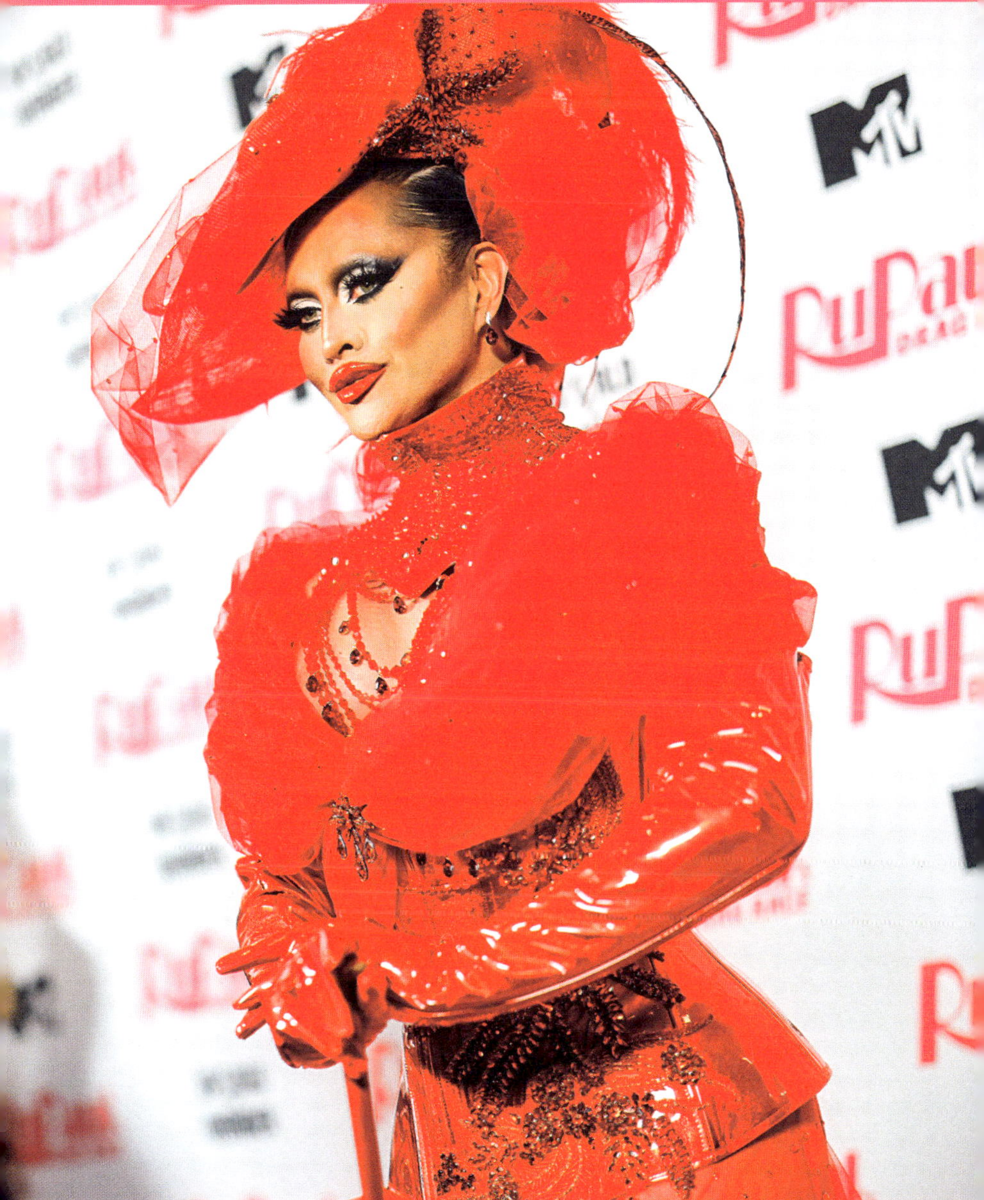

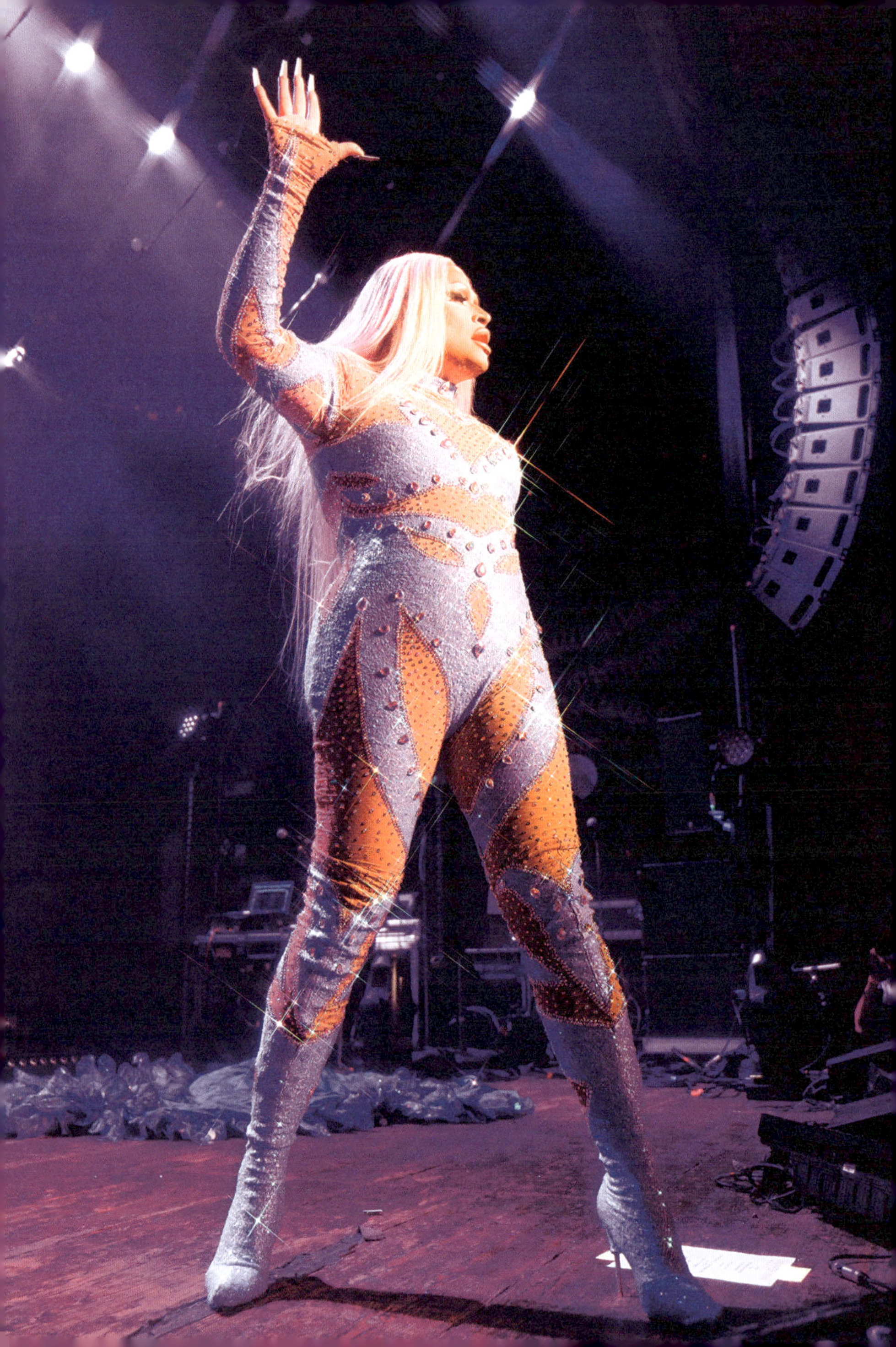

“Drag is camp and camp is the most fun thing in the world, and that is what I want my project to feel like.”

CHAPPELL ROAN TO ANTHONY KOZLOWSKI, *ATWOOD MAGAZINE*, AUGUST 2024

Drag artist Veronica Pop opens for Chappell Roan at the House of Blues in Chicago on 5 October 2023.

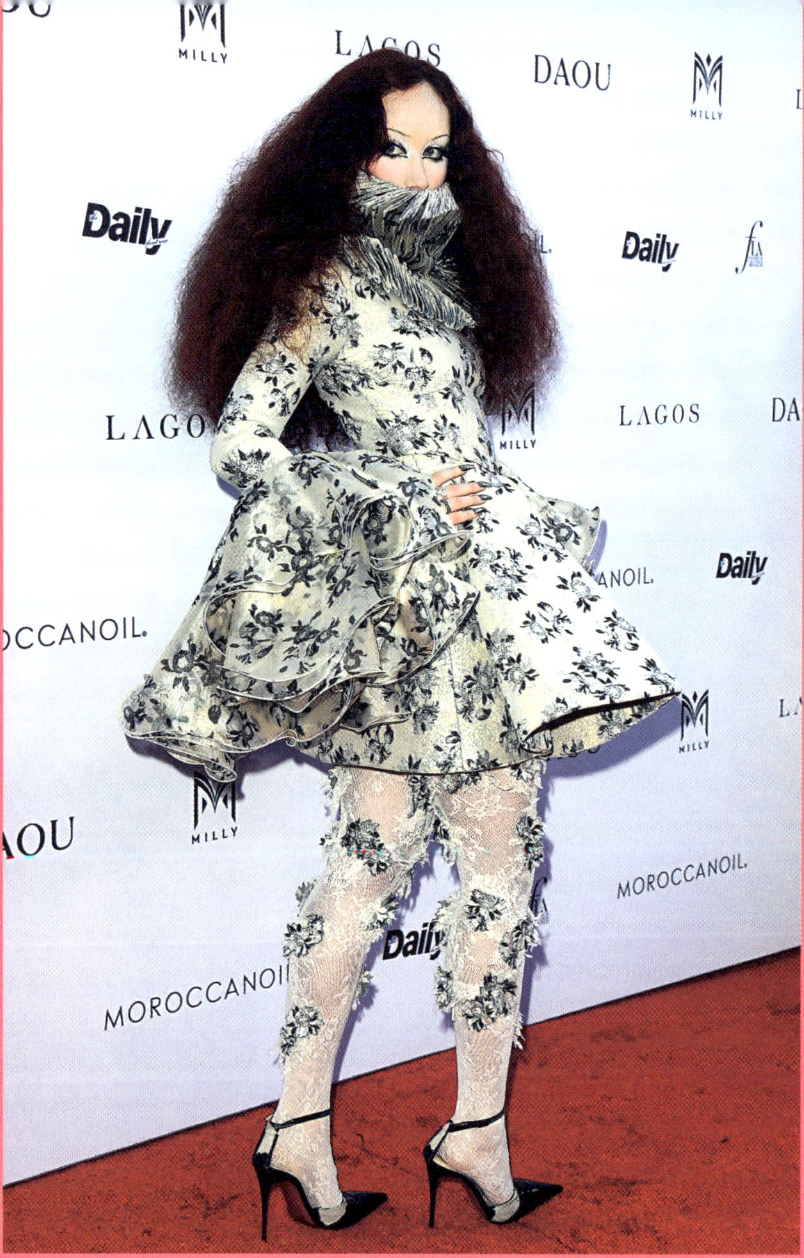

Roan attends the Annual Fashion Los Angeles Awards in April 2025, wearing an Alexander McQueen dress with pumps by Christian Louboutin.

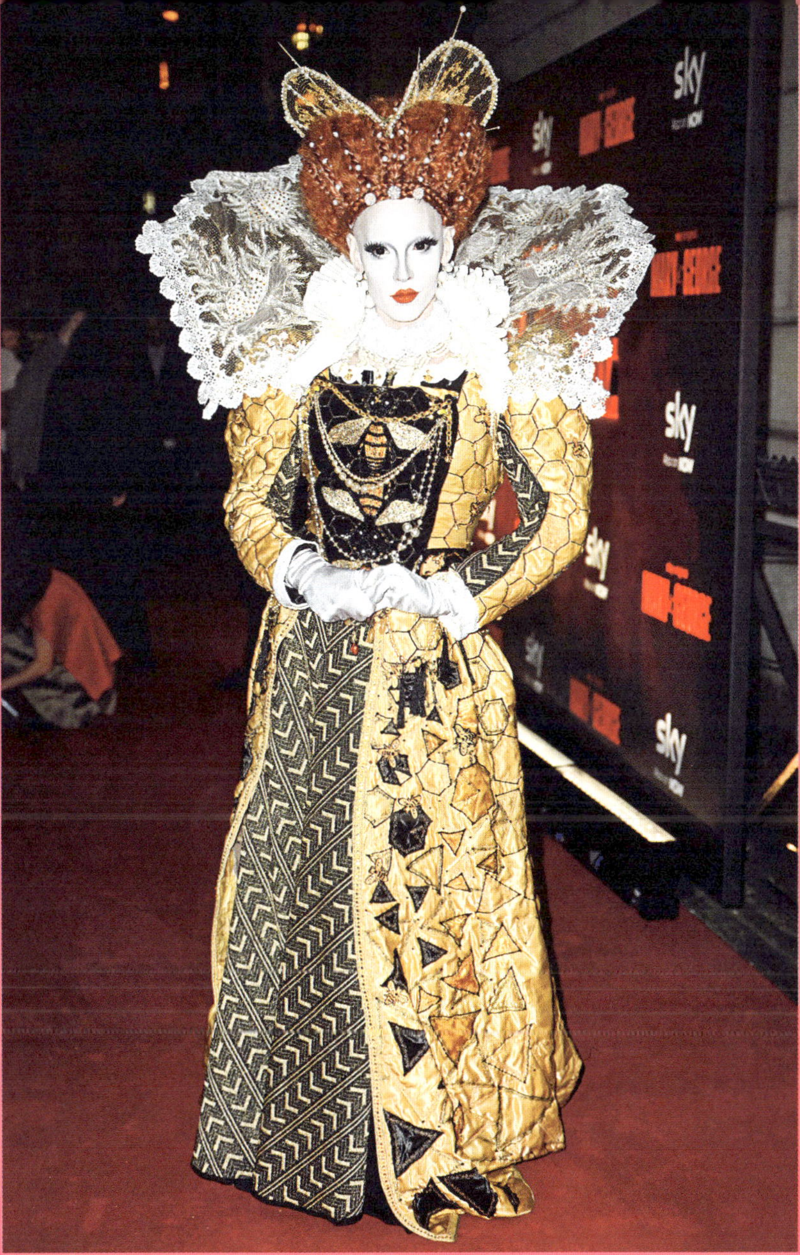

Drag artists have long looked to bygone eras and iconic historical figures for inspiration, proven here with British drag queen Cheddar Gorgeous referencing Queen Elizabeth I at the premier of *Mary and George* in London, on 28 February 2024.

“Drag allows me to feel free, and it makes me unafraid to be loud, queer and hyperfeminine. I’ve never fully understood why women shouldn’t be allowed to do drag, because – yes, I do drag! It makes me feel good and free”, Roan shared in a 2024 interview with Vanja Kadic of *Annabelle* magazine. When browsing through many of Roan’s looks, drag can easily be pinpointed as a key theme worthy of analysis. Roan has spoken about her personal relationship with drag many times, including on the Canadian podcast *Q with Tom Power* where she recalled a pivotal conversation with London-based drag queen Crayola. Roan recalls that by Crayola referring to the Chappell Roan character as a drag queen, partially due to the transformational element of stepping into the persona, Roan has been able to adopt the identity as a drag artist and see it as a project which she can tap into as a performer.

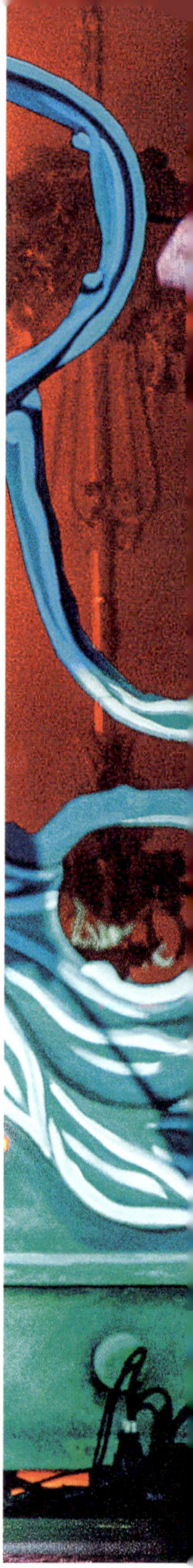

Design duo James Nguyen and AC Gottlieb crafted this layered look for Roan’s 2025 Visions of Damsels & Other Dangerous Things tour, seen here onstage at Way Out West in Gothenburg, Sweden, on 9 August 2025.

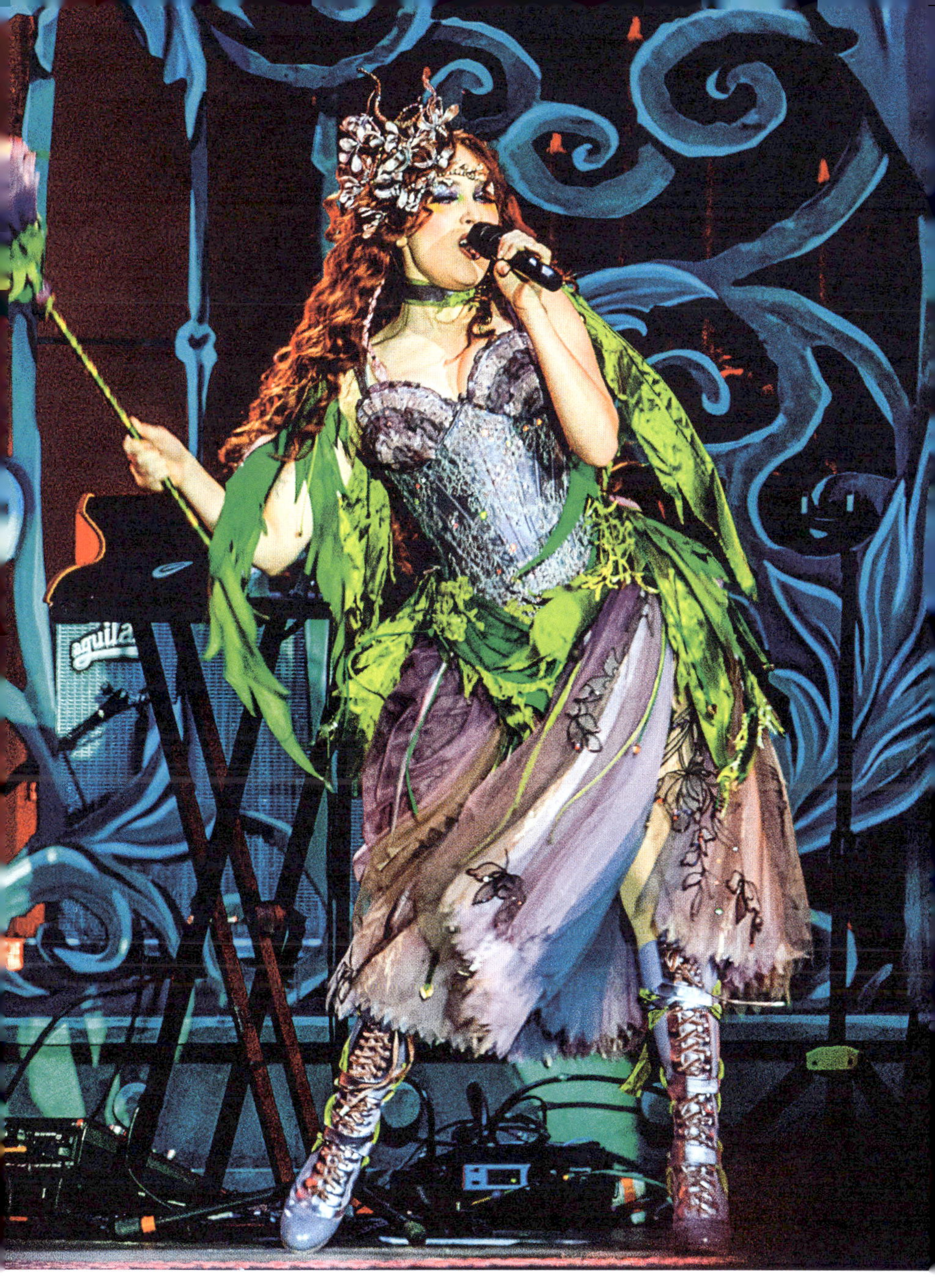

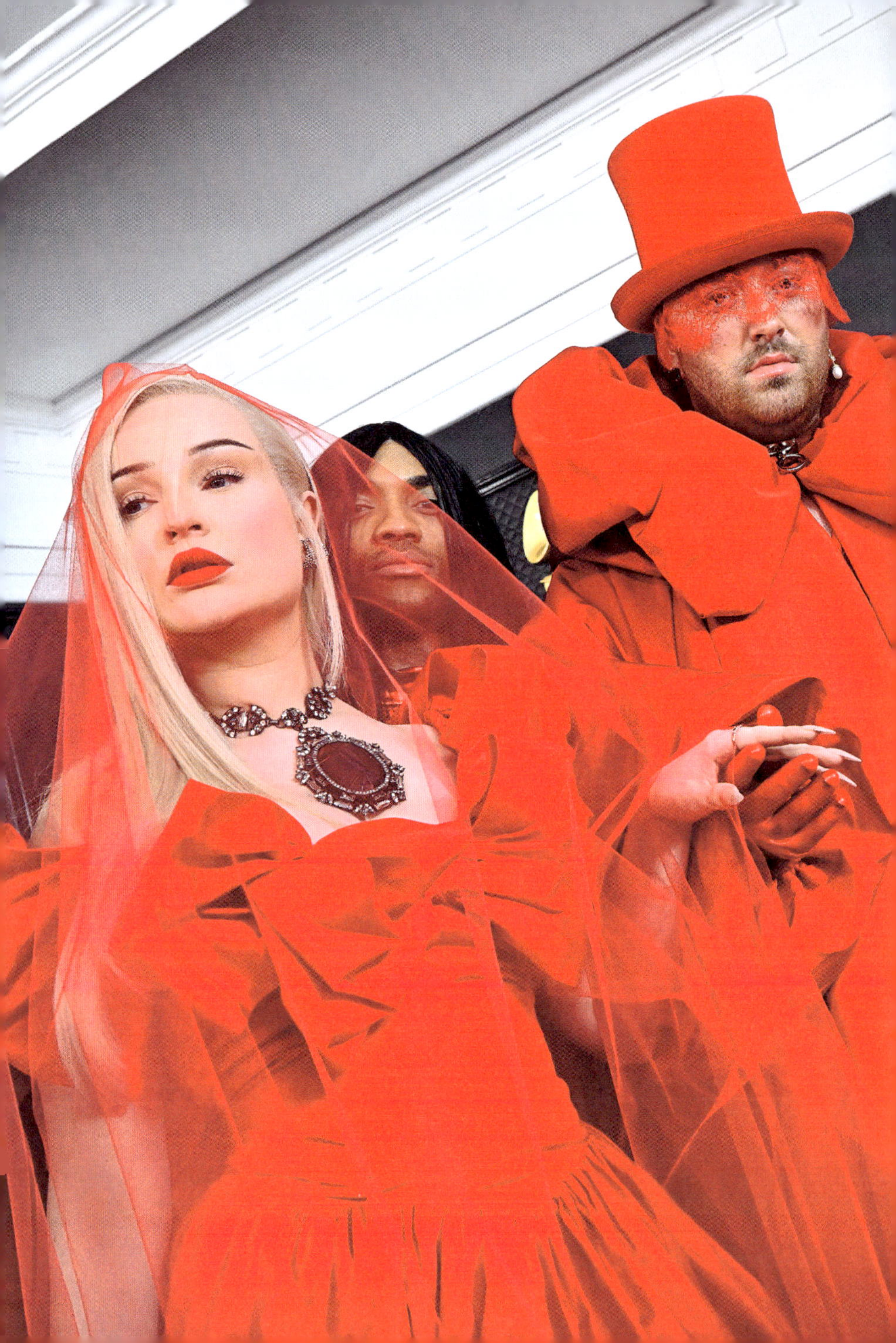

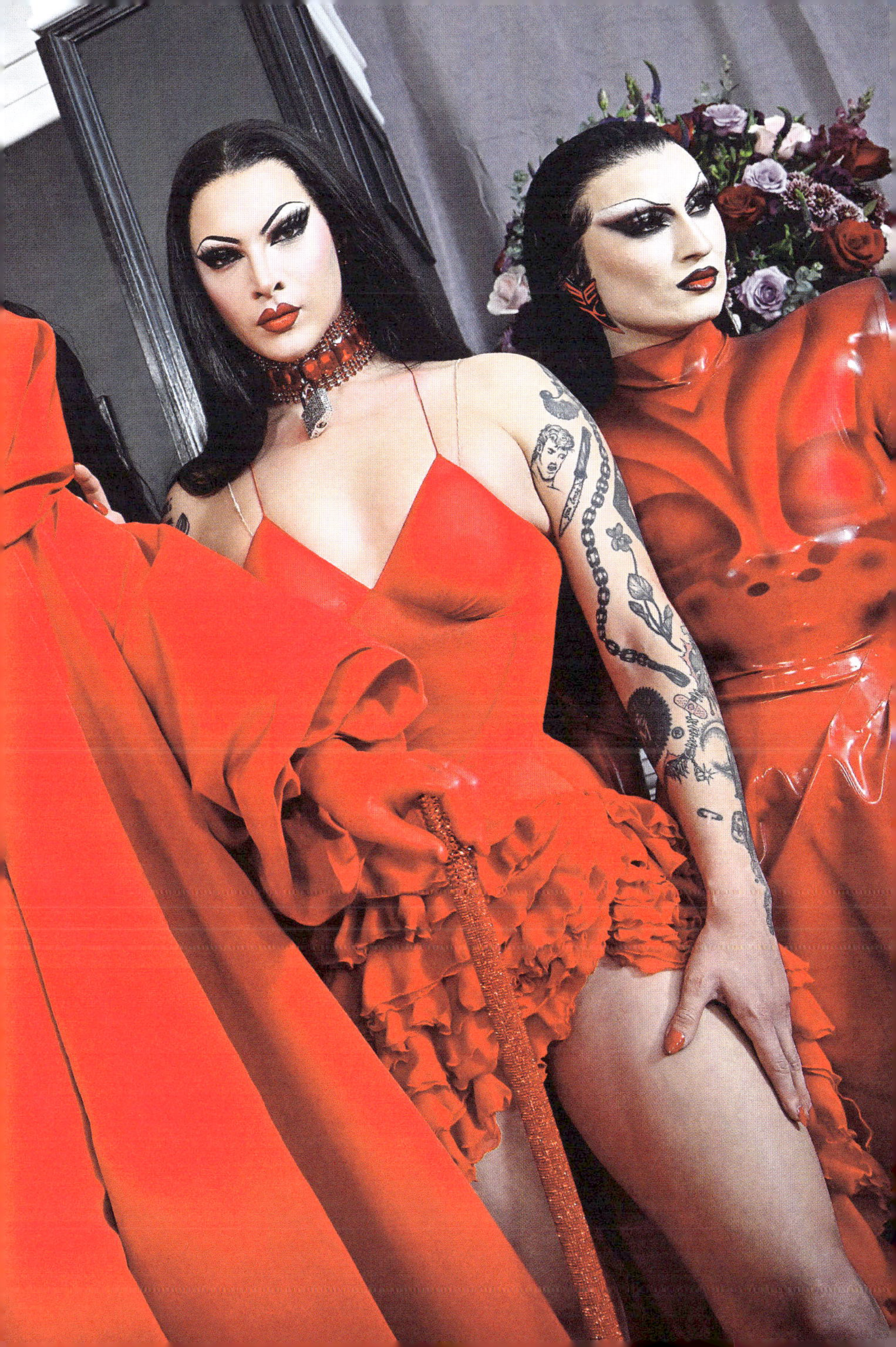

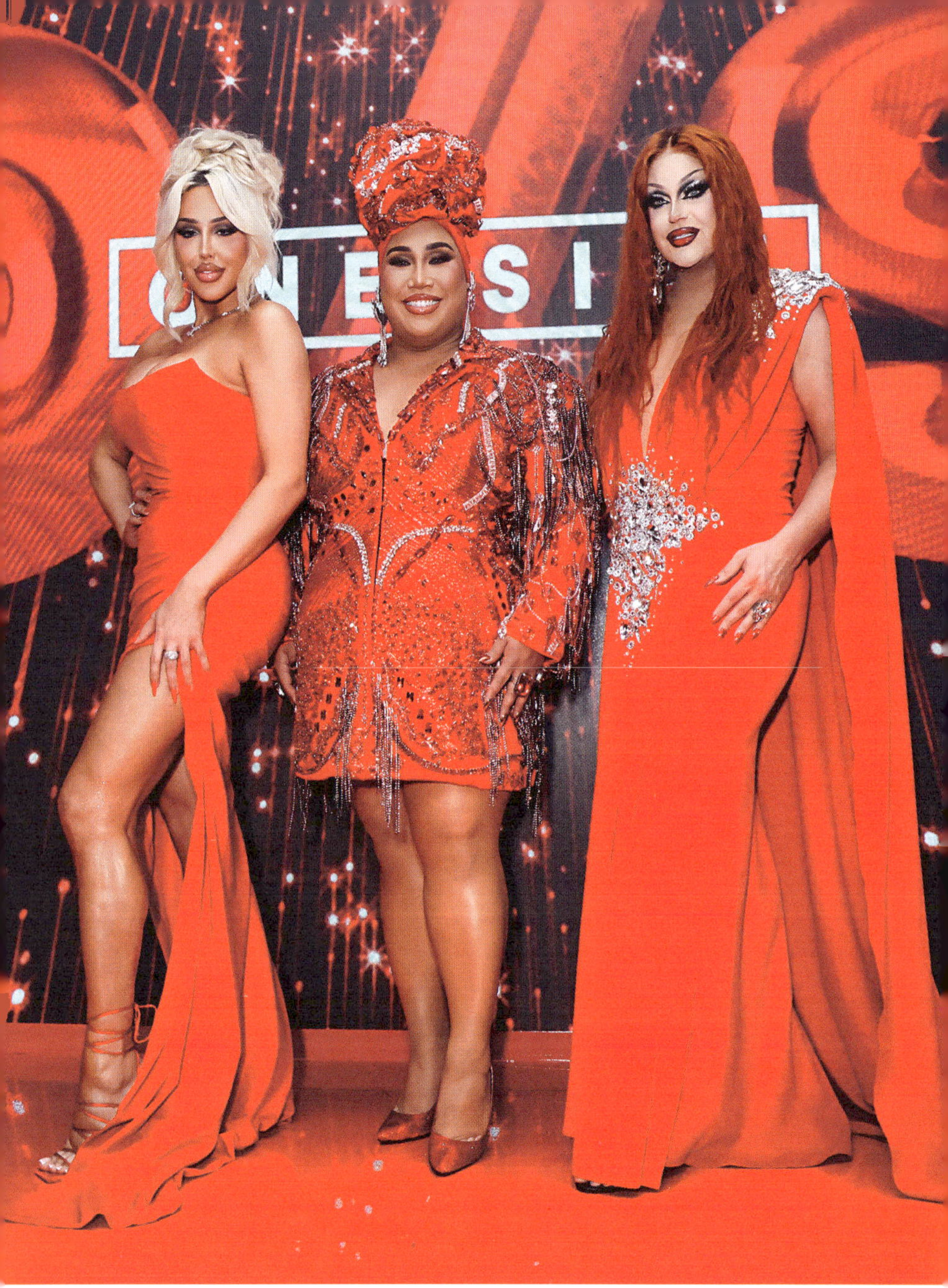

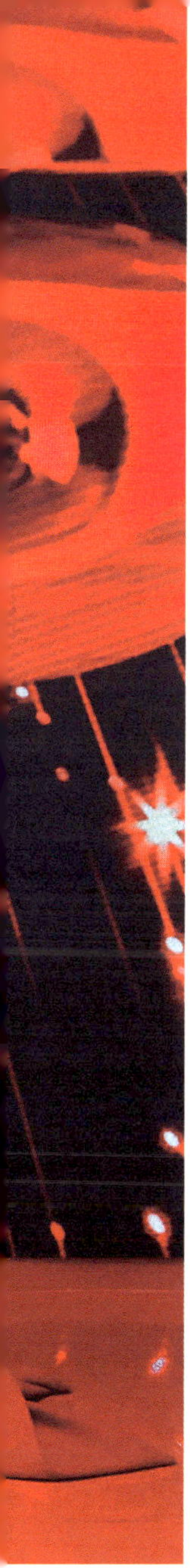

In May 2022, Roan released the video for her single "My Kink is Karma", where she leaned heavily into her drag influences, reportedly looking to the expertise of drag queen Patrick Starrr and their YouTube make-up tutorials for guidance on how to achieve her looks. Roan took to TikTok to break down many aspects of the looks featured in the video, sharing images of drag queen looks from her Pinterest boards and even giving one of her favourite cartoon villains a shout-out, too (the demon simply called "Him" from *The Powerpuff Girls*). Fans have been quick to point out how this video marked a key point in Roan's developing image and her relationship with drag looks.

PREVIOUS Kim Petras, Sam Smith, Violet Chachki and Gottmik pose in bold queer fashion at the 2023 Grammys, celebrating creative drag and pop collaboration.

LEFT La Demi, Patrick Starrr and Shannel pose together at the ONE/SIZE launch. Starrr's artistry has directly inspired Chappell Roan's signature bold make-up looks.

"I think the songs themselves have drag elements," Roan shared in a 2023 interview with Pittsburgh LGBTQI+ publication *QBurgh*, going on to say, "but more so in the visual aspects of how I do my make-up. All the songs are very camp, and I think if you're taking it seriously, you see it as tasteless, but the reality is that's just drag; it's supposed to be tacky."

From dressing up as Divine herself (one of the most famous examples of a drag queen in modern pop culture) to her countless bodysuit looks – which seem as if they came straight from the wardrobes of her favourite queens – and the make-up looks that would make *RuPaul* stars green with envy, Roan's drag-inspired expressions are endless.

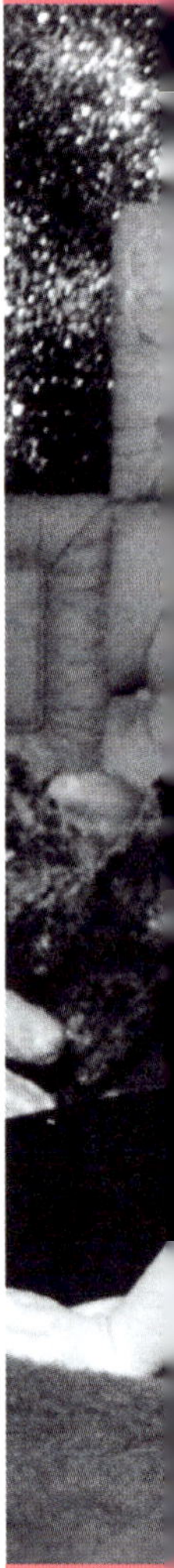

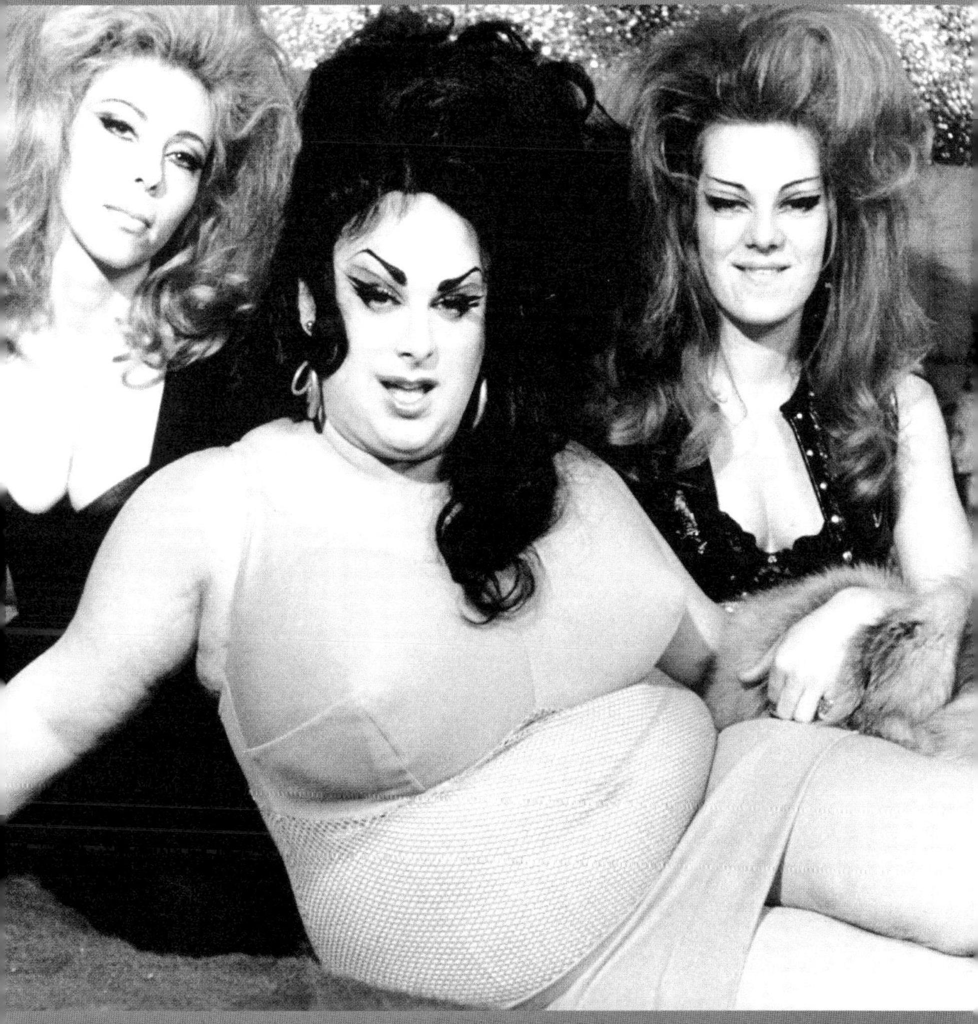

Drag artist Divine poses with co-stars of the 1974 cult classic film *Female Trouble*, directed by John Waters.

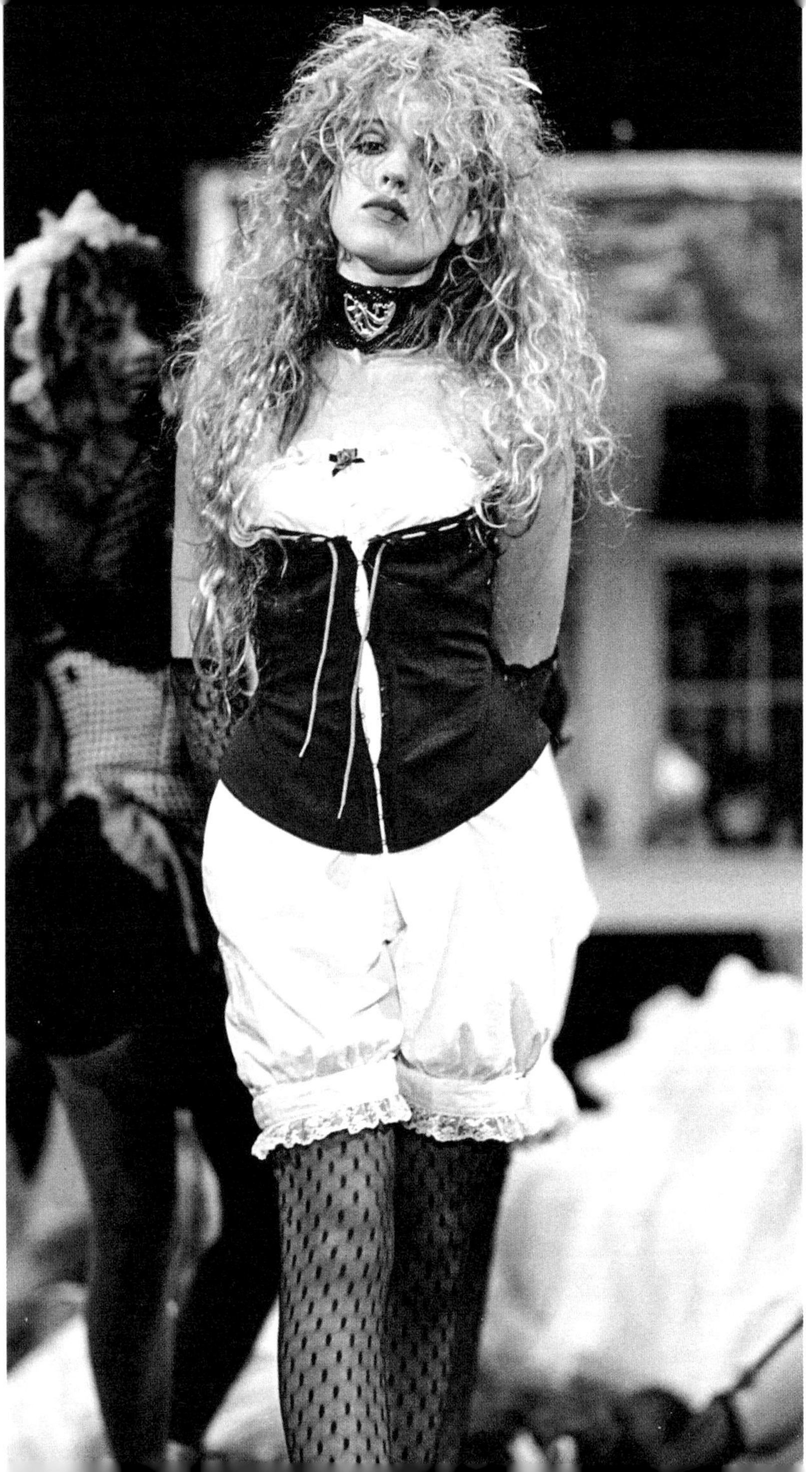

One of the looks that is most associated with Roan and her drag expressions is her Tiny Desk performance in March 2024. Roan sported a look that got the attention of folks across the world, including James Factora of *Condé Nast*'s LGBTQI+ outlet *Them,* who referred to Roan's persona as "very much an exercise in femme camp" and the performance as "the perfect encapsulation of that, at once elaborately constructed and deeply unserious." Roan sported a vintage Betsey Johnson dress featuring floral ruffles in a bold fuchsia hue. Betsey Johnson, though not considered a drag queen herself, also has a deep connection to the drag world with many drag queens being fans of Johnson's work, earning her a place as a guest judge on *RuPaul's Drag Race* on multiple occasions. Genesis Webb has also spoken of her love for Johnson, and Roan and Webb have notably appeared on the red carpet with Johnson at various fashion events. The hair and make-up for the Tiny Desk concert, however, were the real show-stoppers. Roan wore a towering, teased wig accessorized with a tiara, silver butterfly clips and, of course, cigarette butts. The New York-based make-up artist Sterling Tull painted Roan's face a stark white with bright blue eyeshadow, ultra skinny brows and bright red lips. Many noticed that Roan's teeth also appeared to have lipstick on them, prompting conversations online over whether or not this was intentional. Later, Tull shared the look on her Instagram later with the caption "80's Prom gone drag with a blue glitter cut crease, and yes, the lipstick on the teeth is intentional", putting the rumours to rest.

Model poses on runway of Betsey Johnson Fall 1990 Ready to Wear collection show.

It is fitting that another one of Roan's make-up artists extraordinaire is also a drag queen, the iconic Andrew Dahling. Dahling is credited with transforming Kayleigh into Chappell for a number of her most dramatic looks, from her *Rolling Stone* cover in 2024 to her "Pink Pony Club" performance at the 2025 Grammys.

This fusion of aesthetics works with the rough template of looks found in old Hollywood films, fused with Americana Westernwear and tragic pageant queen. One of the key points of reference behind some of these looks lies in the iconic films of John Waters. Roan's stylist and close collaborator, Genesis Webb, has openly referenced Waters' films as a source of inspiration behind a number of Roan's looks, notably that of the red dress she wore on stage at Kentucky Pride in June 2024. Many fans instantly recognized the look as a homage to the late drag queen Divine, who starred in several films directed by Waters from the 1970s to the 1990s. The *Pink Flamingos*-inspired outfit featured a fitted red dress with tulle trim and a leopard-print bodysuit that poked out from the bust. The mastermind behind the dress is one of the hottest up-and-coming designers behind some of the most talented queer artists in the spotlight at the moment, Irish designer Oran O'Reilly.

Chappell Roan's dramatic look for the cover of *Rolling Stone* in 2024.

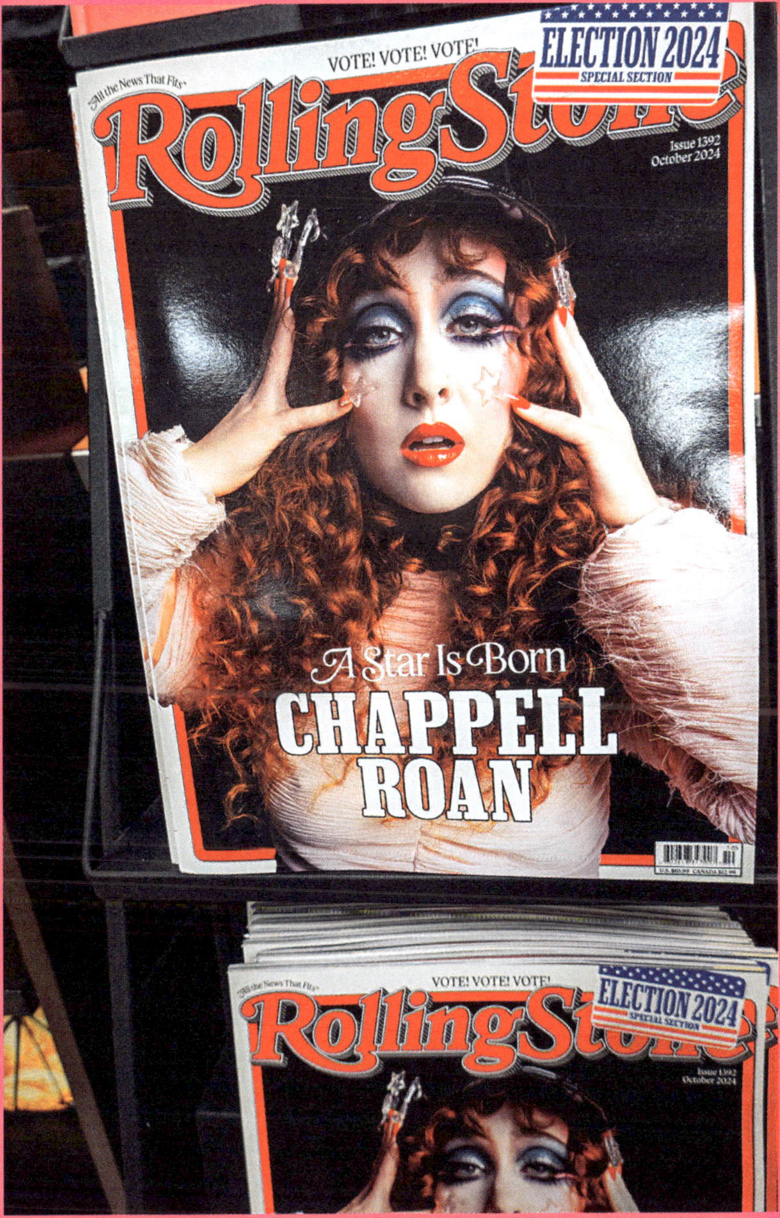
VOTE! VOTE! VOTE!
ELECTION 2024
SPECIAL SECTION
"All the News That Fits"
Rolling Stone
Issue 1392
October 2024
A Star Is Born
CHAPPELL
ROAN
VOTE! VOTE! VOTE!
ELECTION 2024
SPECIAL SECTION
Rolling Stone
Issue 1392
October 2024

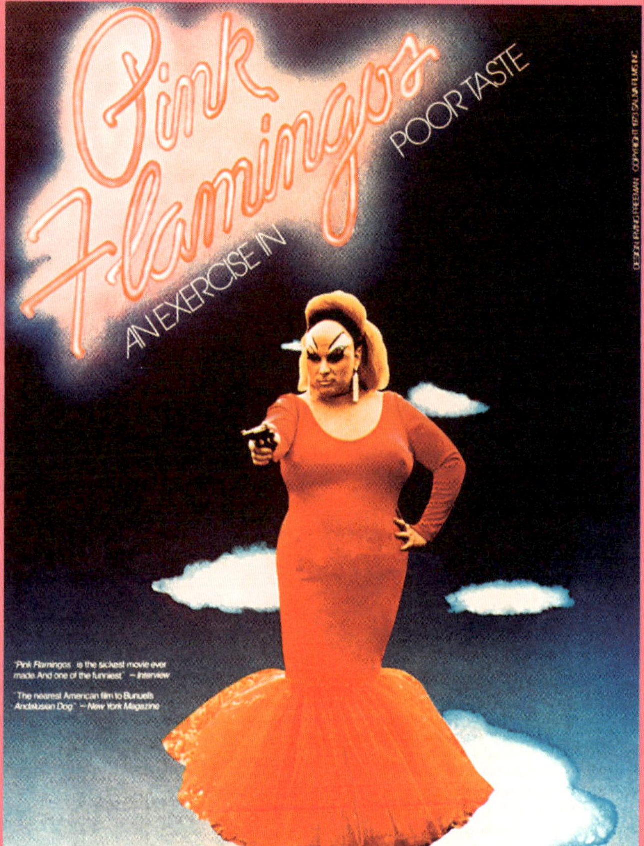

ABOVE Poster for John Waters' 1972 film *Pink Flamingos*, starring drag artist Divine.

OPPOSITE Roan wears a dress inspired by Divine in *Pink Flamingos* and designed by Oran O'Reilly while onstage at Kentucky Pride, in June 2024.

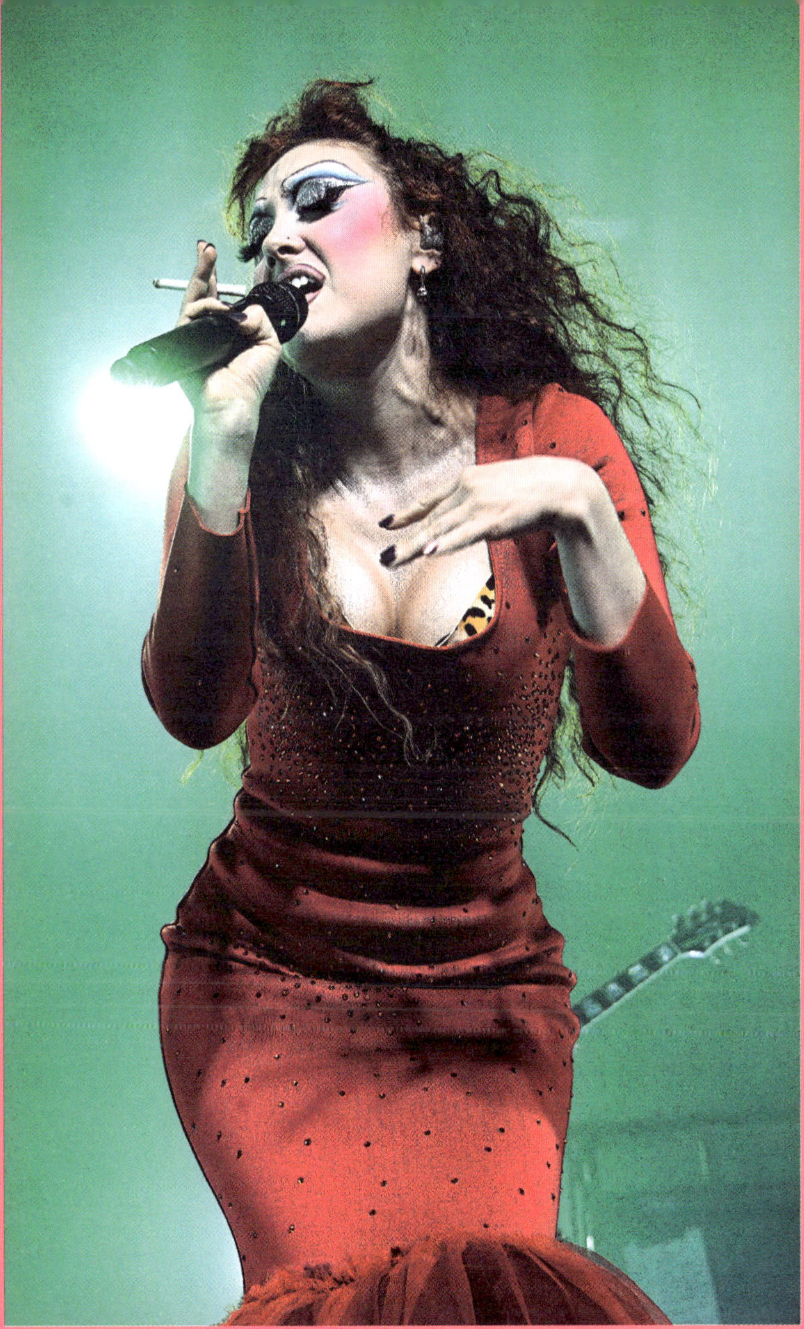

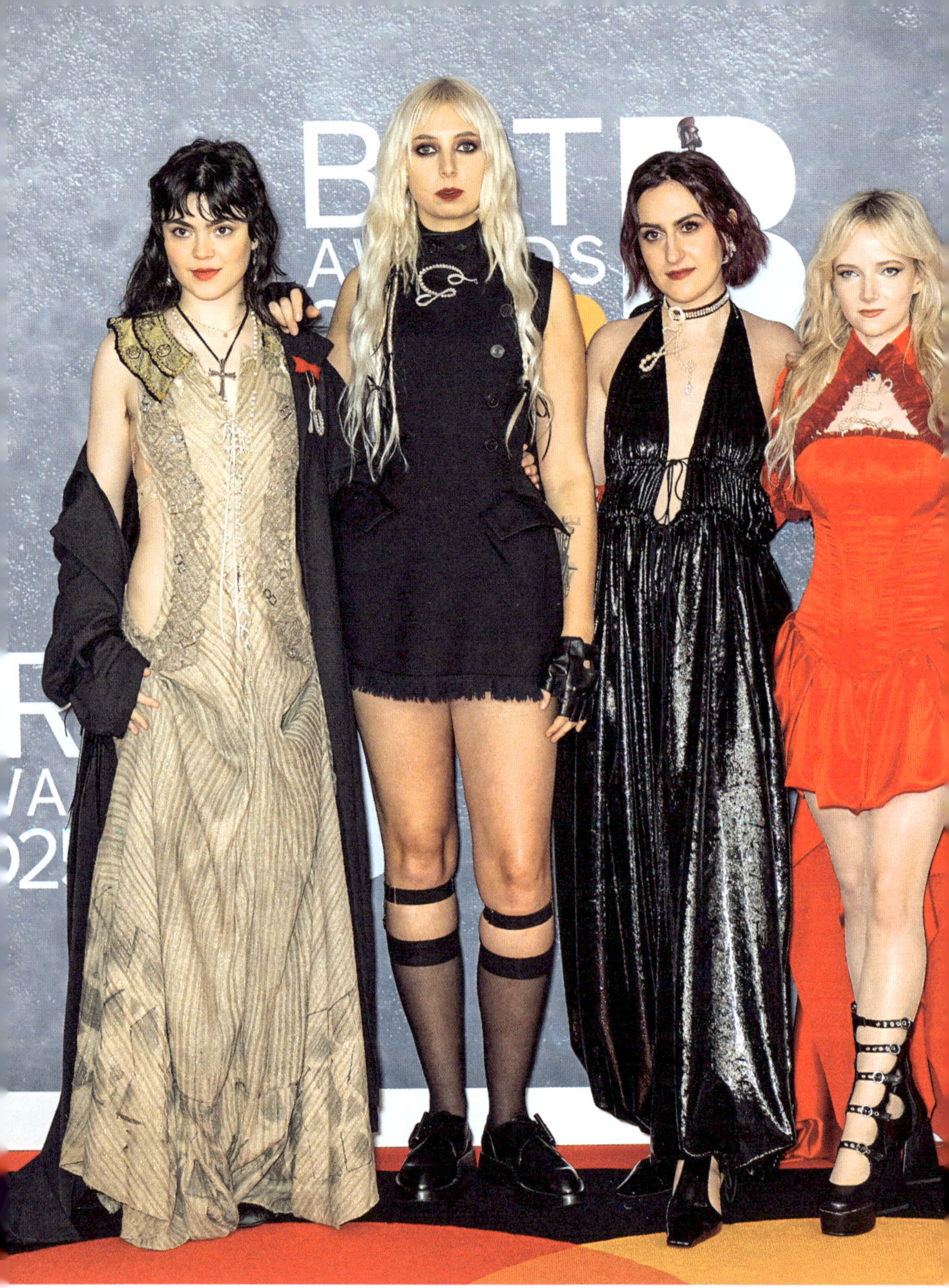

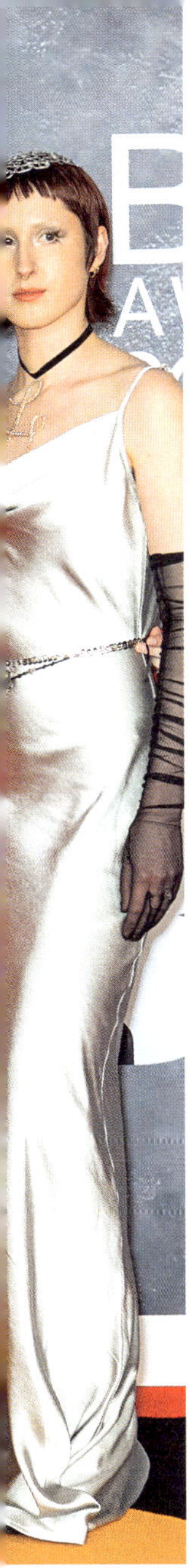

O'Reilly's designs can be seen on fellow LGBTQI+ stars such as Bimini (of *RuPaul's Drag Race UK*), CMAT and The Last Dinner Party. The make-up look was also a nod to Divine and was executed by Kentucky native Andrew Dahling himself. Juiccy Misdemeanor, one of the many drag artists that Roan has invited to open for her over the years, remarked on the look in a 2024 interview with *Salon*, saying "Her playing homage to Divine for instance in drag – it's like a simultaneous connection because drag is a protest. I feel like she's protesting in her own way through her music and her looks ... Also just a really beautiful thing that she's keeping an open space for the LGBTQ community."

London-based band The Last Dinner Party have, like Roan, drawn comparisons to acts such as David Bowie and Kate Bush for their theatrical dress and varied influences. They have also worked with Oran O'Reilly, who designed Roan's Divine-inspired look in 2024.

New Romantics

For those who may be unfamiliar, New Romantics were a subcultural group that sprouted from the punk movement in the UK in the 1970s. Some say that the formation of the scene was a reaction to punk moving away from its origins of challenging the establishment and stuffy social norms through provocative clothing and energy-fuelled guitar riffs and into something that attracted anyone who simply liked the look or wanted an excuse to push people around. The New Romantics took some of the key elements of punk but infused a Victorian charm and flamboyancy that put much of the 1980s in a chokehold. Teased locks and frilly frocks filled the Blitz Club in London's West End, where names such as Boy George and David Bowie were regulars and "gender-bending" looks were the norm. The group appropriately garnered the nickname "peacock punks" due to their dedication to the extravagant looks they proudly strutted through the streets of Soho. Vivienne Westwood's earliest collections are often referred to as key artefacts for the group, too. And just as Roan found herself becoming a household name, a New Romantic resurgence was under way. "The return of the New Romantics feels true to the spirit and nature of what's happening here with Chappell and her team", make-up artist Andrew Dahling noted in a *Dazed Beauty* article in July 2024.

Boy George, pictured here in 1984, is widely regarded as one of the key figures in bringing the New Romantic movement to the mainstream.

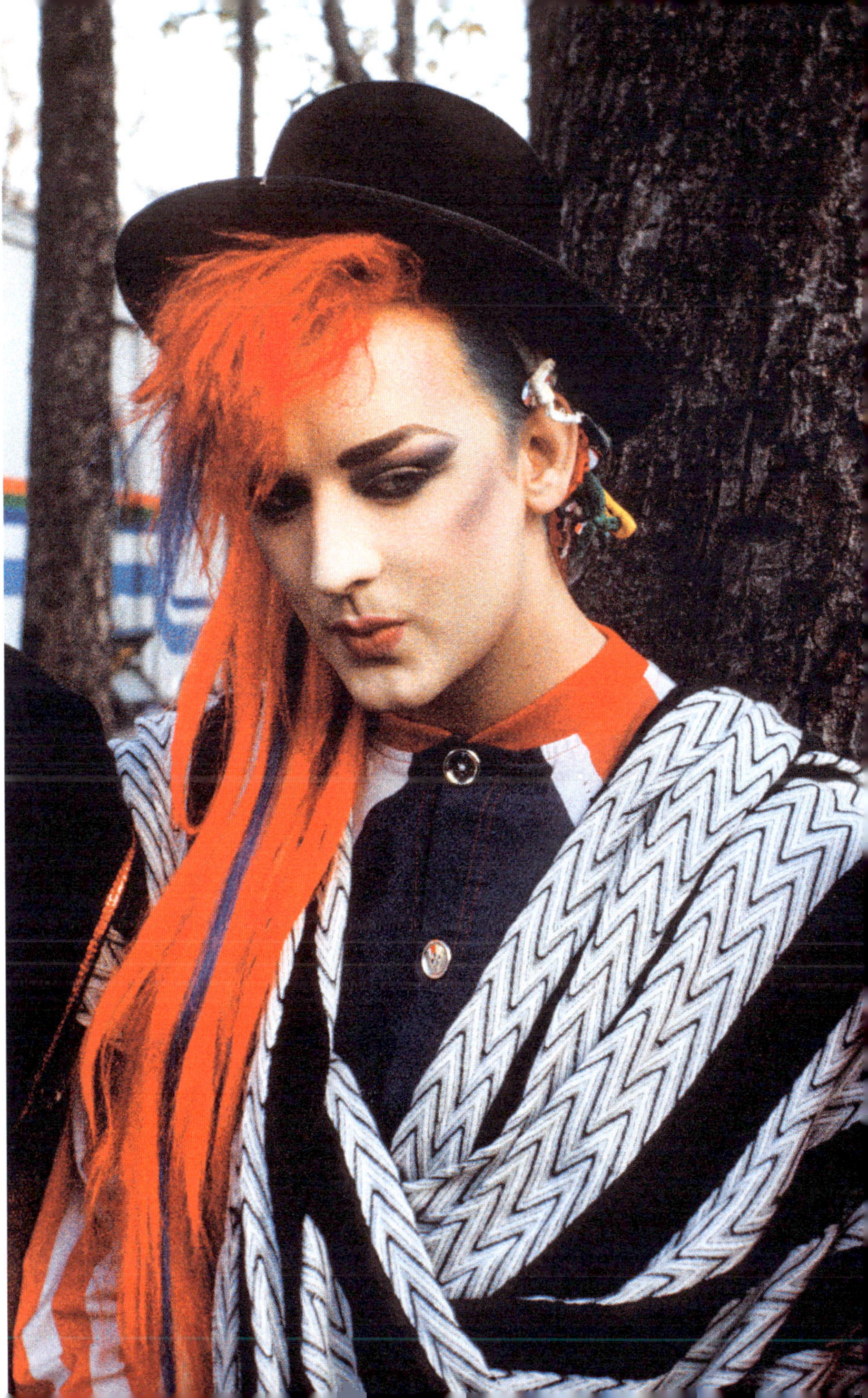

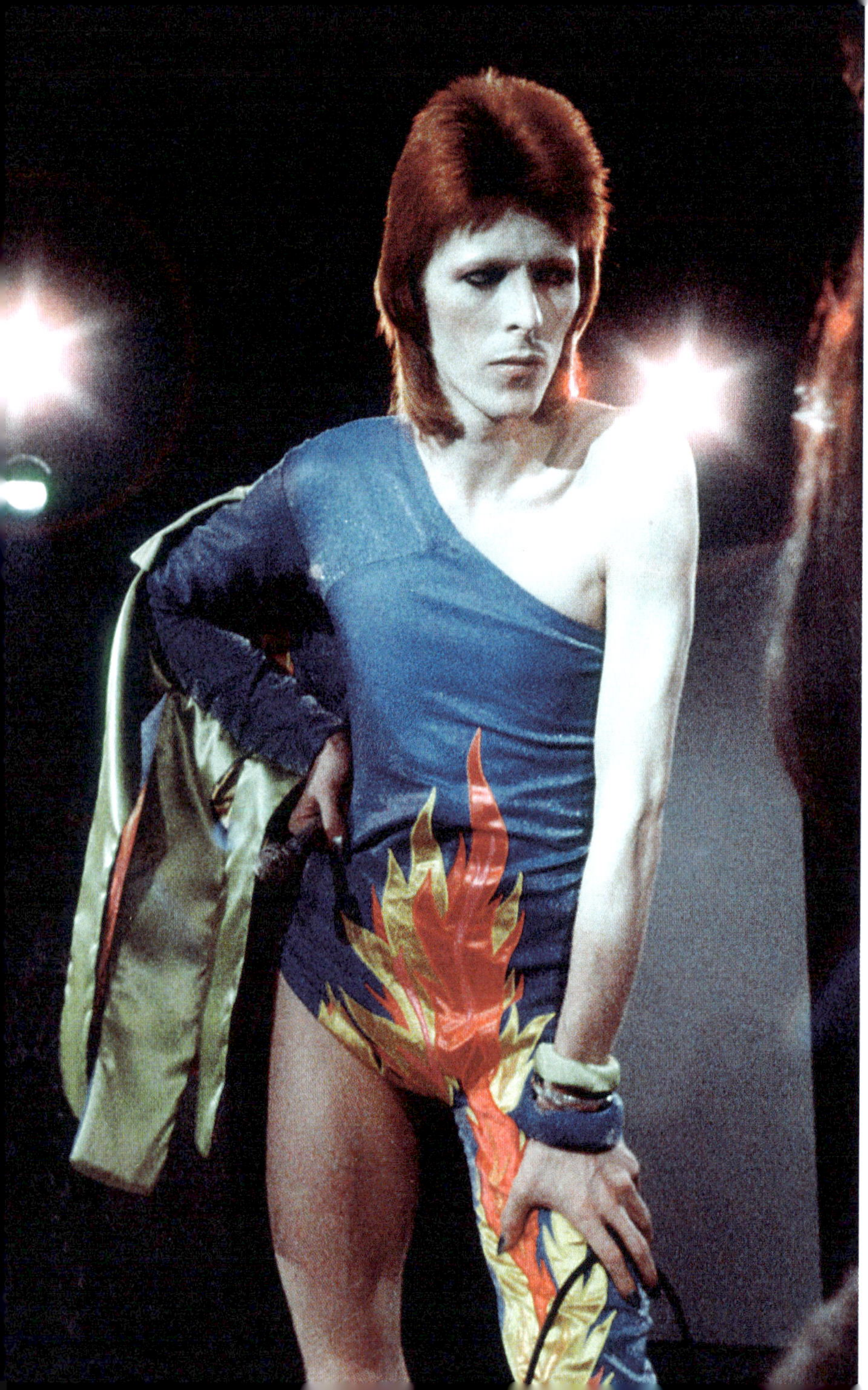

Madeline Hirsch of *InStyle* is one of the many fashion journalists who were quick to note Roan's connection to the 1980s movement, saying in a 2024 piece on the singer: "Roan is like if Boy George and Cyndi Lauper had a baby – only cooler. And much like those '80s pop idols, her look is no less revolutionary." Other icons of the scene that have drawn comparisons to Roan include the Glasgow duo Strawberry Switchblade, who would not only often appear wearing bold make-up looks and back-combed hair for serious volume but, like Roan, also made headlines by speaking out against the lack of privacy and personal respect that often comes with fame. Singer Rose McDowell shared in a 2015 interview with *The Quietus*, "It's ridiculous, you don't belong to anyone. I will write what I've got to say in a song, and if I wanted to say any more I would've written it in the song."

Many compare Roan's work to that of David Bowie and his Ziggy Stardust persona, a likeness evident in Roan's debut album title, *The Rise and Fall of a Midwest Princess*, which is easily seen as a nod to Bowie's *The Rise and Fall of Ziggy Stardust and the Spiders from Mars*.

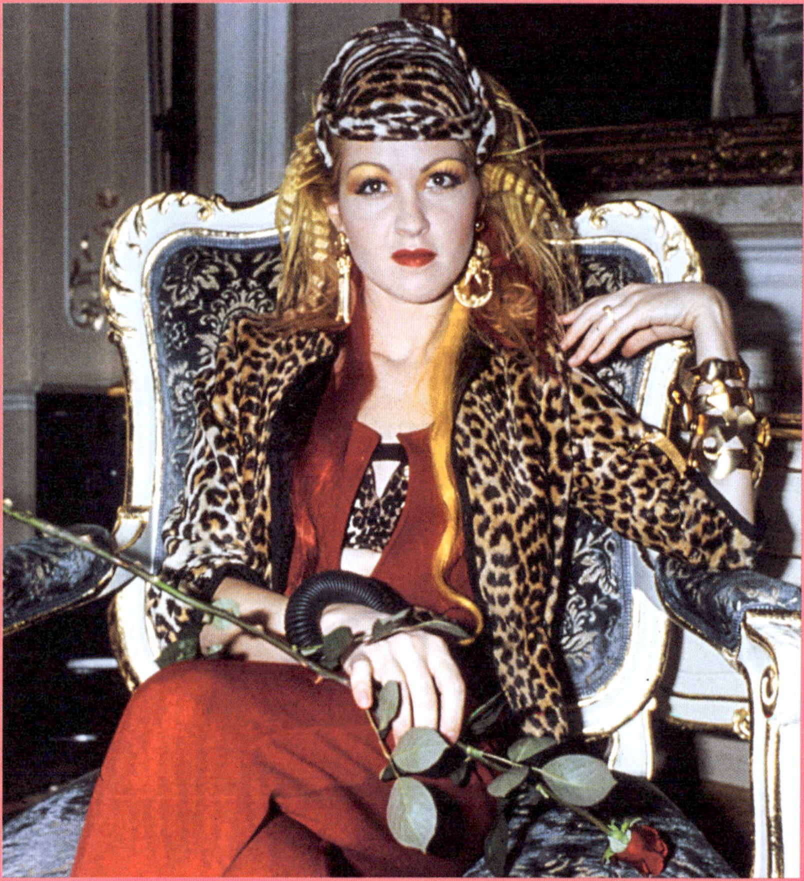

ABOVE Cyndi Lauper, pictured here in 1986, has been an inspiration to Roan, thanks to her bold style that celebrates self-expression and individuality.

OPPOSITE Kate Bush, pictured here in 1979, is another name that often comes up when speaking of Roan, due to their shared theatrical performance styles and impressive vocal range.

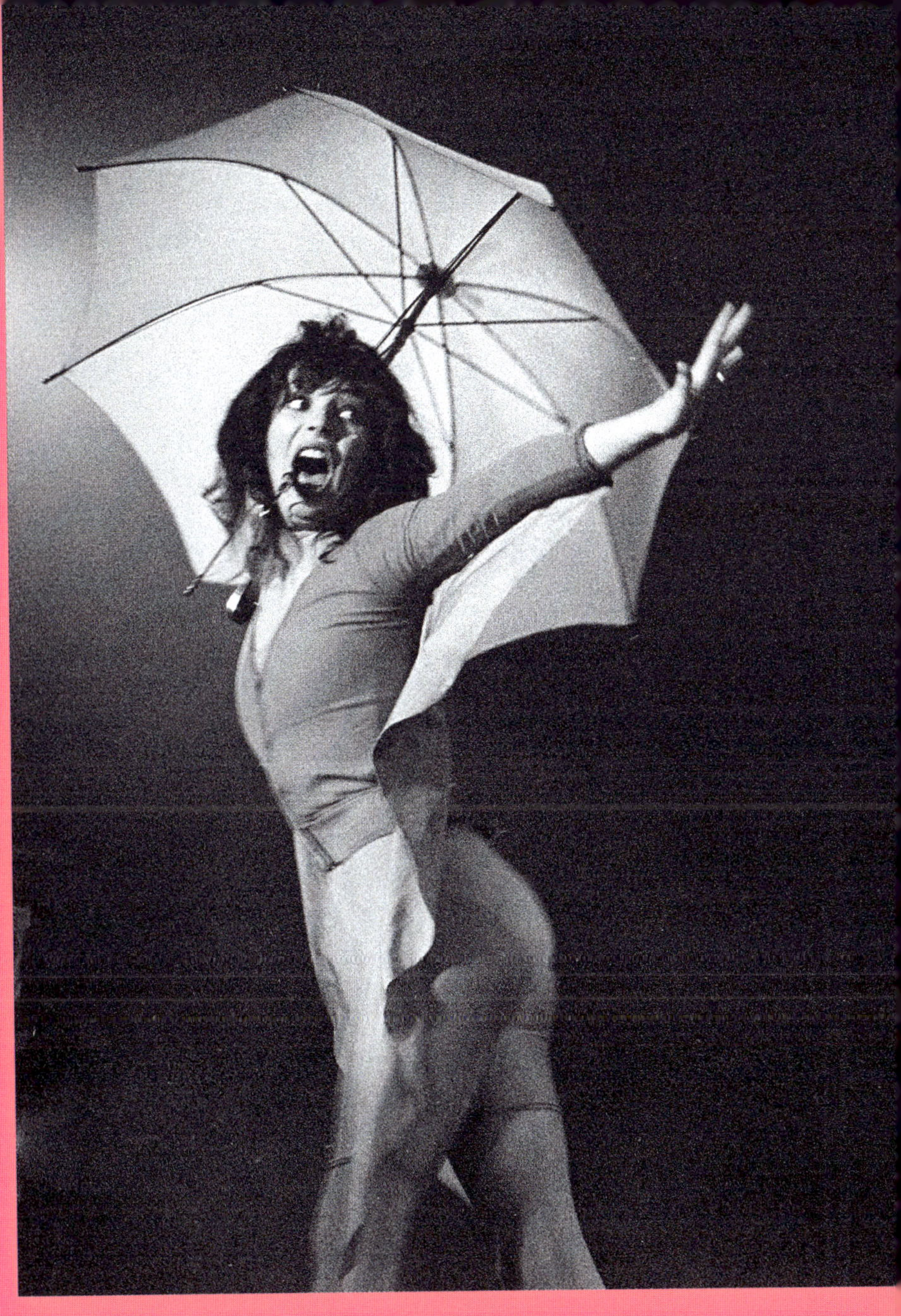

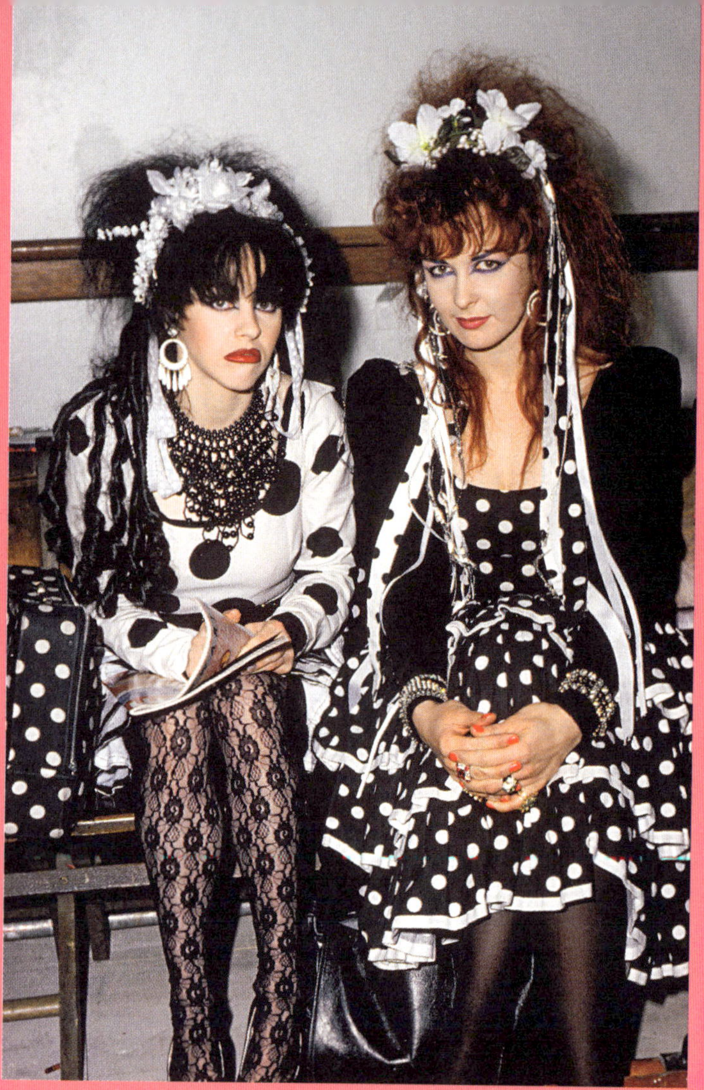

ABOVE Strawberry Switchblade were known for their dramatic looks, demonstrated here in an image from 1984.

OPPOSITE Cyndi Lauper's playful approach to dressing, seen here in an image from 1983, helped pave the way for artists such as Chappell Roan to experiment with their appearance in a way that previously had been seen as less palatable for the mainstream.

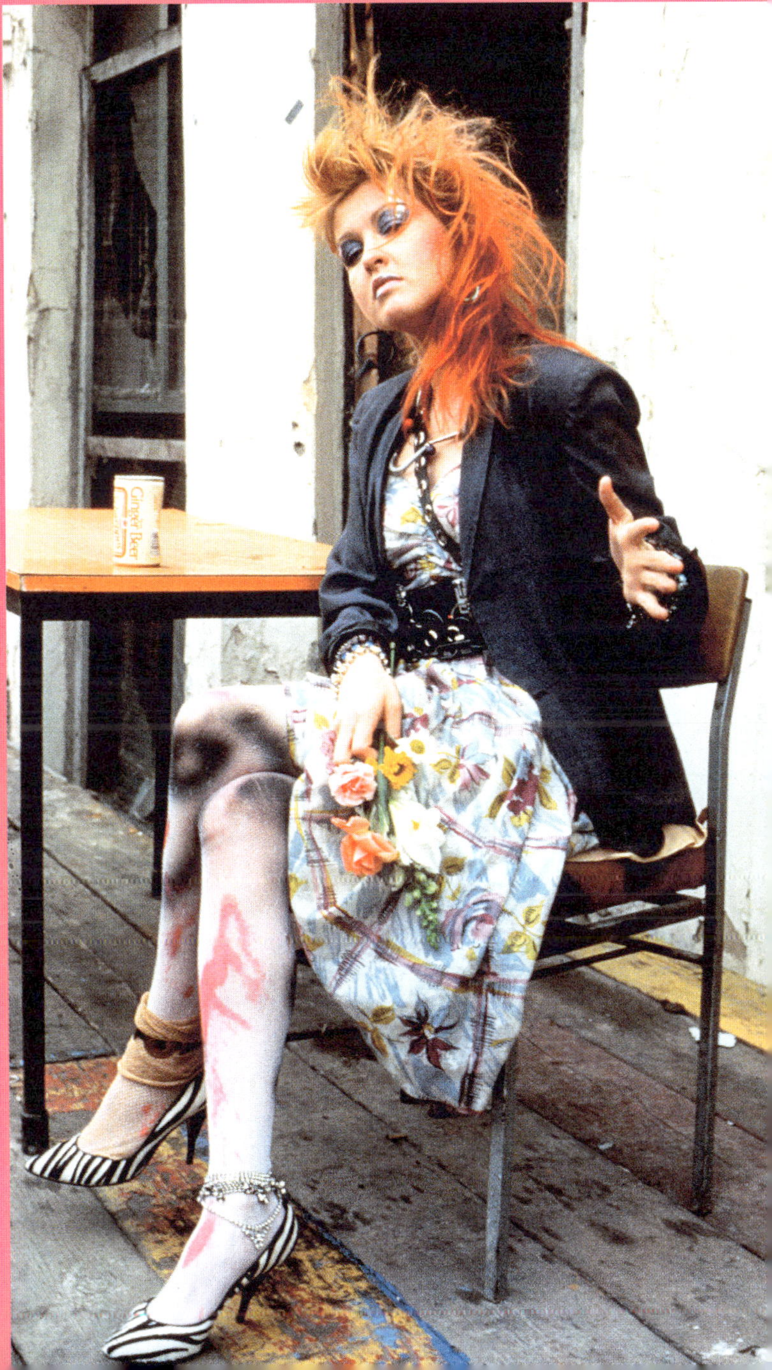
Ginger Beer

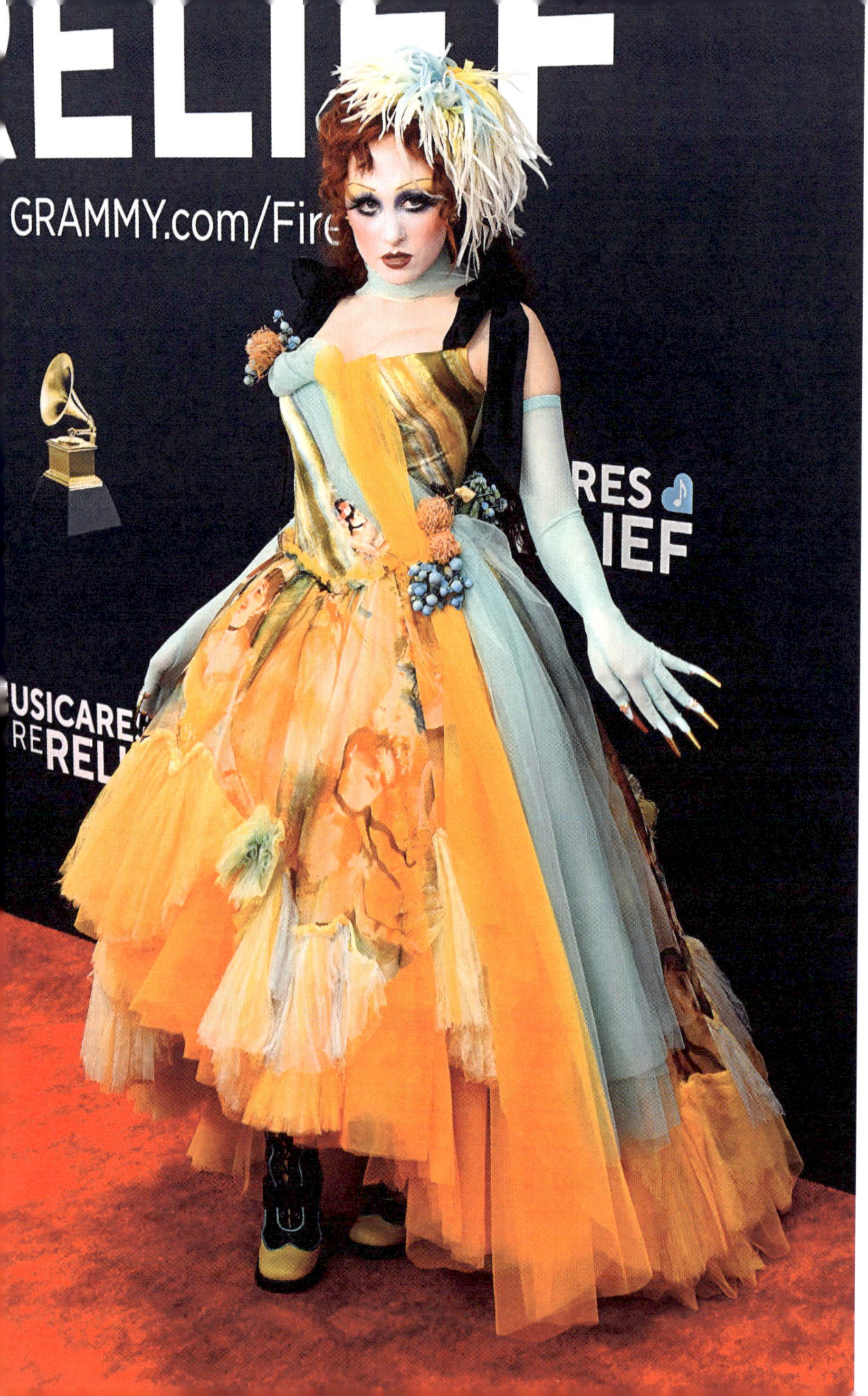
GRAMMY.com/Fire

Though the references to her likeness of New Romantics had already been coming in hot, Roan's appearance on the red carpet at the 67th Annual Grammy Awards on 2 February 2025 can be seen as one of the clearest examples of being influenced by the British subculture. The singer arrived at the event in a vintage Jean Paul Gaultier gown from the French designer's 2003 couture collection. The dress presented blue and yellow tulle layers with elements from Edgar Degas paintings across the skirt, including 1877's *Dancer with a Bouquet*. The look was complemented with matching gloves and footwear, courtesy of Canadian label Fluevog. When *Vogue* asked Webb about the look, she replied, "I wanted something with history; something that carried weight beyond aesthetics. Gaultier had been on my mind for her for some time, so I reached out, and when this particular archival piece was presented, I had an immediate visceral reaction. It wasn't just an option, it was the dress. While I had several looks prepared for the fitting, this was the only one that truly aligned with the vision." The make-up look was executed by Andrew Dahling who told *Byrdie*, "I wanted to keep the make-up in the same world of the Victorian romantic aesthetics". And the hair? "Bigger, longer, more – everything was about taking her look to the next level", Roan's hairstylist for the evening, Dom Forletta, told *Elle* following the event – a sentiment surely shared by many of the participants in the New Romantic scene as they prepared for a night out at the Blitz.

In February 2025, Roan attended the 67th Annual Grammy Awards wearing a vintage 2003 Jean Paul Gaultier gown.

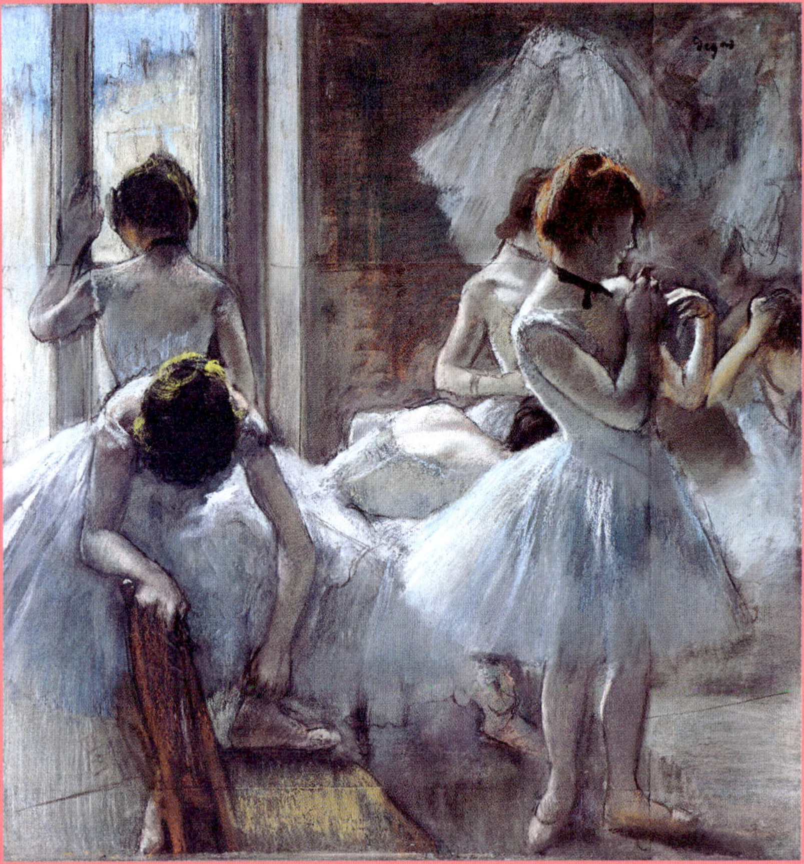

ABOVE Edgar Degas's 1877 *The Ballet Class*, *c*. 1877, one of the paintings featured across the skirt of the Gaultier gown on page 100.

OPPOSITE A stark white base, dramatic drawn-on eyebrows and neon eyeshadow, the foundation for many make-up looks associated with the New Romantics scene, were a clear influence for many of Roan's looks, including this one worn to the 2025 Grammys.

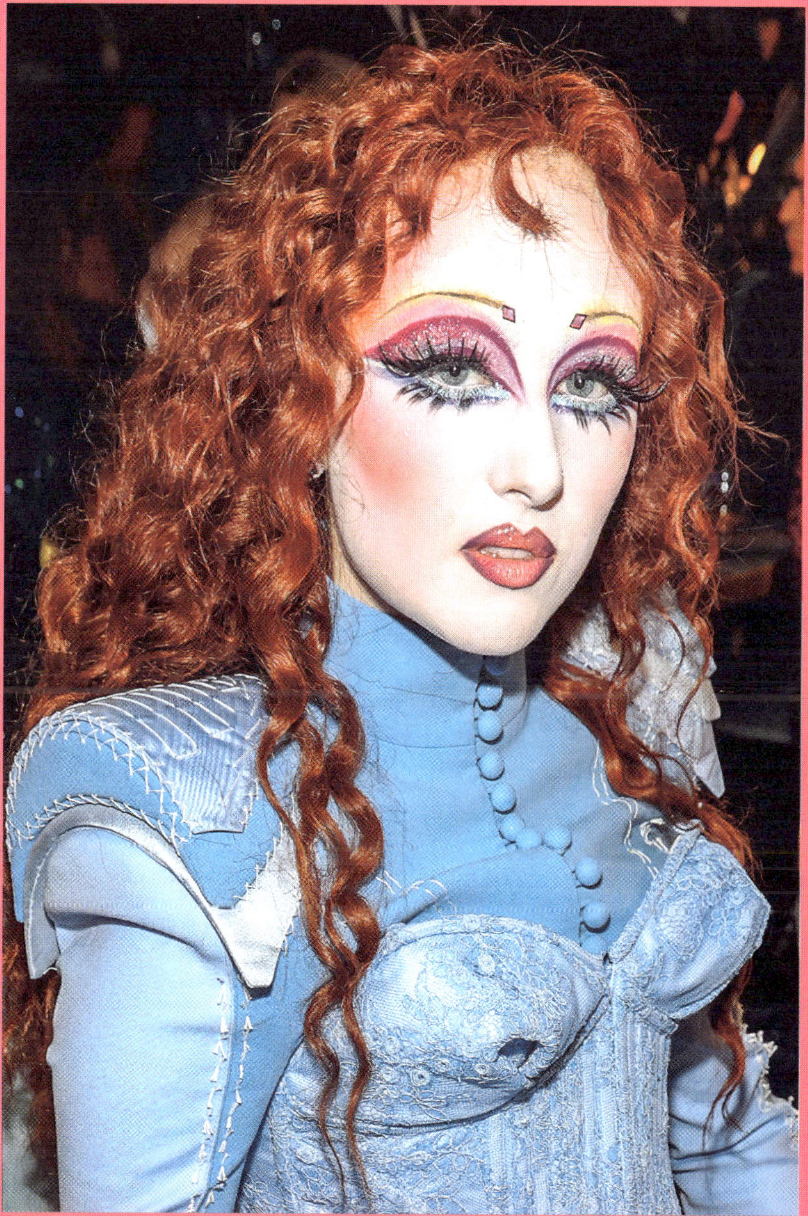

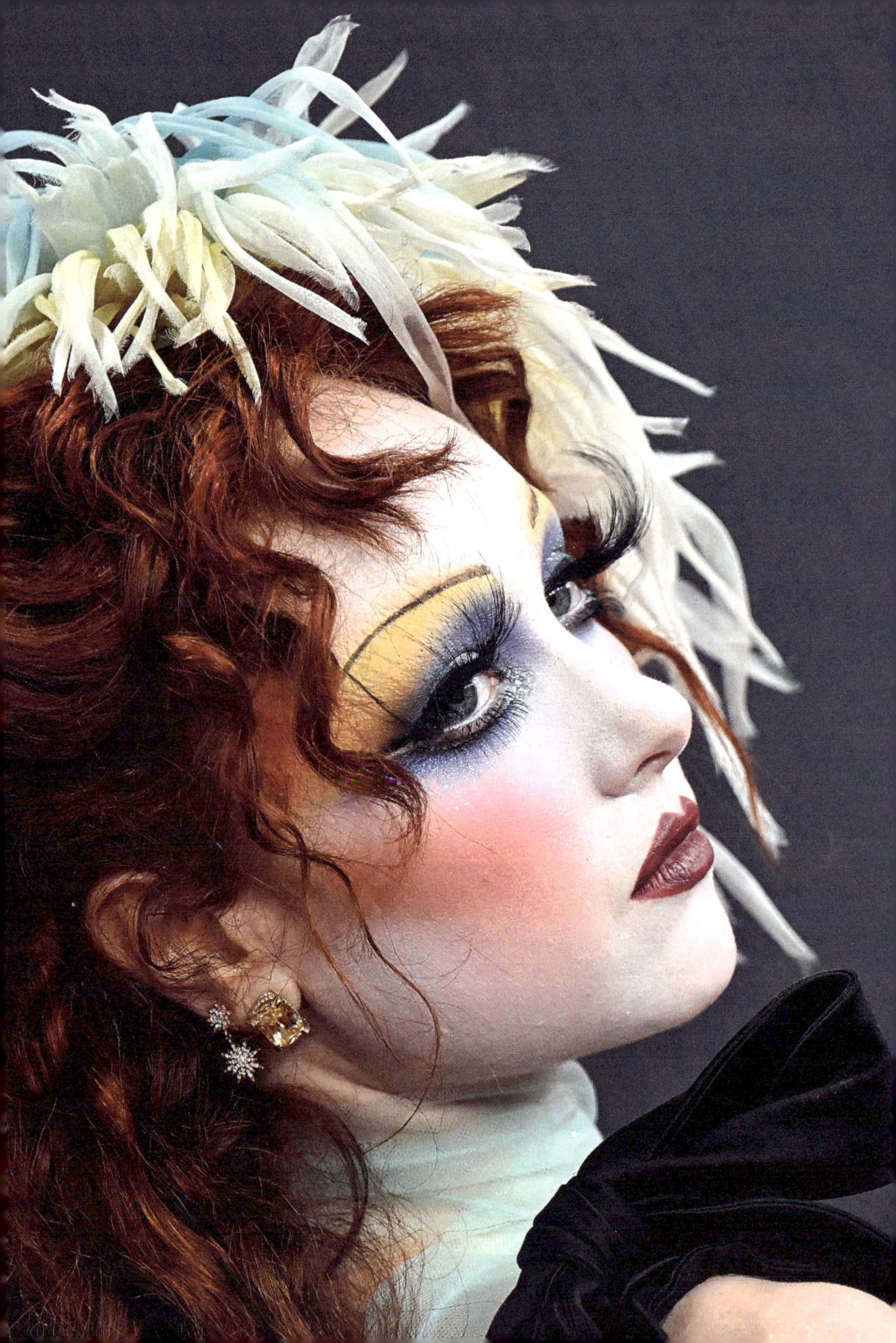

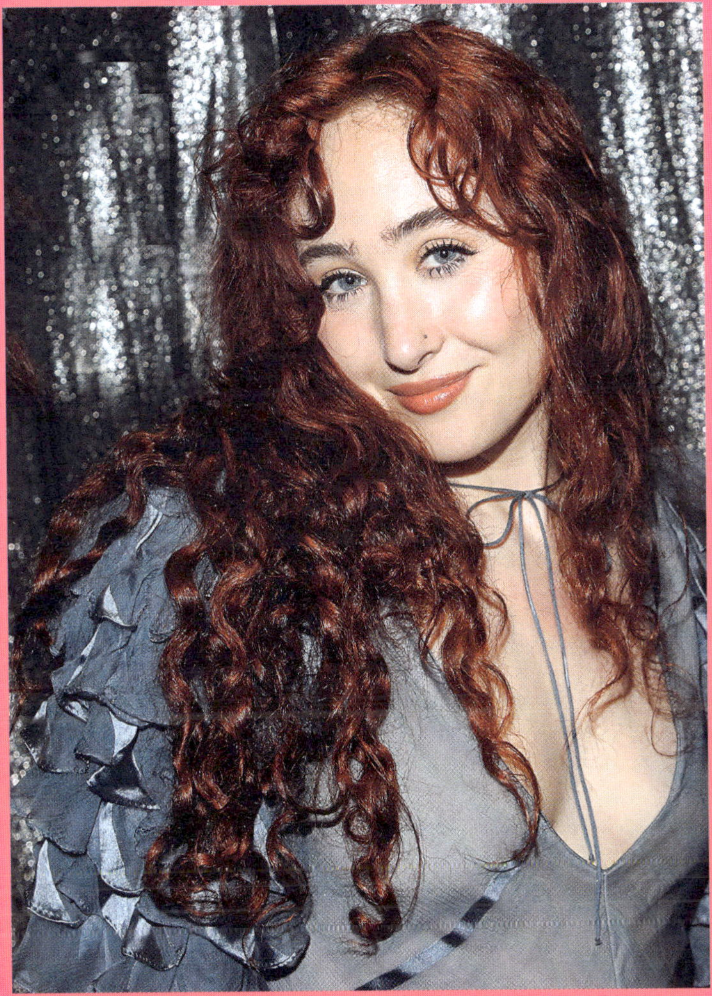

OPPOSITE The evening's make-up look was executed by Andrew Dahling and her hair by New York-based hair stylist Dom Forletta.

ABOVE Roan wore understated make-up and a vintage 1930s gown to the Broadway play *Oh, Mary!* on 7 May 2025.

Club Kids

Roan's stylist Genesis Webb has spoken about her love for 1990s Club Kids looks on numerous occasions, citing the 2003 film *Party Monster* as the inspiration behind a number of her looks. The film depicts the story behind one of the most infamous club promoters in New York in the 1990s – Michael Alig – and the Club Kids scene, which was famous for its extravagant and subversive approach to fashion and sexual expression, and often combined with the heavy use of class A drugs. One of the most notable looks inspired by this iconic scene was the one Roan wore on stage at Bonnaroo Music and Arts Festival in Manchester, Tennessee in the summer of 2024. The look was heavily inspired by an outfit worn in a scene from the film by Chloë Sevigny's character Gitsie, as the character handed out pills in small paper cups on a tray. The latex look was crafted by latex label Aimless Gallery, who reached out to Genesis Webb to design the look for Roan and her band for the performance.

OPPOSITE Key figures of the Club Kids scene, Club Kids Michael Alig, Christopher Comp and Waltpaper (aka Walt Cassidy), pose for a picture during a 1992 rave at Macy's in New York.

OVERLEAF Michael Alig, Richie Rich, Nina Hagen, Sophia Lamar and Genetalia at the Tunnel Club in New York, on New Year's Eve 1993.

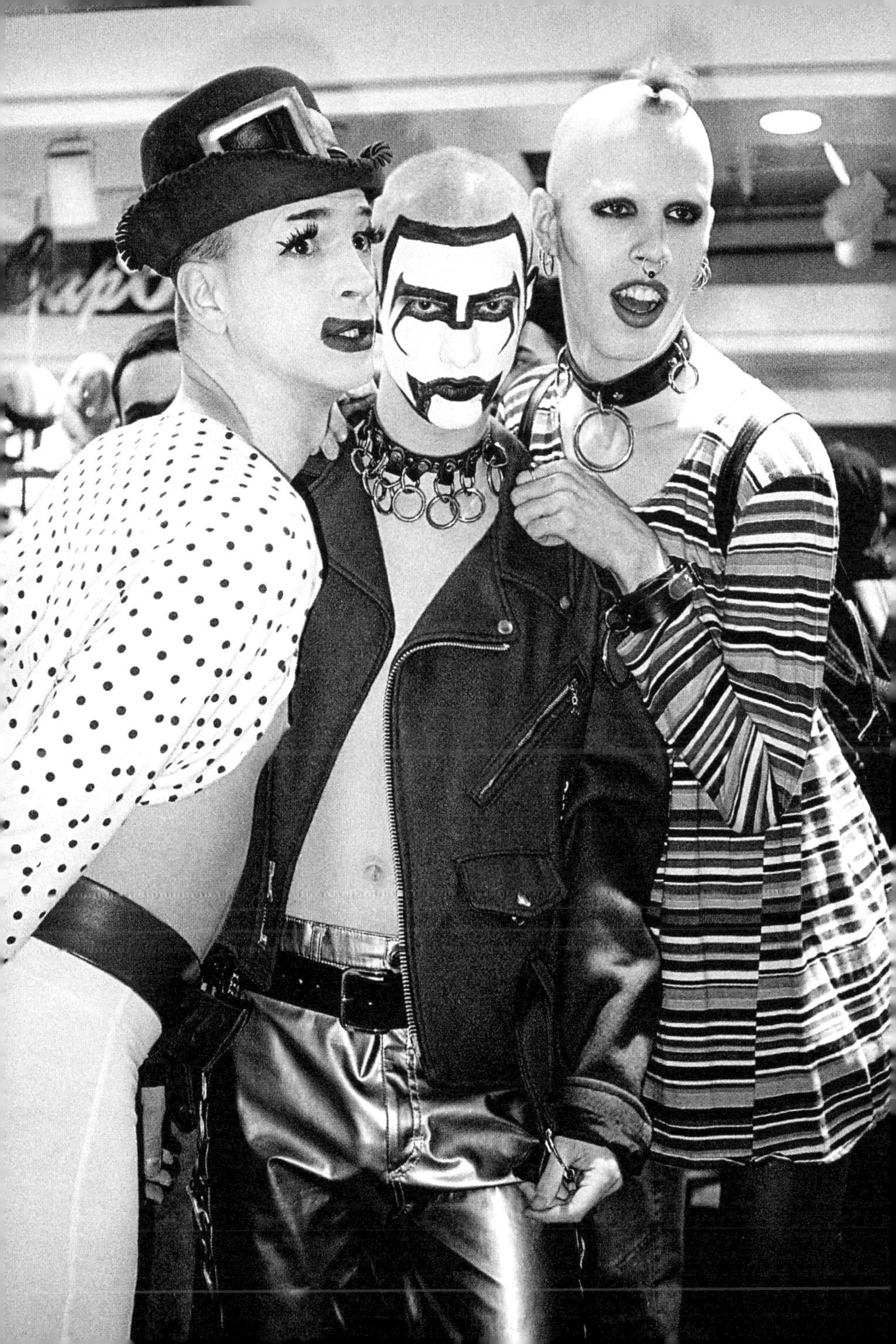

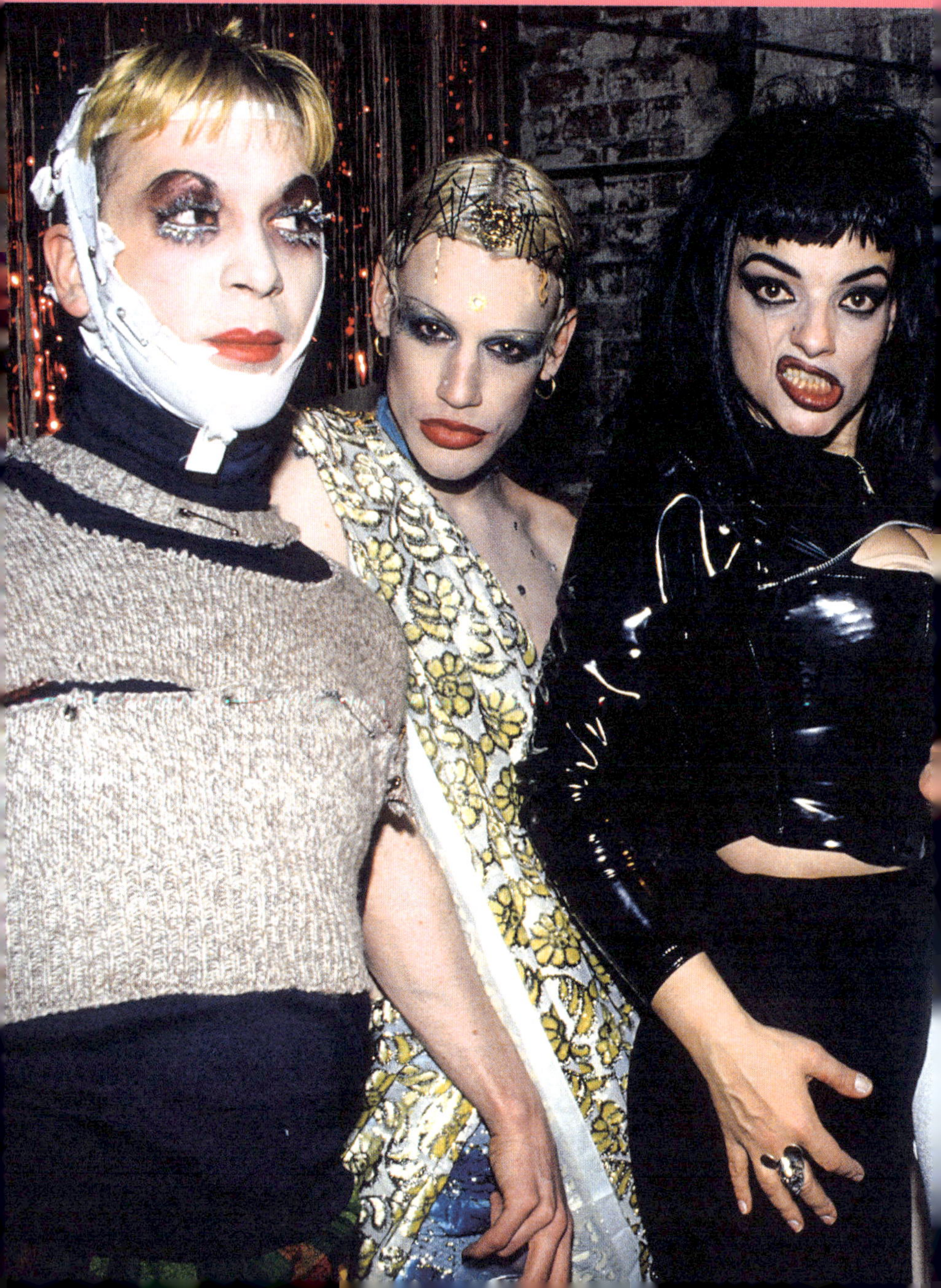

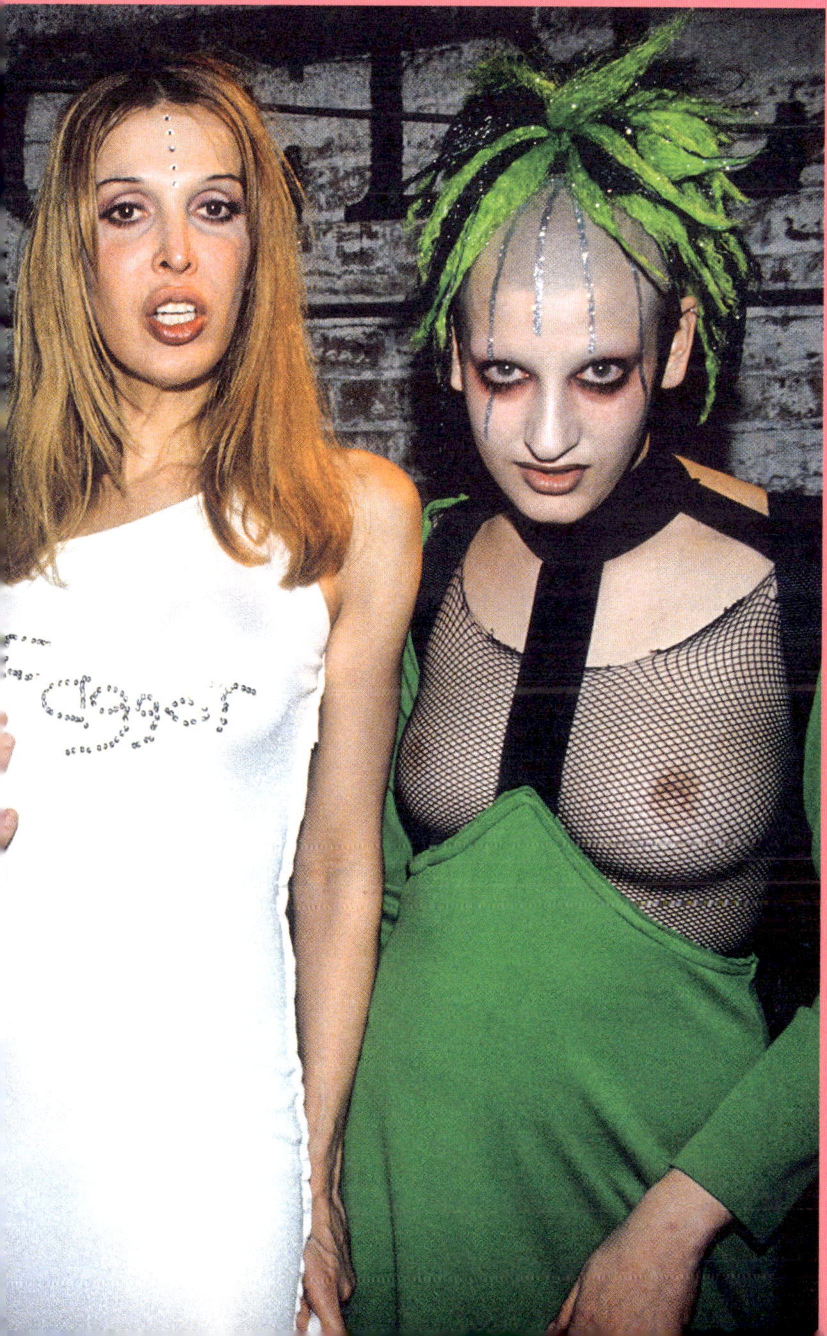

"She obviously loves drag and comes from a more glam drag background, where I loved the Club Kid scene. Coming from a punk scene is just a little harsher ... She taught me just that glam and colour and glitter can be just as avant-garde and just as high fashion as anything."

GENESIS WEBB, CHAPPELL ROAN'S STYLIST, *BRITISH VOGUE* 2024

One of Roan's key Club Kid-inspired looks onstage at the Bonnaroo Music Festival in Manchester, Tennessee, in 2024.

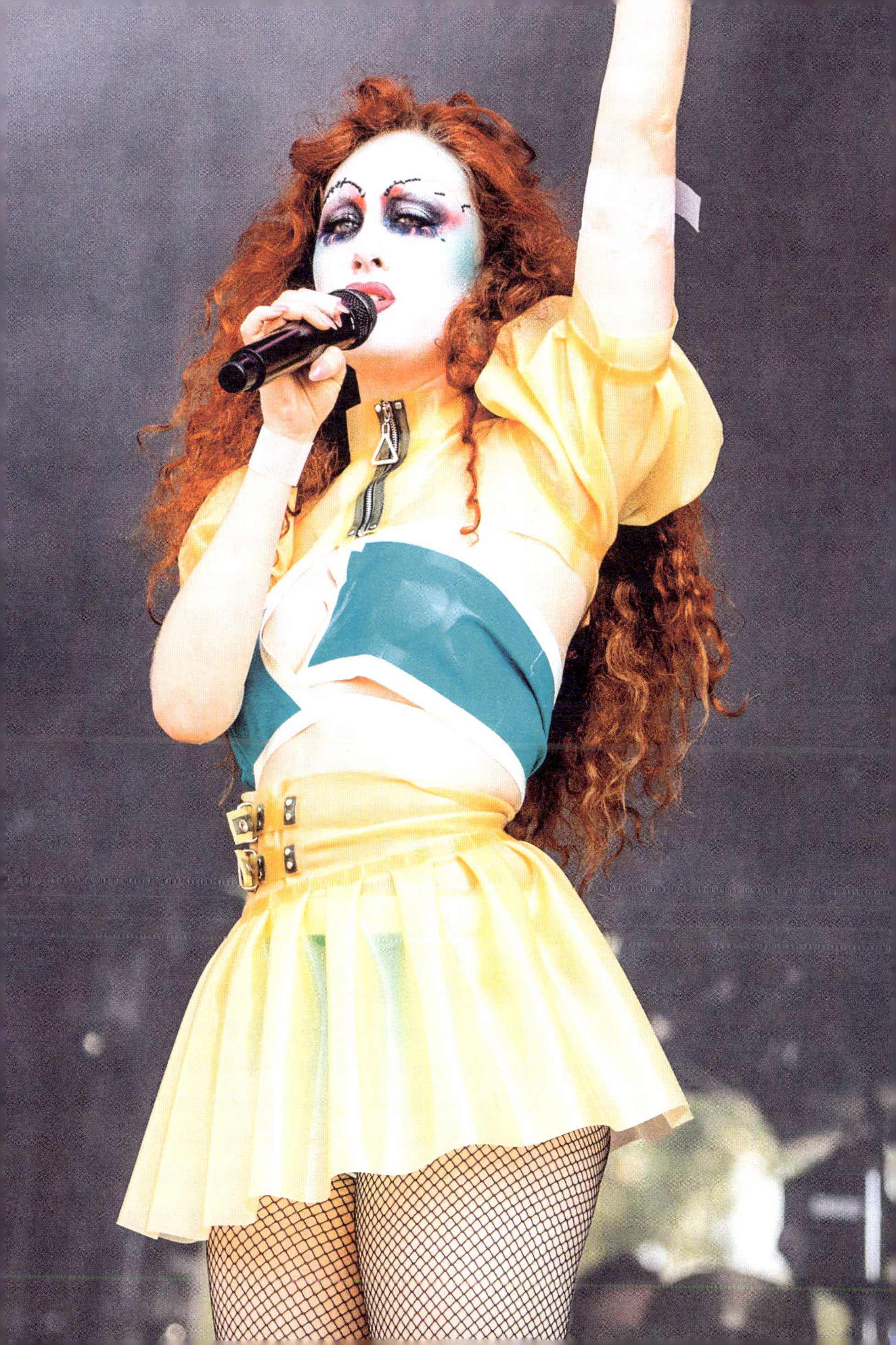

But even before that Bonnaroo performance, Roan had already proved her love for the Club Kids scene in another format. On 22 September 2023, the music video for her track "Super Graphic Ultra Modern Girl" was posted to Roan's YouTube channel, sending fans into a frenzy. The three-minute eight-second video shows Roan roaming around some of LA's tourist spots wearing a number of looks that appear as if they could have been plucked directly from a blurry photograph taken at the Limelight: a latex mini dress with corset back closure from Buster Brand, metallic opera gloves, Buster Brand cut-out bodysuit and skirt combo and shimmering knee-high boots that catch the eye as they reflect the hot sun on the Hollywood Walk of Fame. The garments are complemented by Roan's cherry red locks, which are styled in a high pony and V-cut fringe, topped with an alien-esque antennae hairband. Much of the video also features Roan in stark white face paint and dramatic skinny brows climbing up her forehead. These looks appear to take serious inspiration from some of Walt Cassidy's looks in particular, with many of his most widely recognized photos depicting his hair fashioned into two antennae-like pieces and sporting drawn-on brows in a very similar manner.

Roan often works with drag icon Andrew Dahling, who has often talked about his involvement in the Club Kids scene, something that can be seen in many of his looks for the pop artist. He also continues to work with the legendary Suzanne Bartsch – the unofficial reigning queen of New York nightlife, famous for her unparalleled parties and over-the-top outfits for the occasions. When discussing the inspiration behind his work with Roan, Dahling told *Highsnobiety* in a July 2024 interview, "Each look is going to really reference and pay homage to the people and the subcultures that have gotten us to where we are now."

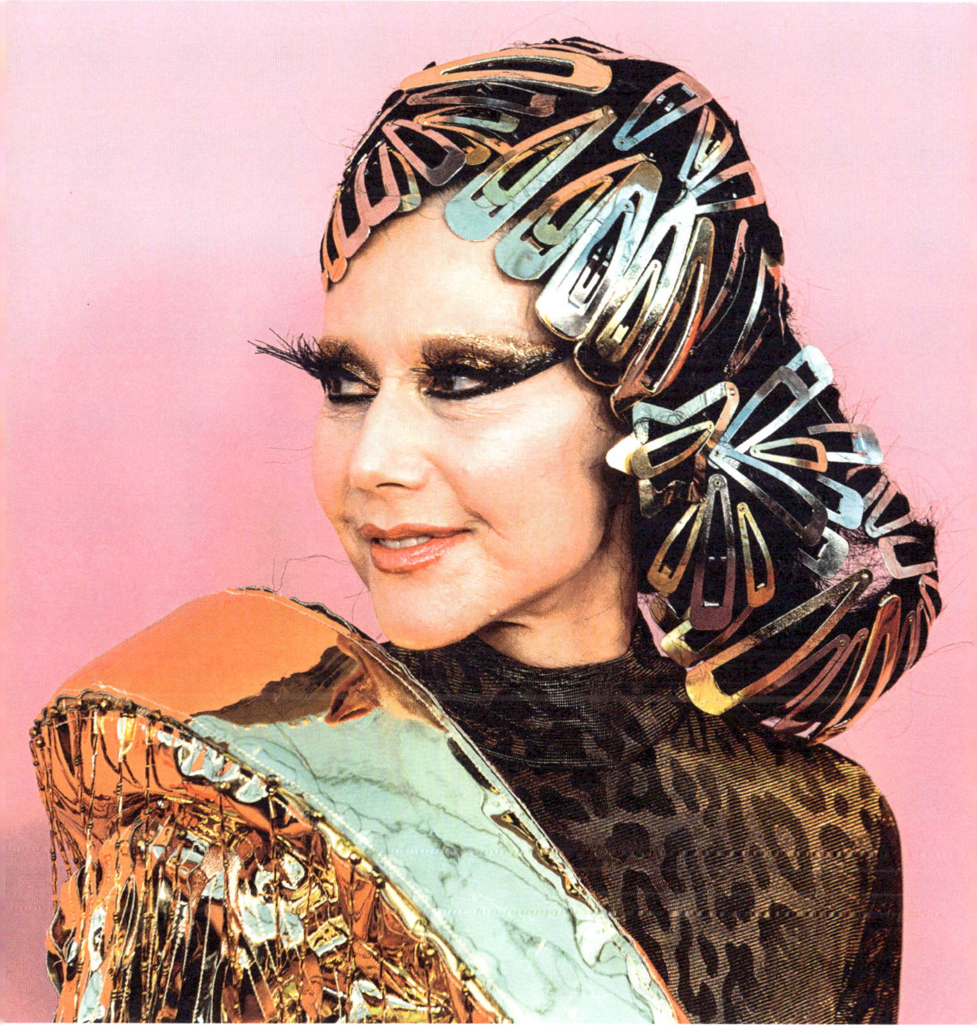

Often called “the mother of all Club Kids”, Susanne Bartsch remains a key player in the nightlife scene, inspiring many artists and performers, including Andrew Dahling, the creative mind behind many of Roan’s famous make-up looks.

Another look of Roan's that was heavily influenced by the Club Kids scene was that of her 2024 Coachella performance. Roan told *Vogue* beforehand that the inspiration behind the look came from asking, "What if Paris Hilton and James St. James or Walt Cassidy became one and put on a drag show?" James St. James and Walt Cassidy were two of the most recognized characters from the Club Kids scene in New York, both known for their dramatic make-up and DIY looks which often incorporated BDSM gear such as leather, latex and harnesses. For her Coachella debut, Roan brought in the talents of Busted Brand for the latex top that read "EAT ME" across the chest. The leather-studded thong and belt were courtesy of Zana Bayne. Eagle-eyed fans quickly recognized the choker style as similar to one previously sported by one of Roan's favourite drag queens, Violet Chachki. Make-up artist Donni Davy has also noted Chachki as one of her influences for Roan's make-up on the day, alongside 1980s punks and Boy George.

Roan graces the stage in a custom latex look for the first day of Coachella in April 2024.

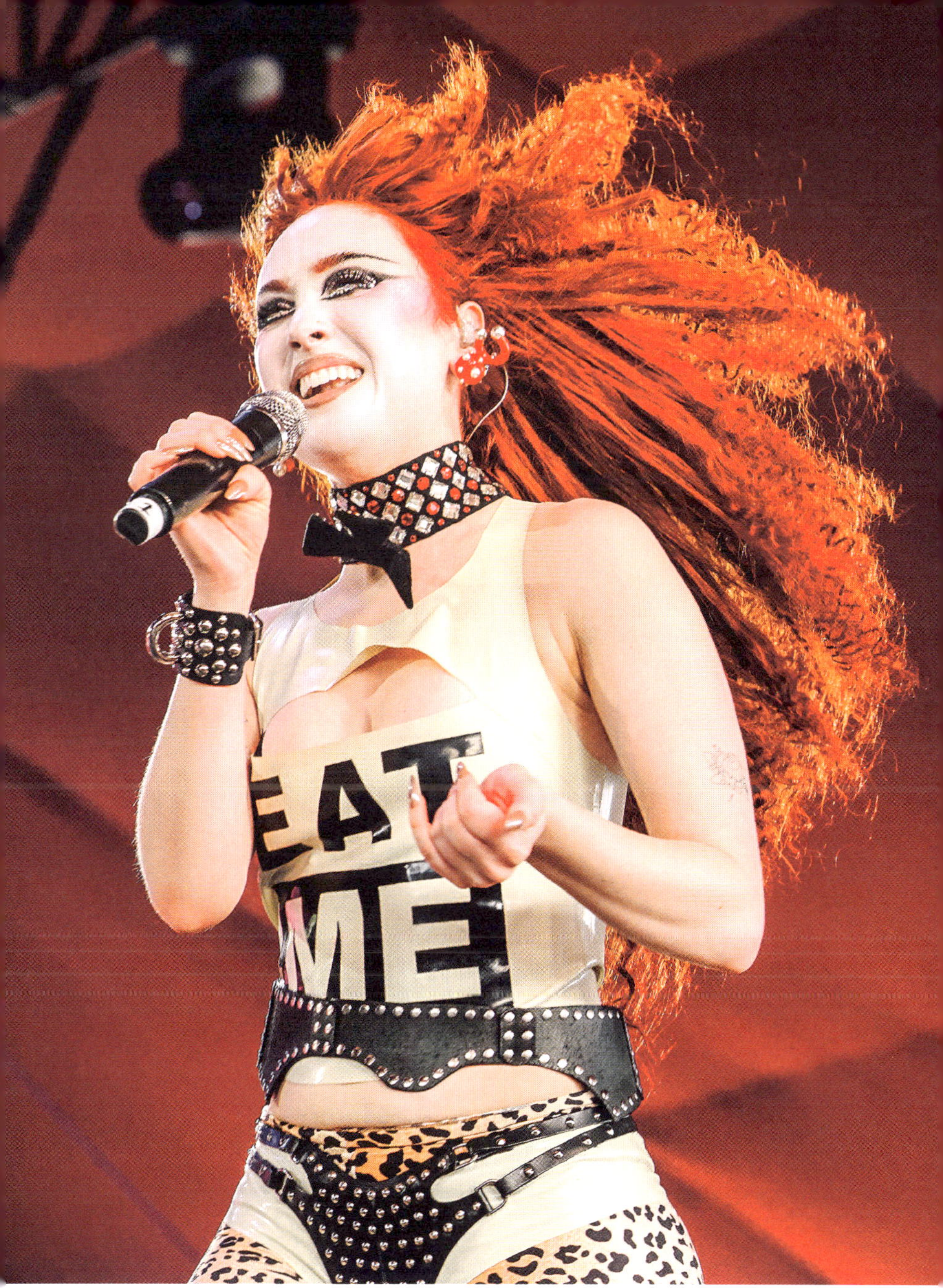
EAT
ME

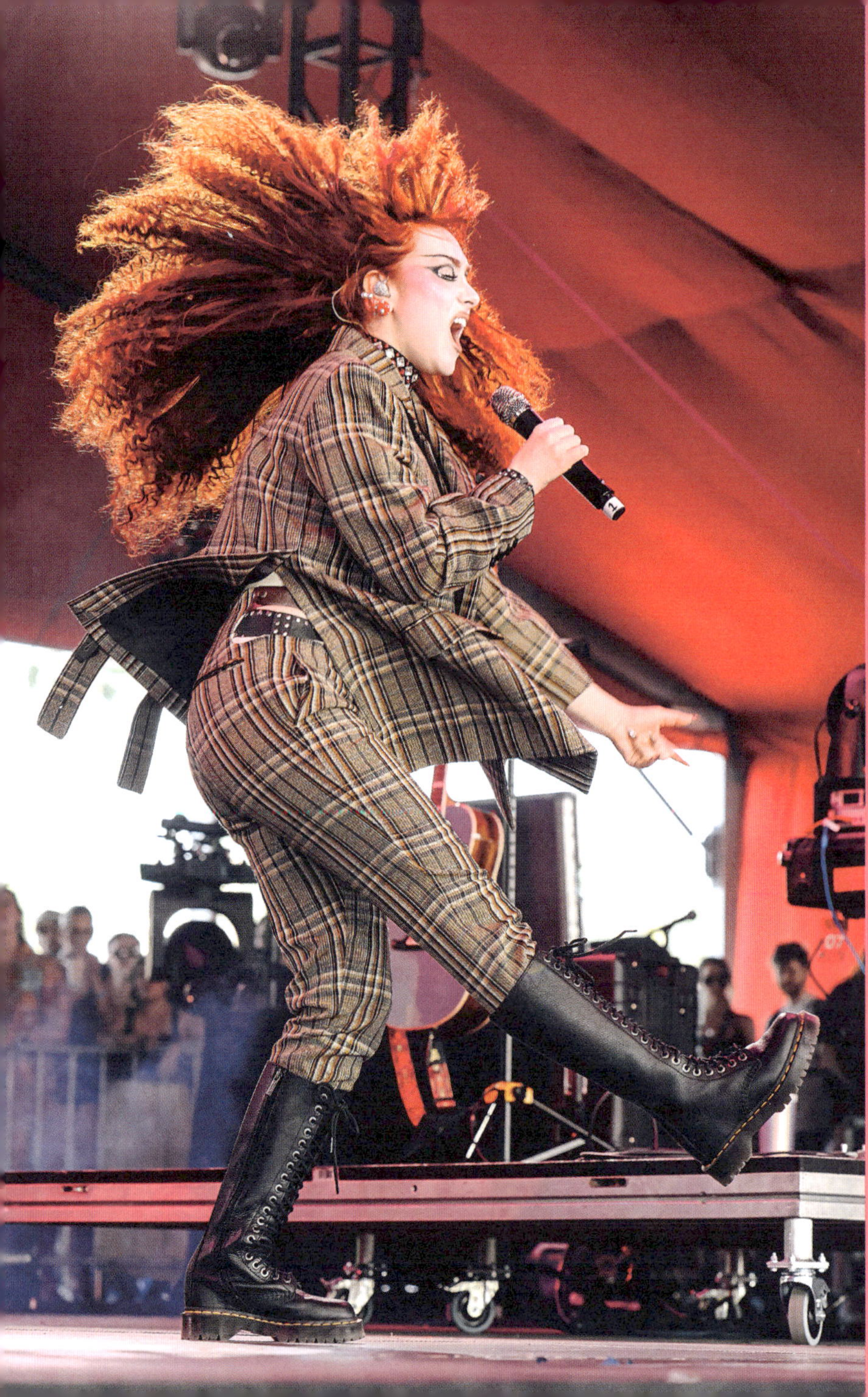

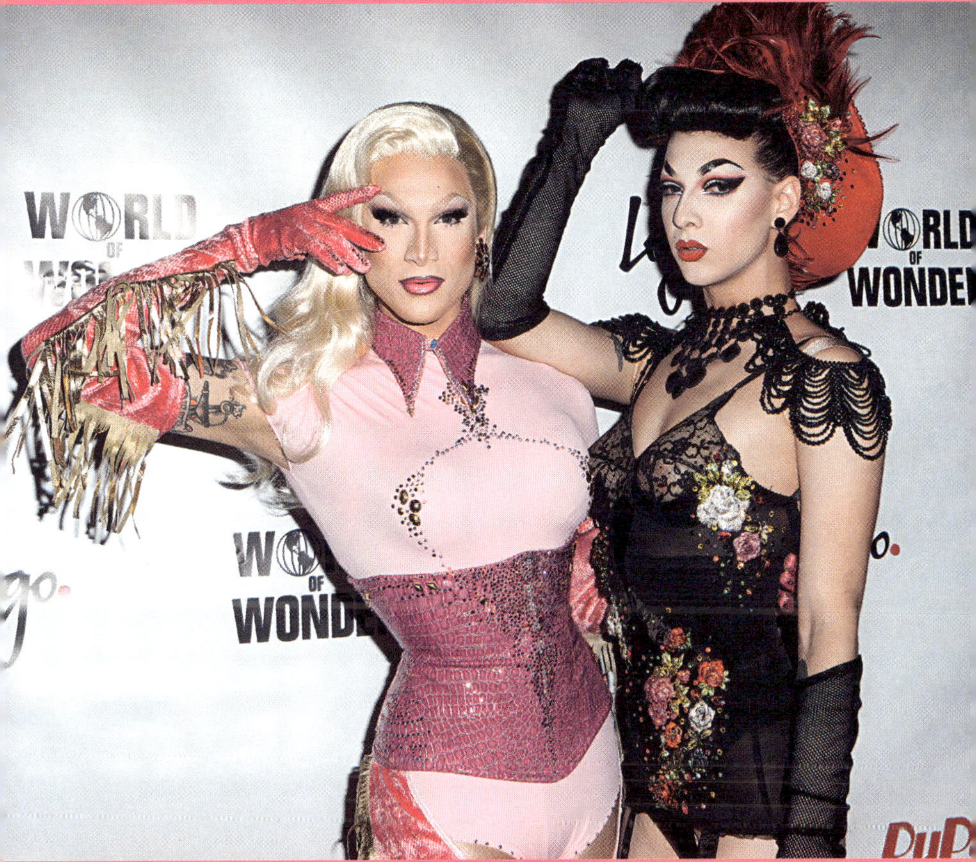

OPPOSITE Roan wears a plaid suit look from Japanese label TOGA, paired with knee-high boots from Dr. Martens at Coachella 2024.

ABOVE Both Miss Fame and Violet Chachki (pictured here at a *RuPaul's Drag Race* event in 2015) have openly discussed their involvement in the Club Kids scene and its role in their development as artists and performers.

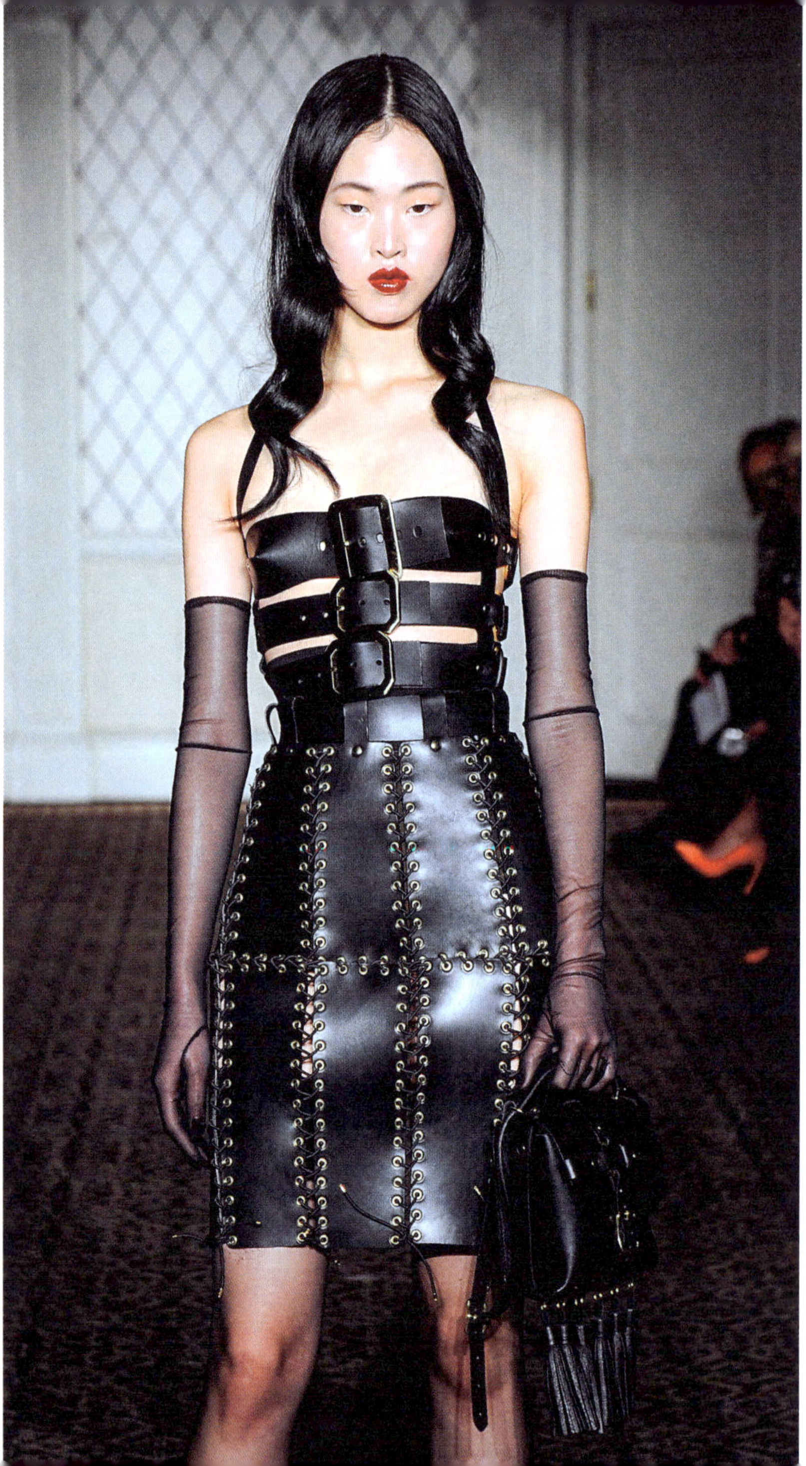

Kayla Kumari Upadhyaya of *Autostraddle*, one of the leading online publications for sapphic-related content, ranked this look at number four in her preferred queer looks from the pop star. Upadhyaya noted that she saw it as "a perfect distillation of Chappell's trashy, campy aesthetics ... it feels so distinctly her. It's textural chaos." She went on to say, "The EAT ME top with the boob-highlighting cut-out is just the cherry on top. Webb cites Vivienne Westwood as an influence here, and it shows!" In January 2025, Guy Trebay of *The New York Times* spoke to vintage clothing shop owner Dani Cabot, who also remarked on Roan's Club Kids influence: "What's brilliant about Chappell Roan is that what she's doing hearkens back to the club kids of the '90s." And when discussing Roan's themed concert approaches, Cabot highlighted, "They're a way to bring into real life communities most people only get to experience online."

Zana Bayne's designs have long been influenced by her involvement in the Club Kids scene, playing with latex and leather, as seen here in a look from the label's 2014 collection.

History, her way

Other key areas that Roan and her team have pulled inspiration from include bygone centuries, with one of the first examples coming in the form of the headpiece for Roan's "Good Luck, Babe" single cover, which she also wore to the UMG Grammys after-party in February 2024. The horned design has historically been referred to as an escoffion and was usually associated with women of great wealth and social standing through the late Middle Ages in Europe. The style of headpiece was somewhat controversial during that period, as Katherine Morris Lester shared in her book *Accessories of Dress:*

"So ridiculous were these extravagances that they were denounced by preachers and condemned by lay moralists. One bishop preached a sermon against the outrageous fashion and directed the people, upon the approach of a woman so dressed, to cry, 'Beware of the ram! Beware of the ram!' He promised ten days pardon to all who should in this way show their indignation." Lester went on to relay, "Other moralists started the cry, 'War to the hennin! War to the hennin!' All these attacks, however, only led to greater extravagance on the part of the ladies."

Jacqueline de la Grange, wife of Jean de Montagu, Grand Minister of France under Charles VI, wearing an escoffion head piece in an illustration from 1827.

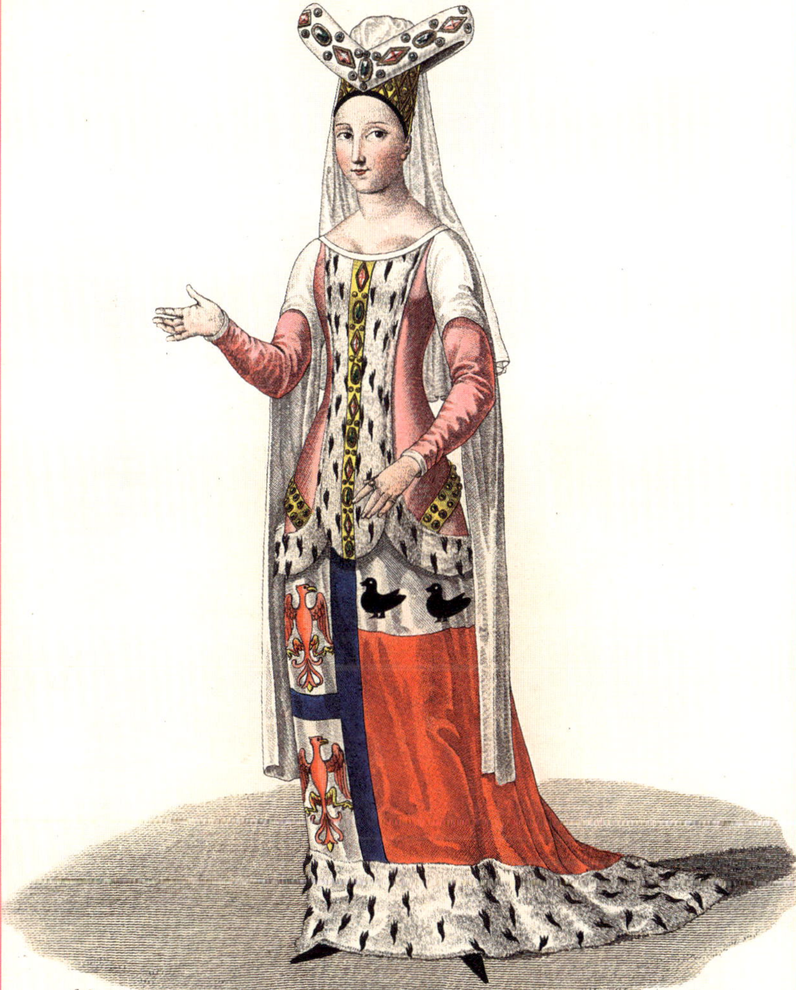

Lanté del.t Gatine sculp.t

JACQUELINE DE LA GRANGE,

FEMME DE JEAN DE MONTAGU,

Grand Ministre de France, sous Charles VI.

D'après une Statue en pierre, peinte dans le Temps.

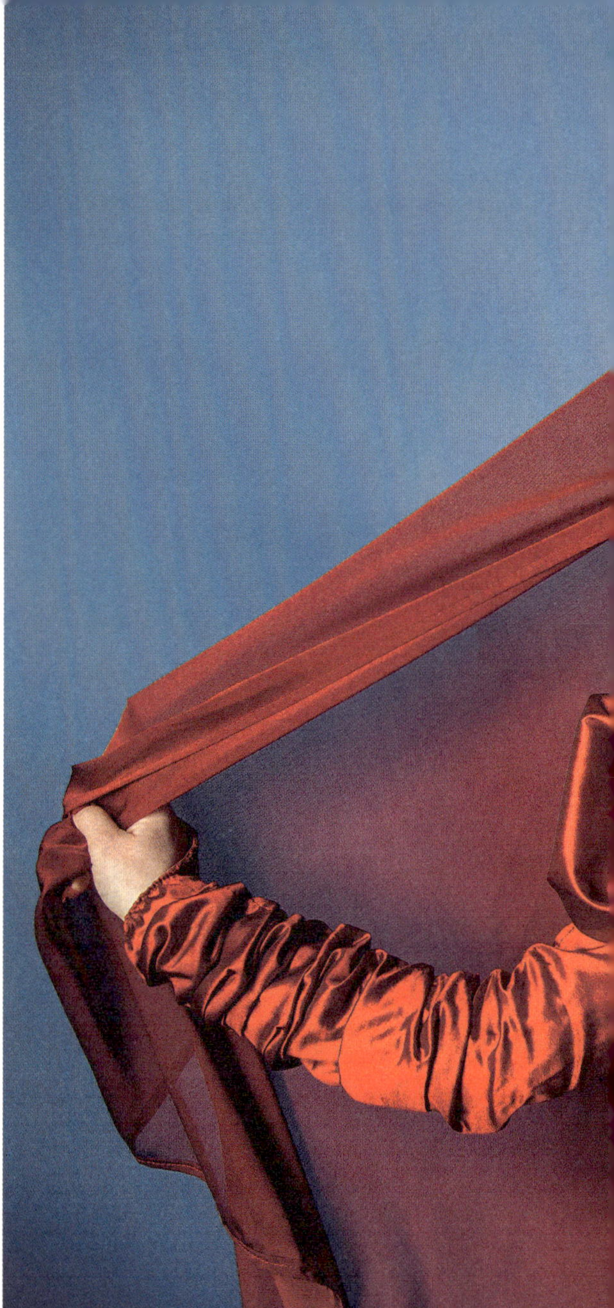

Roan's look for the Grammy Awards after-party gained the nickname the "Penelope look" due to its similarities between the 2006 film of the same name starring Christina Ricci in a prosthetic pig snout.

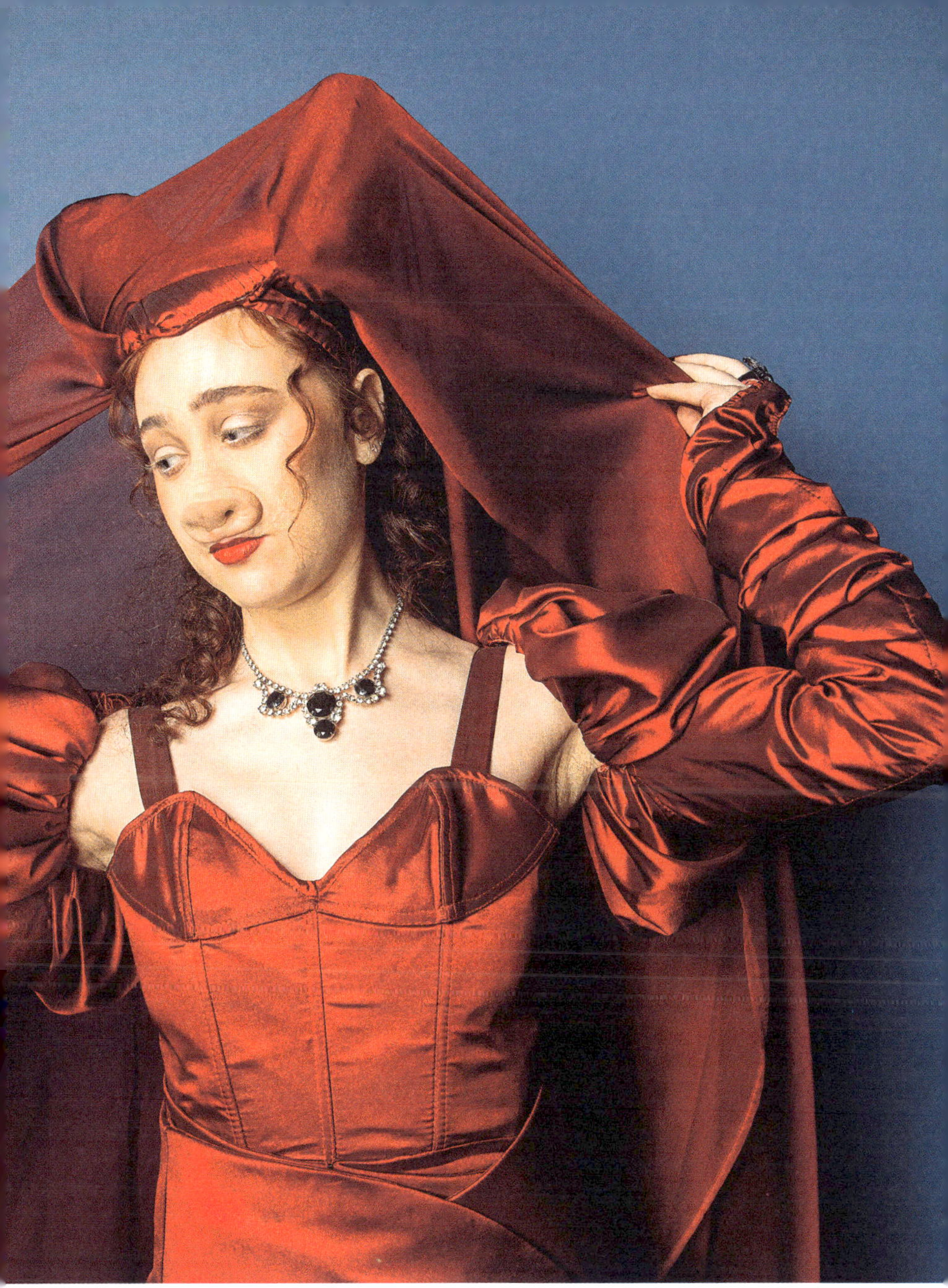

"The *inspiration* came from Chappell and [stylist] Genesis's medieval *royal fantasy* visions!"

MARGAUX ANBOUBA, *VOGUE*

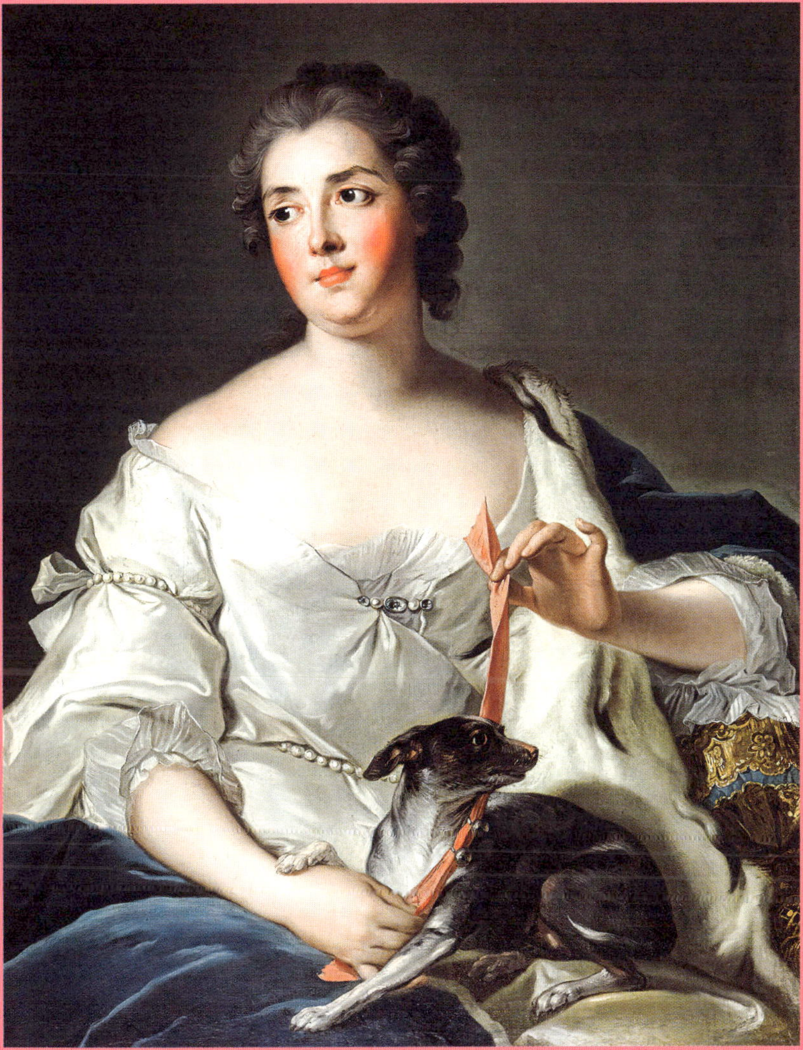

Historical images don't just inspire Roan's outfits: some of her softer make-up styles have been compared to looks seen in eighteenth-century French portraiture, such as the one seen here in *Portrait of a Woman and her Dog* (1750) by Jean-Marc Nattier.

Roan's headpiece was crafted by independent designer Manny Robertson, while the matching dress was courtesy of Efrain Nava. When asked about the look by *Vulture*'s Caitlin Wolper, Genesis Webb shared that this look was pulled from a variety of sources, including "*Gummo* and Chris Cunningham visuals, but also screen grabs from *The Tales of Hoffmann*. I feel like I'd had that headpiece on a mood board for a while." When asked about the meaning behind the prosthetic nose, she shared that it was Roan's idea: "I don't know if it's my secret to tell why she chose it. That one felt right for a variety of reasons", she said. Though this book attempts to categorize some of Roan's most iconic looks through their main sources of inspiration, this insight from Webb demonstrates the breadth of influences that can go into one single look.

The next demonstration of how Roan looks to the historical periods of yesteryears was one of her most career-defining performances yet: the 2024 MTV Video Music Awards. It was at this star-studded event that Roan further cemented herself as a true style icon through three distinct outfits, all of which garnered their own headlines from leading fashion publications across the globe. These looks played a key

Poster for the 1951 film *The Tales of Hoffmann*, said to have inspired Roan's stylist Genesis Webb for Roan's "Penelope look".

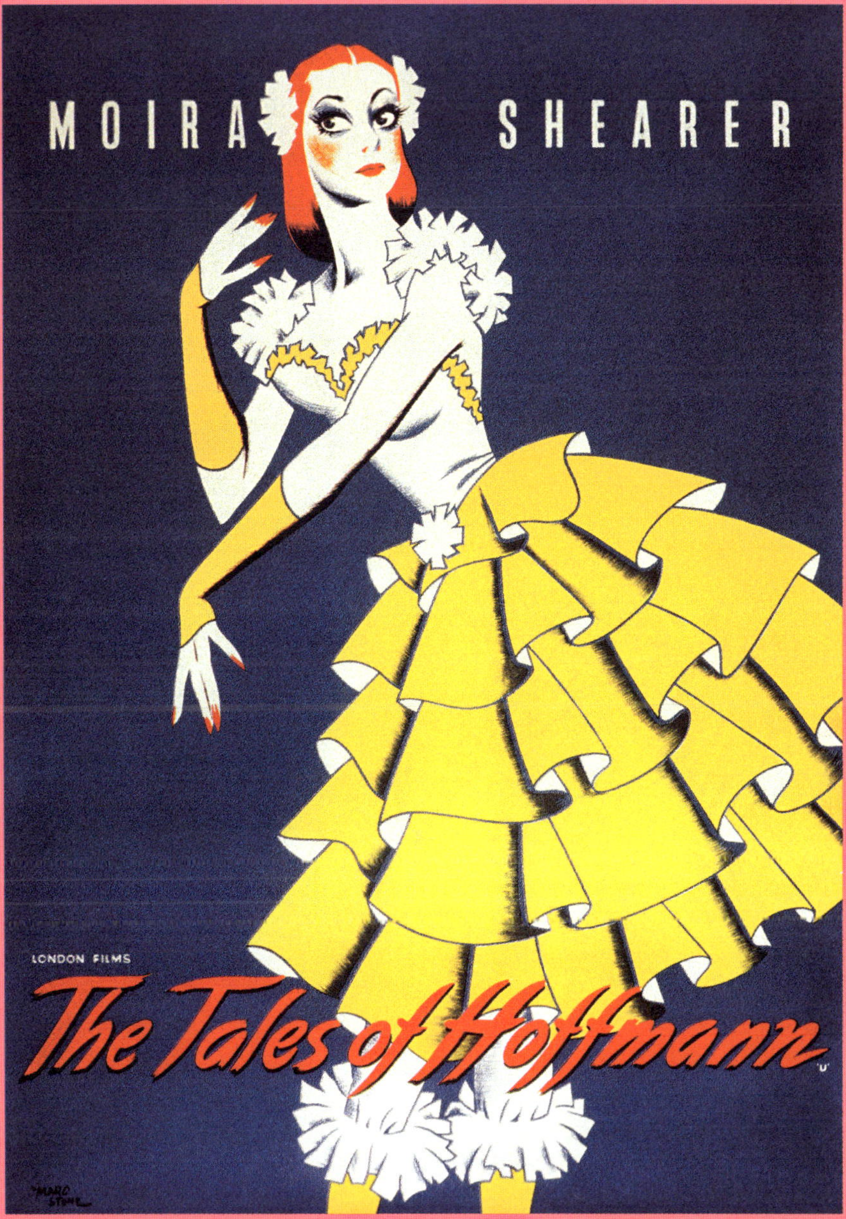
MOIRA SHEARER
LONDON FILMS
The Tales of Hoffmann
'U'

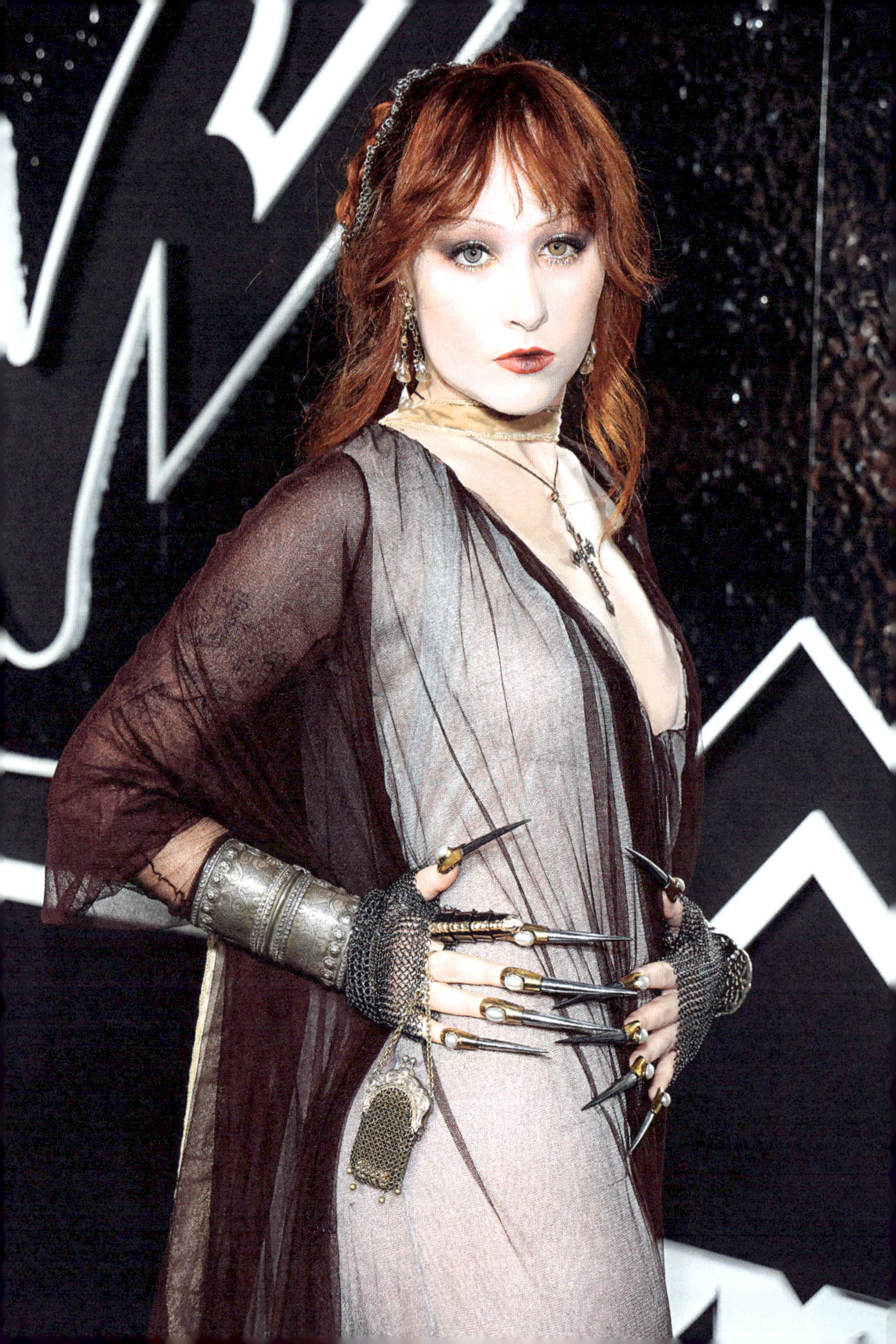

role in Roan becoming a household name and an instantly recognizable pop star who approaches fashion in a way that defies expectations. Her first look of the evening was the red carpet style that Chelsey Sanchez of *Harper's Bazaar* interpreted as "channelling a medieval warrior queen". The Missouri native stepped out in a sheer-panelled dress from Y/Project's Fall/Winter 2024 ready-to-wear collection, initially worn under a velvet green robe that Roan told Nessa Diab was 300 years old, dating back to the seventeenth century. But the oldest piece of the night was the rug, which was rolled out for Roan (and only Roan) to step onto as her own personal red carpet of sorts. Webb spoke about the symbolism of the look with *Interview* magazine: "It was this intensely theatrical moment showing her femininity, but also the power that she holds. The knight gives her the sword, and she gives it back. And then, the actual performance where she becomes the knight and accepts the award."

Vogue's Margaux Anbouba reported on her look that night, dubbing the team behind her beauty approach as the "genius glam trifecta", referring to Dom Forletta on hair, make-up by Andrew Dahling and her nails being taken care of by Juan Alvear. Dahling told Anbouba about the look: "The inspiration came from Chappell and [stylist] Genesis's medieval royal fantasy visions!"

Draped in a sheer dress from Y/Project, Roan's first look for the 2024 MTV Video Music Awards was completed with accessories that included a cross necklace, wrist cuffs and a ring by American designer Lillian Shalom.

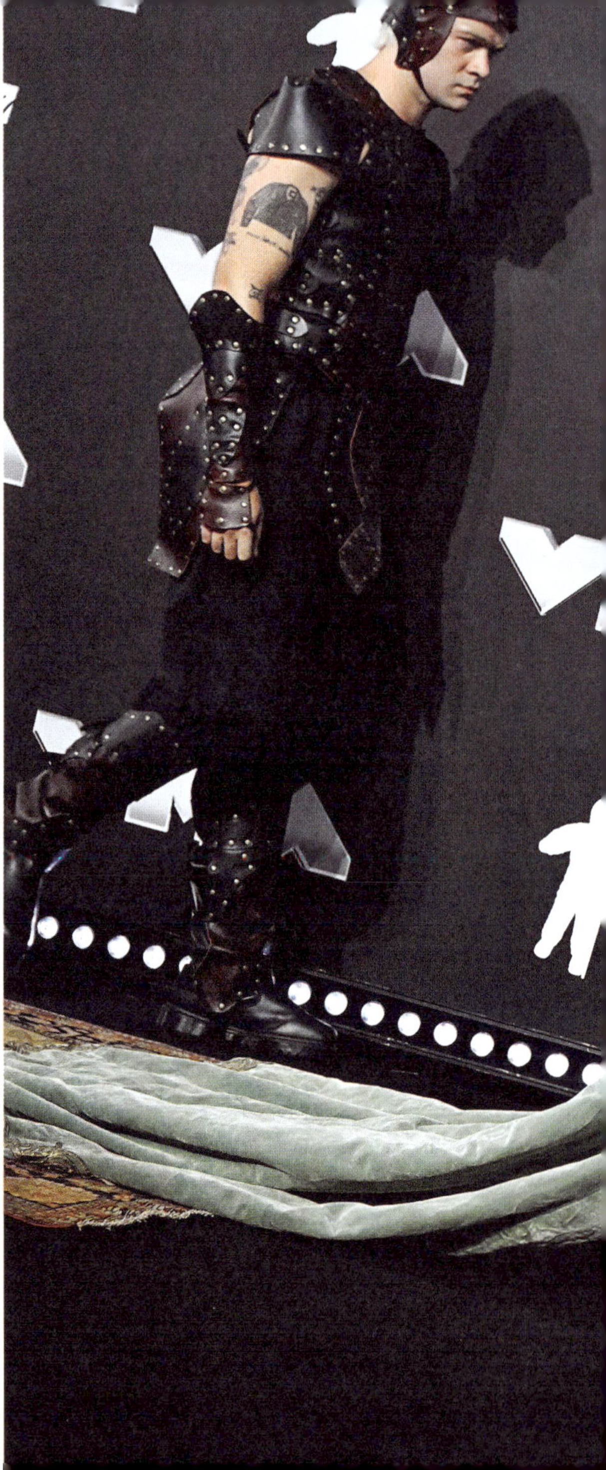

"It wasn't just a fashion statement – it was a full-on character transformation", proclaimed fashion journalist Catherine Kallon for Red Carpet Fashion Awards, regarding Roan's 2024 MTV Video Music Awards entrance look.

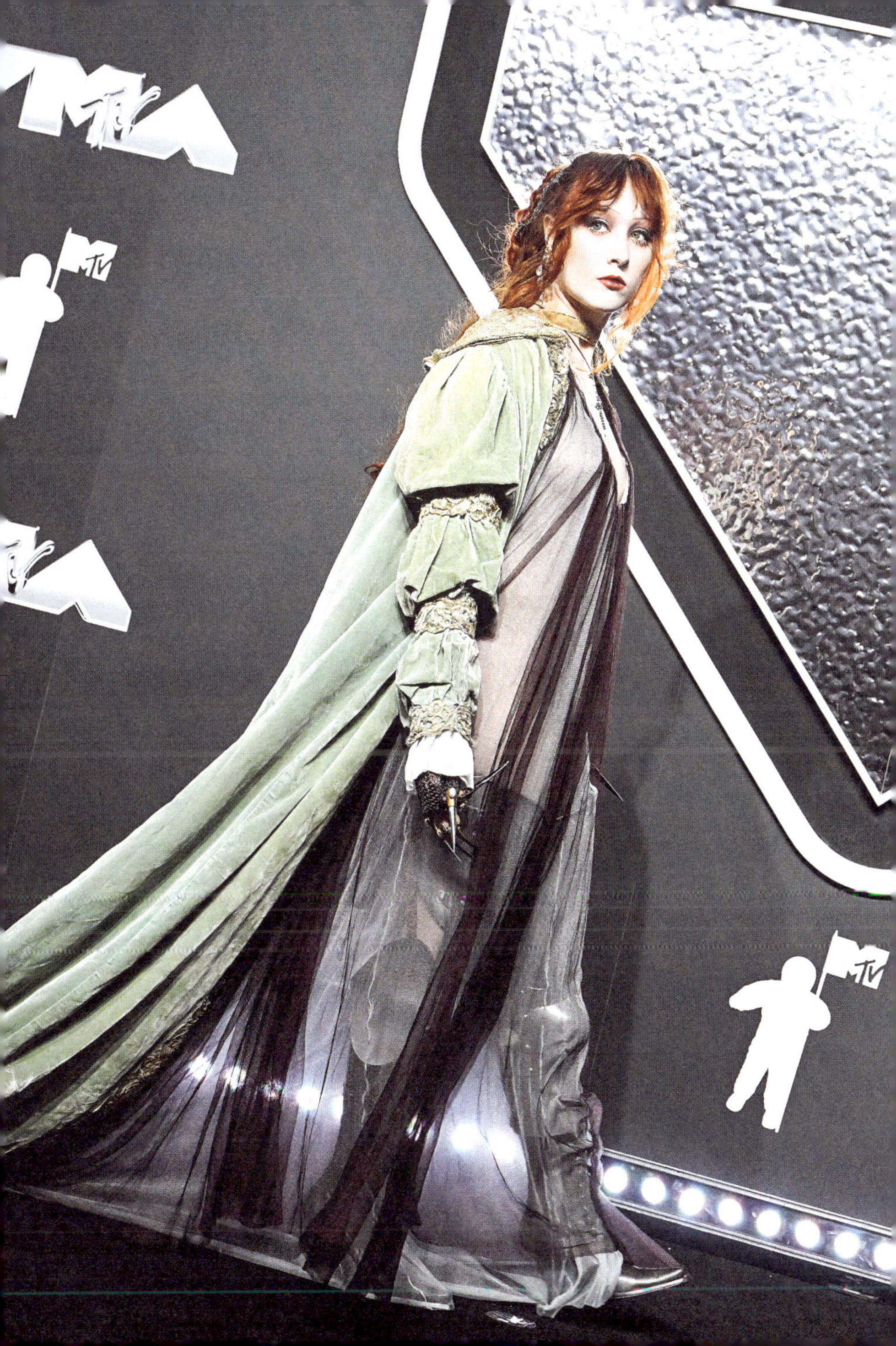
MTV

For her performance on the evening, Roan slipped into a full suit of armour created by the legendary Zana Bayne with chain mail by Thomas Hauth. This look caused many to speculate that the inspiration could be either Joan of Arc or Mademoiselle de Maupin. The latter was a seventeenth-century opera singer who led a colourful life which included plenty of dramatic love affairs, notably one that included Julie d'Aubigny (as she was also known) burning down a convent as a distraction measure to allow her female lover to escape with her into the night. She went on to sing opera in Paris before retiring into oblivion after her French noblewoman lover passed away. Though it is more likely that it was Joan of Arc who inspired the look more directly, Marie-Adélina de la Ferrière for pride.com highlighted the power of the trio, stating, "Whether it's Joan, Julie or Chappell herself, the message is clear: we're here, we're queer and we've been setting the world on fire for centuries."

As she accepted the Best New Artist award later in the evening, Roan appeared in a Rabanne Spring 2024 chain mail dress, a nod to the fashion house's long-standing relationship with chain mail since its 1966 debut collection. Independent chain mail designer Juniper Rose of Falconiere provided the gloves. This look grabbed the attention of critics across the globe and would help spark what some referred to as "castlecore" or "medievalcore" – a trend that drew on elements such as chain mail for fashion inspiration. Pinterest shared that this would be a key area of interest throughout 2025, disclosing a 110 per cent increase in searches for "medievalcore" on the platform.

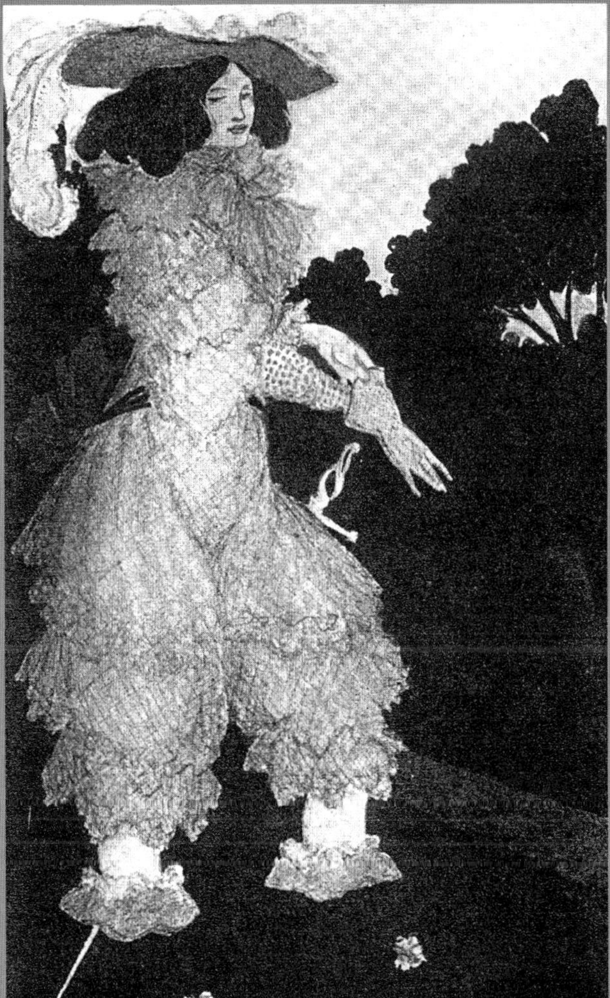

Fans speculated that Roan's warrior look could be a nod to French sapphic icon Julie d'Aubigny, better known as Mademoiselle Maupin.

"Fashion is used as armour for me – Fashion is armour in a protective way but also in a freeing way."

CHAPPELL ROAN VIA YOUTUBE VIDEO FOR *THE MET GALA EBAY COLLABORATION*

Roan takes the stage in Zana Bayne with chain mail by Thomas Hauth at the 2024 MTV Video Music Awards in Elmont, New York, on 11 September 2024.

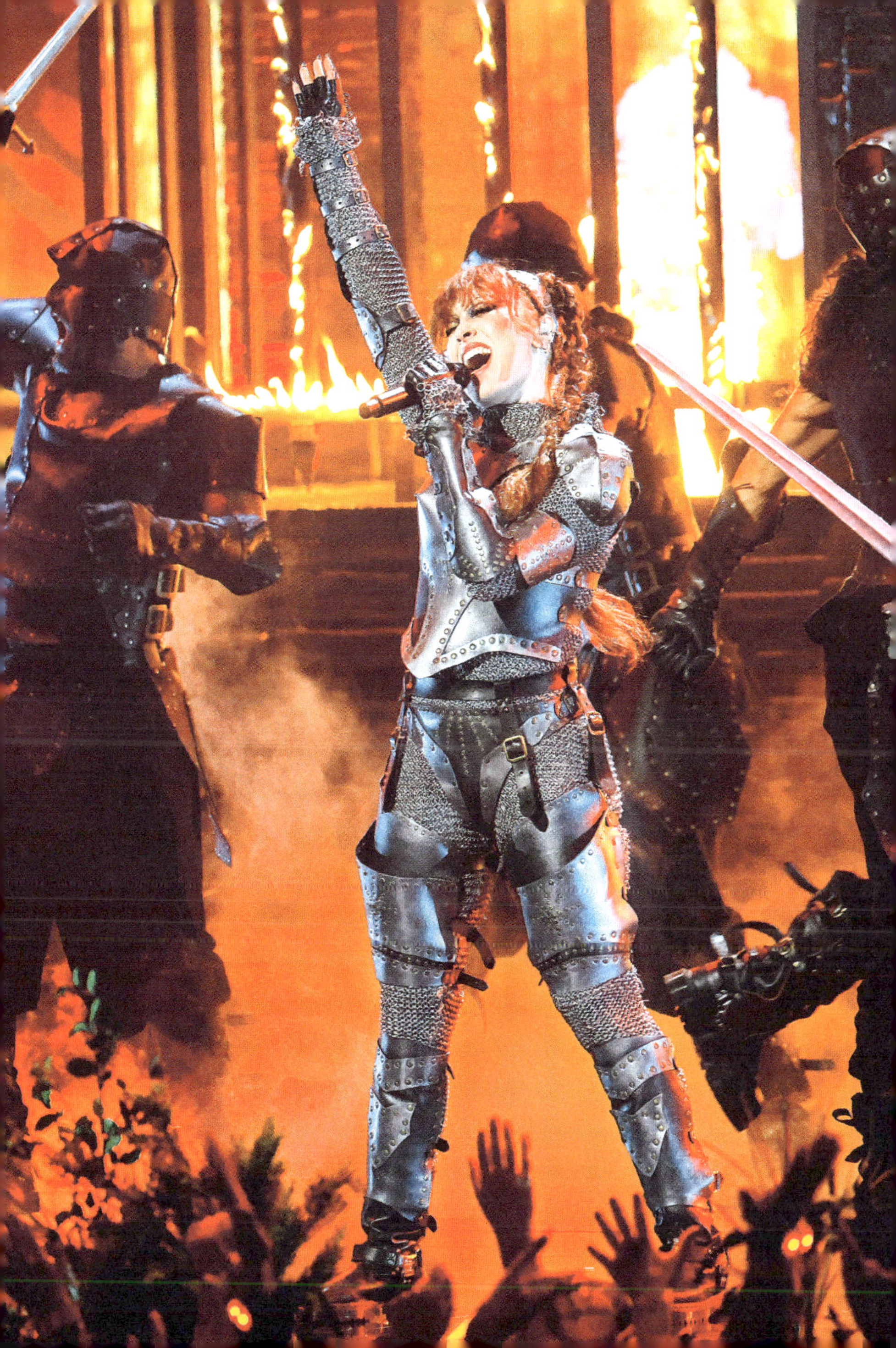

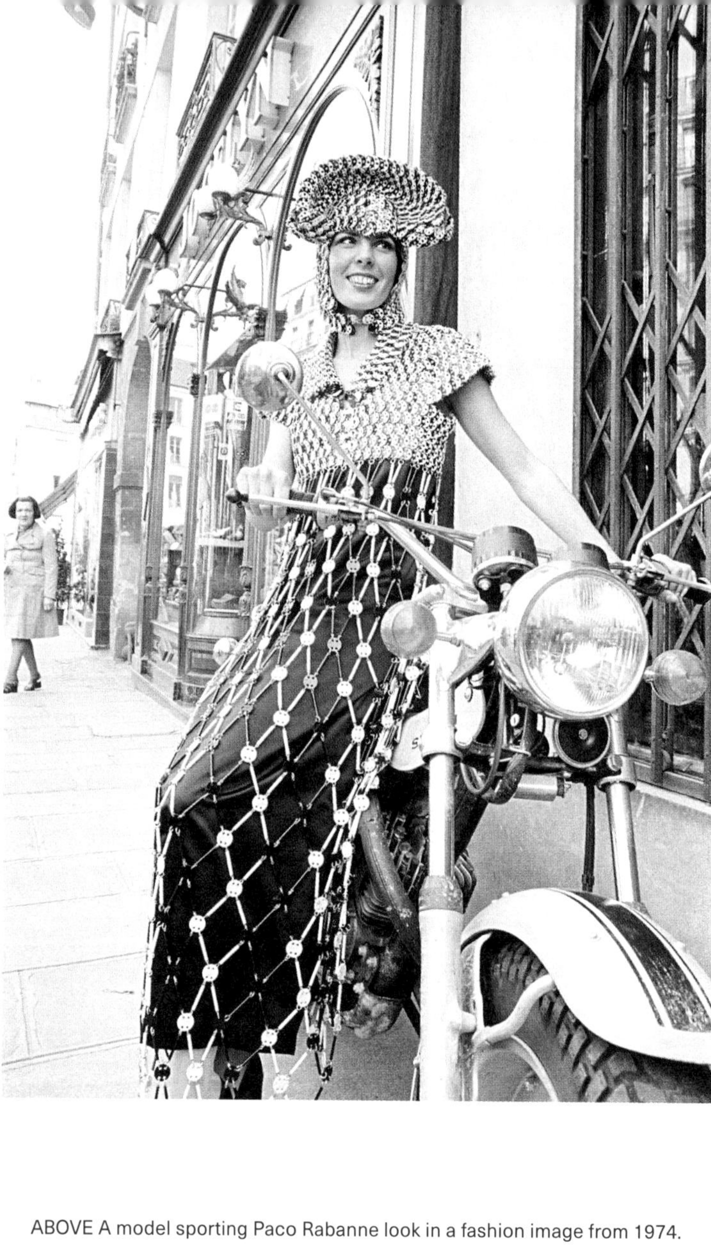

ABOVE A model sporting Paco Rabanne look in a fashion image from 1974.

OPPOSITE Roan wins the Best New Artist award in a Rabanne Spring 2024 chain mail dress, with gloves by Juniper Rose of Falconiere.

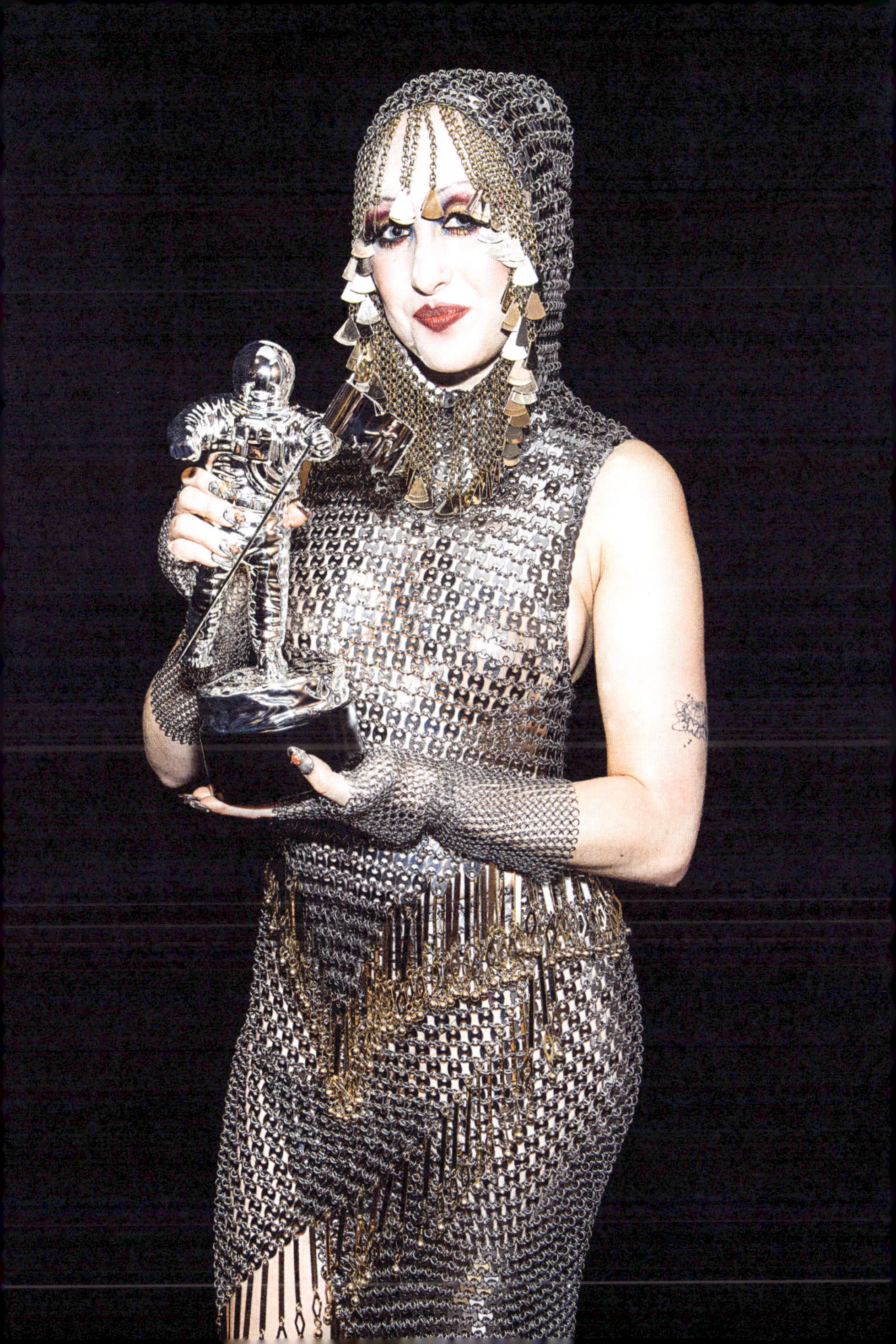

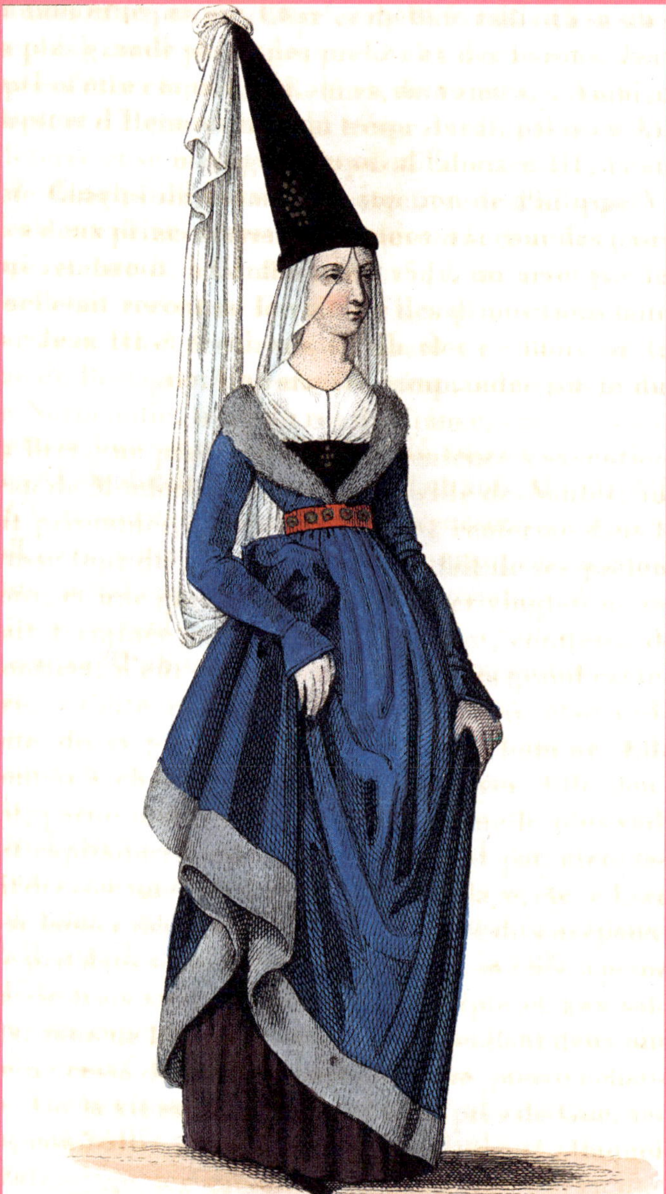

A few months after debuting the chain mail ensemble, Roan won Best New Artist again, this time at the 67th Annual Grammy Awards in Los Angeles, California. Roan returned to the world of historical headwear with a cone hennin designed by British milliner Piers Atkinson. Atkinson used hand-printed vintage fabrics from Zandra Rhodes to wrap the pointed hat, which famously fell off Roan's head mid-speech. The historical relevance of the statement style can be traced back to a number of key characters, though most notably aristocratic women in Europe around the fifteenth century. Over the years, the distinctive headpiece became associated with the character of the princess and cemented itself as a symbol of such, becoming commonly known simply as a "princess hat". This look is something that Roan also played with during a shoot for the Spring/Summer 2024 issue of *Nylon* magazine, though rather than being paired with an avant-garde Acne Studios dress, Roan looked to a bright pink satin gown seemingly fresh from the rails of a local thrift shop.

A tall conical hat (hennin) is seen atop the head of Jeanne la Flammande (Joanna of Flanders) in an illustration from Leopold Massard from 1834.

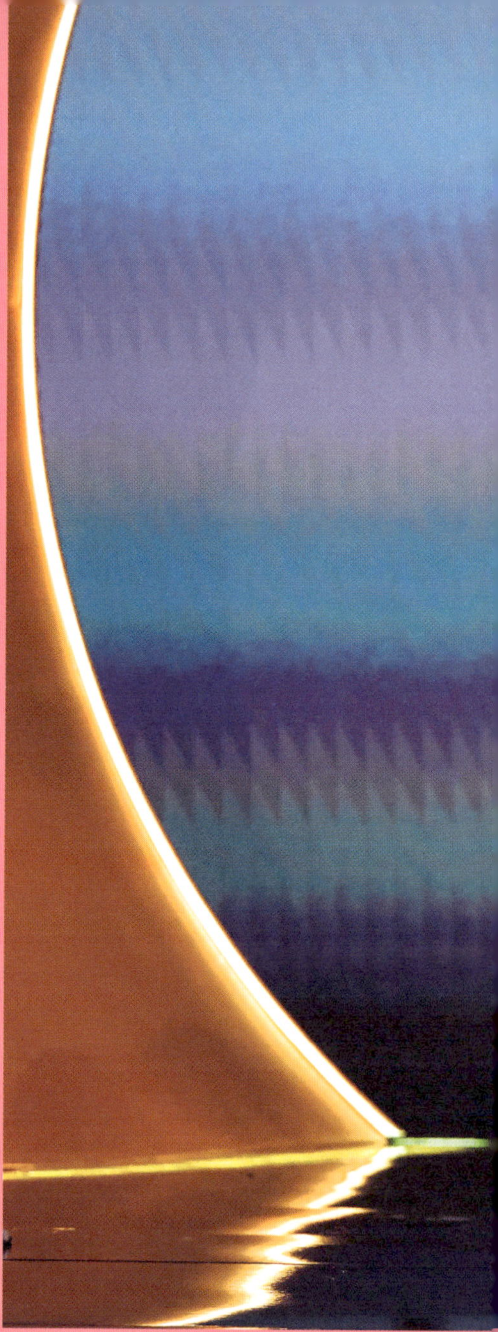

OPPOSITE Roan wearing a cone hennin by British milliner Piers Atkinson, paired with an Acne Studios dress, as she accepts the award for Best New Artist at the Grammys, in February 2025.

OVERLEAF Australian-Taiwanese designer Samuel Lewis is credited with creating this nun-inspired look worn onstage by Roan at the Hinterland Music Festival in Saint Charles, Iowa, in August 2024.

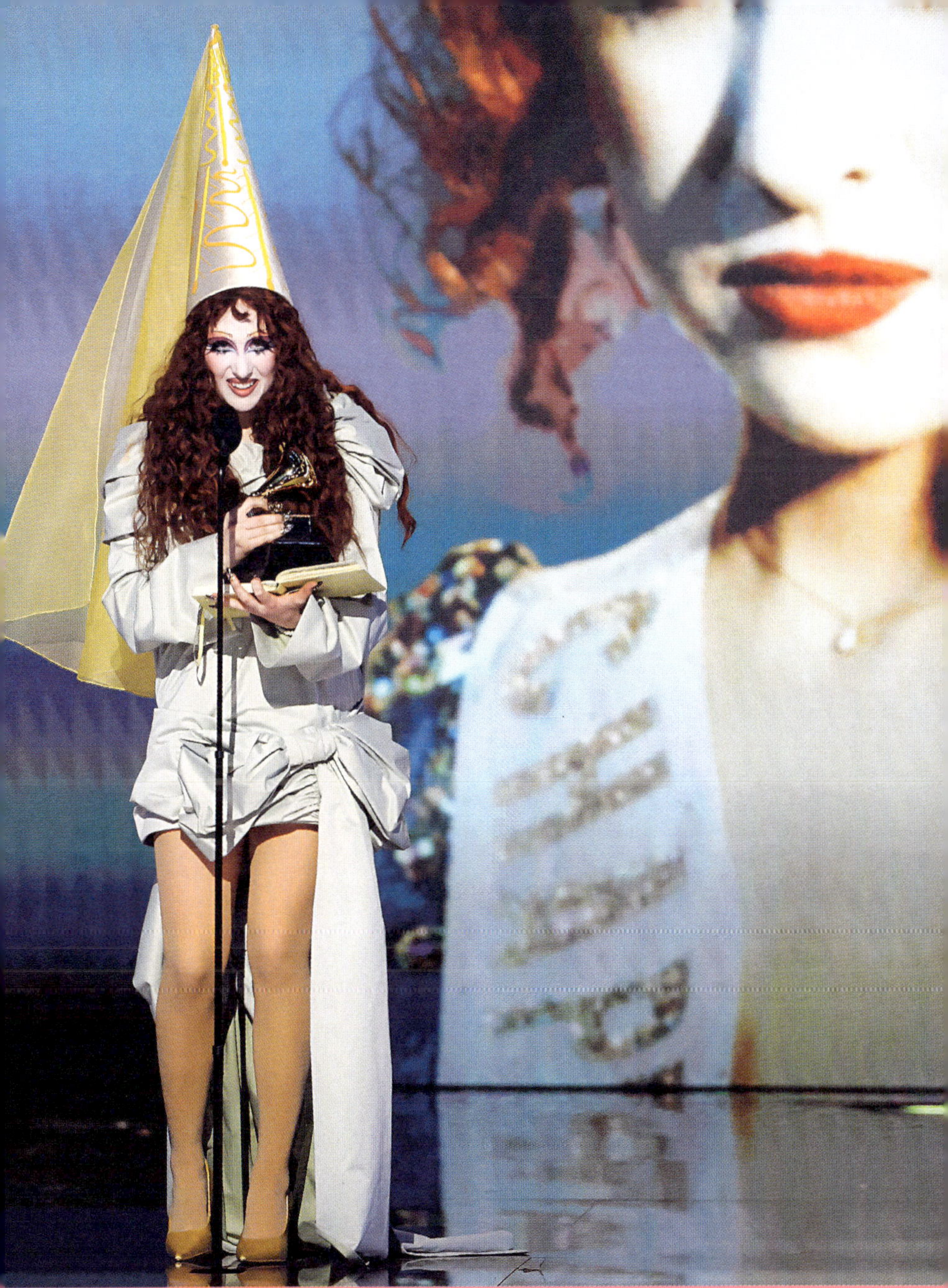

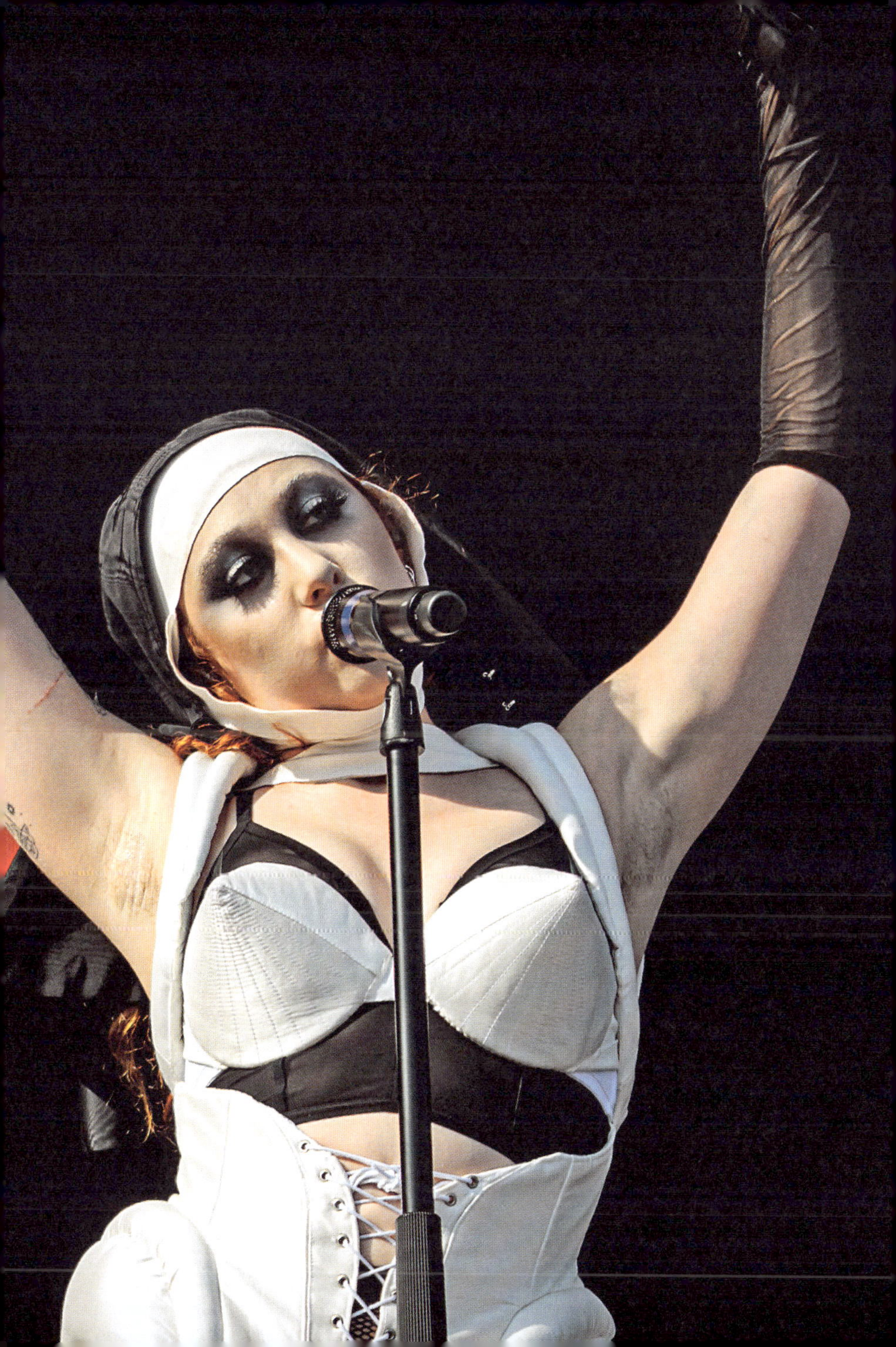

High

CHAPTER 3

Fashion

By spring 2025, Roan had become a bona fide fashion icon with her bright and bold looks that often sent fans into a frenzy with their rich cultural references pulled from nearly every corner of history. But it would be her appearances at Paris Fashion Week in March 2025 that would take her into new realms of fashion and build her wardrobe beyond the playful looks that many associated her with.

Roan attends the Ludovic de Saint Sernin Fall 2025 show at Paris Fashion Week, wearing a leather dress from the French label along with Christian Louboutin heeled sandals.

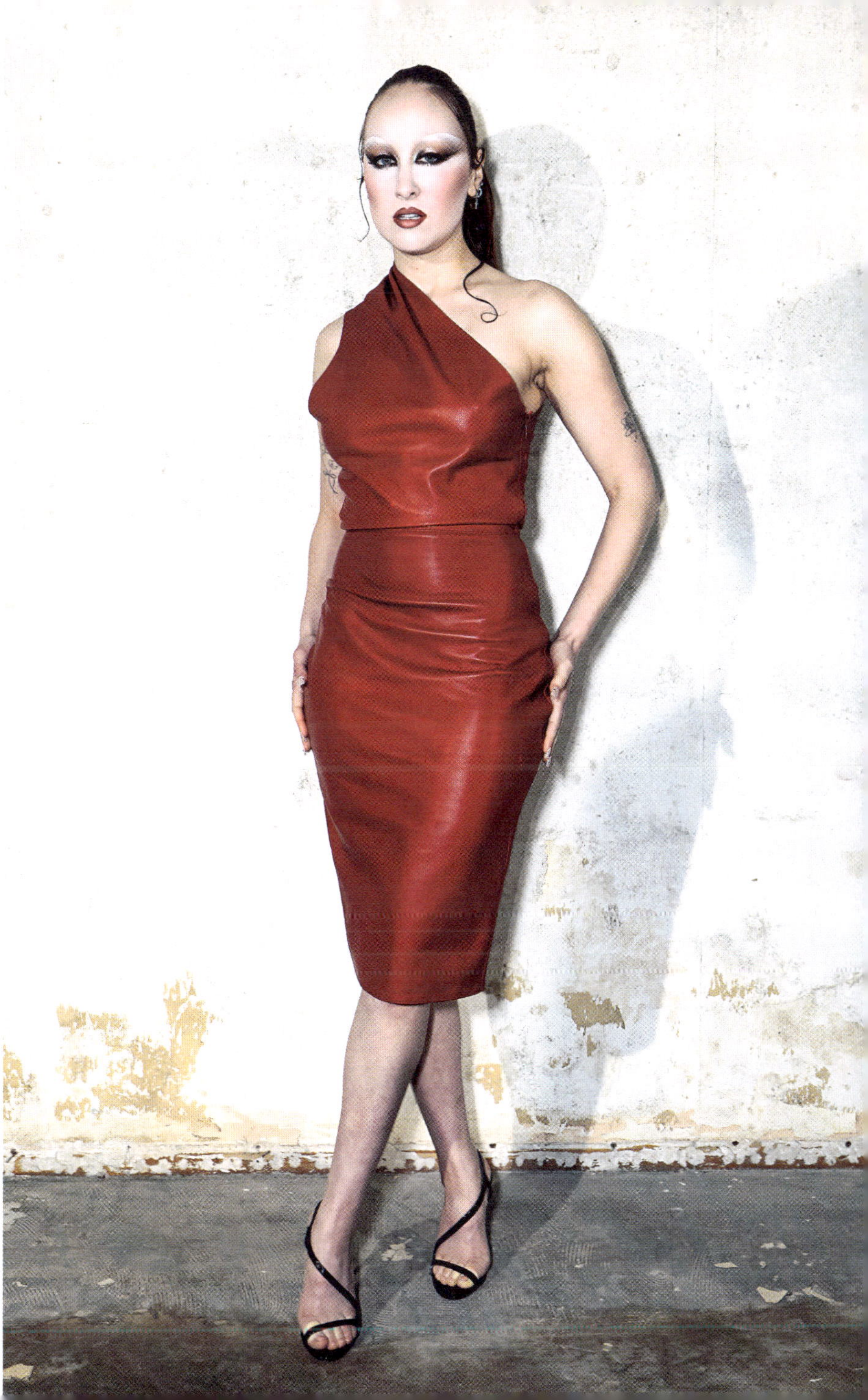

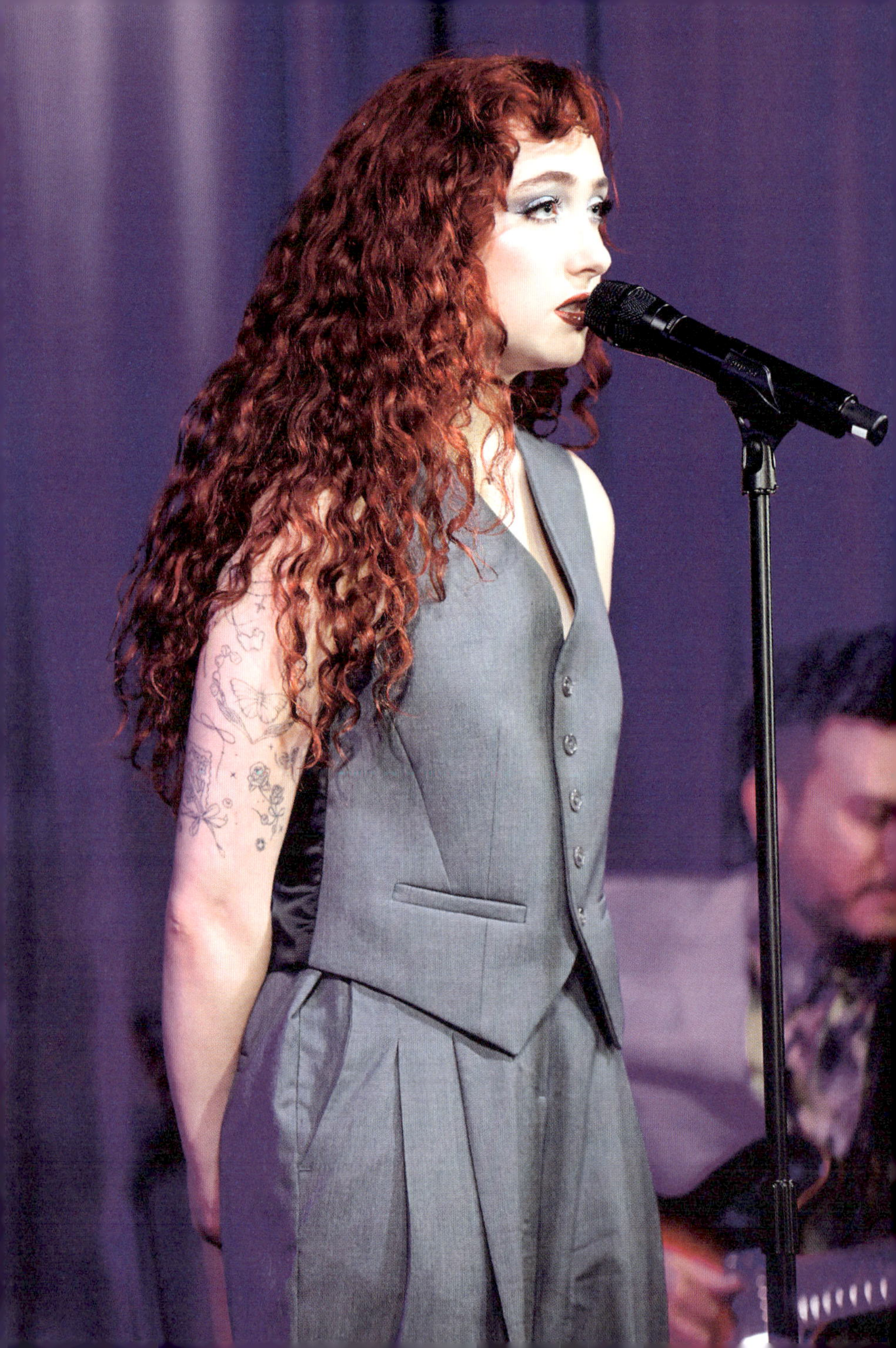

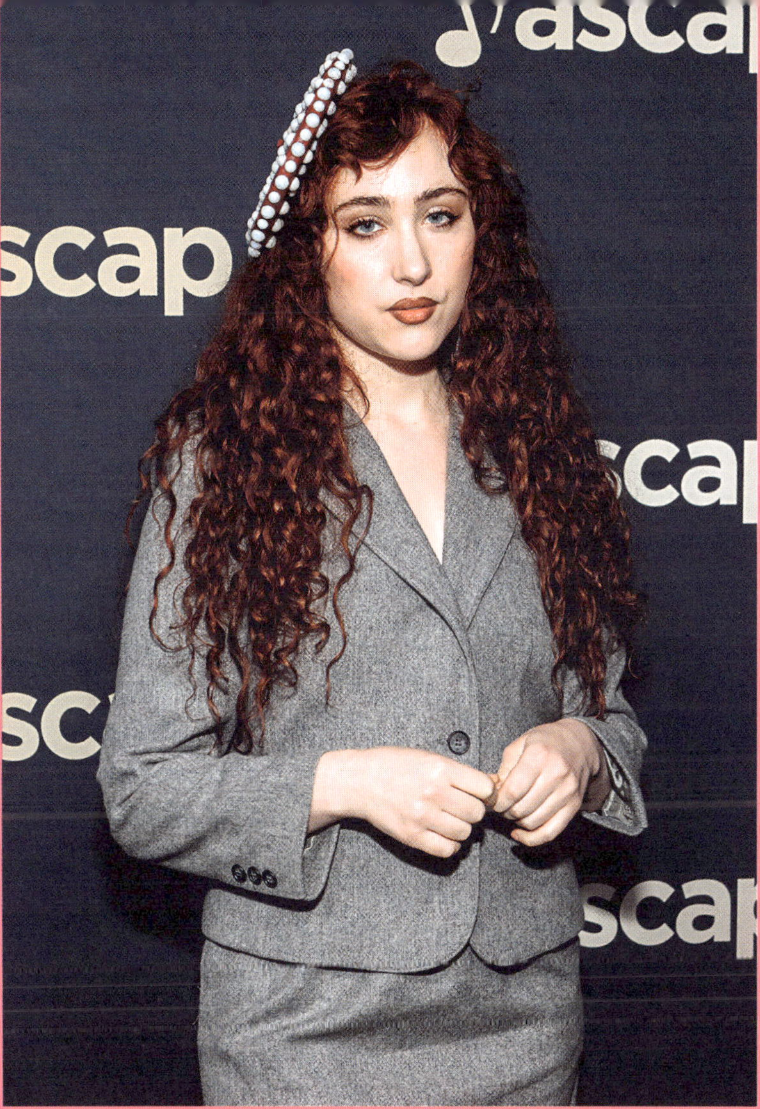

OPPOSITE On 7 November 2024, Roan performed at the Grammy Museum in LA wearing an oversized tailoring set from The Frankie Shop.

ABOVE Stylist Genesis Webb looked again to a tailored style for Roan's appearance at the ASCAP Pop Music Awards in May 2024, this time completing the monochrome look with a beret, courtesy of renowned latex label Vex Clothing.

It is important to note, however, that this shift in aesthetics didn't come out of nowhere. There were a few occasions where Roan has opted for slightly more pared-back looks that leaned away from clown and more towards couture. One such look was seen on the red carpet of the premiere of the Netflix *GUTS World Tour* film in October 2024. Showing her support for her former tour mate Olivia Rodrigo, Roan turned up wearing a sheer floor-length dress in a scarlet red hue, adorned with flower appliqués across the body. The dress featured two thigh-high slits, which showed off Roan's vintage leather boots, and she wore it with matching opera gloves for added drama. The design of the dress is credited to Sam Harper of Harper Collective, a fellow Midwest girl turned New Yorker who has become known for dressing some of her fellow Gen Z fashionistas such as Addison Rae, Kylie Jenner and Emma Chamberlain. Though the dress may have surprised some of her fans for its simple silhouette and nipple-revealing properties, Roan's make-up stuck a bit closer to home as she chose a stark white base, rosy cheeks and deep maroon lips – akin to some of her beauty looks inspired by softer Renaissance painting looks.

Roan wears a sheer Harper Collective dress for the premiere of Olivia Rodrigo's *GUTS World Tour* film in LA on 25 October 2024.

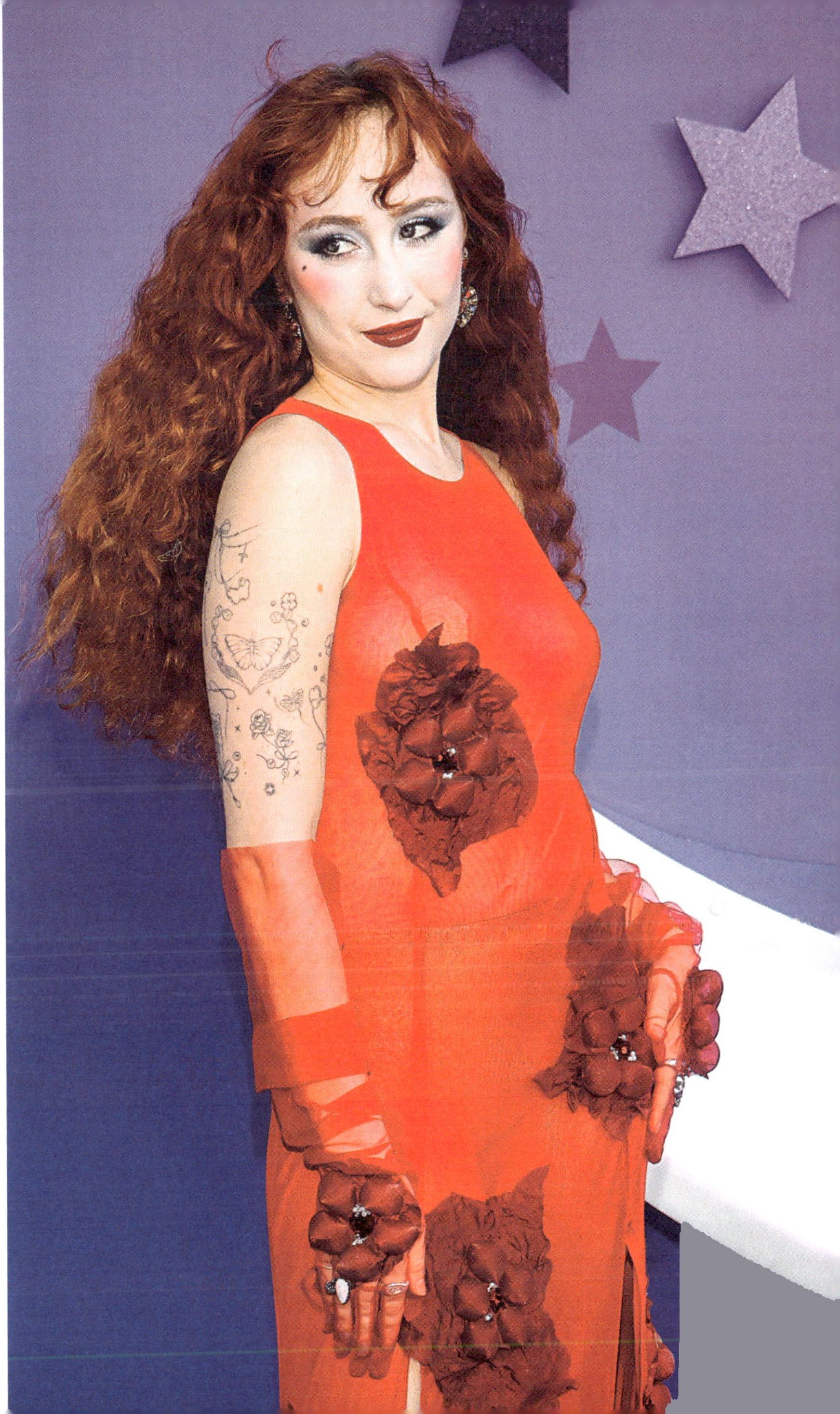

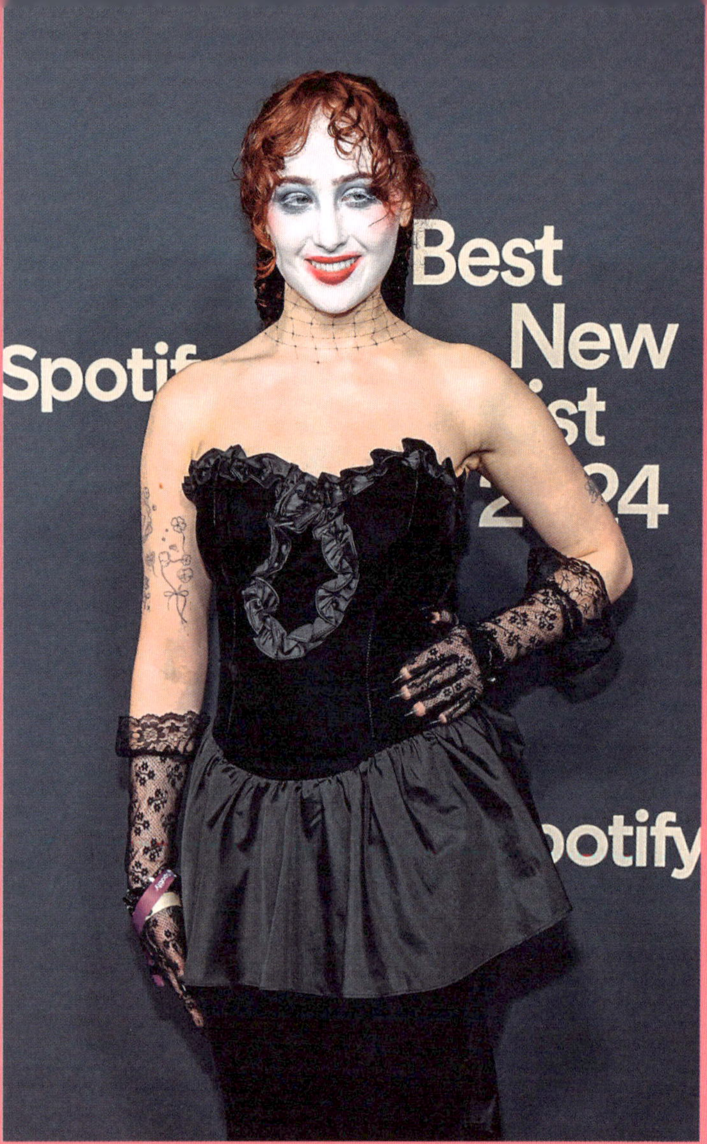

ABOVE For the 2024 Spotify Best New Artist Party in LA, Roan wore a vintage 1980s Scott McClintock dress in black velvet along with lace gloves.

OPPOSITE Nail artist Rachel Sun created Roan's nails using newspaper print and pearl details for Cyndi Lauper's Rock & Roll Hall of Fame induction ceremony, in 2025.

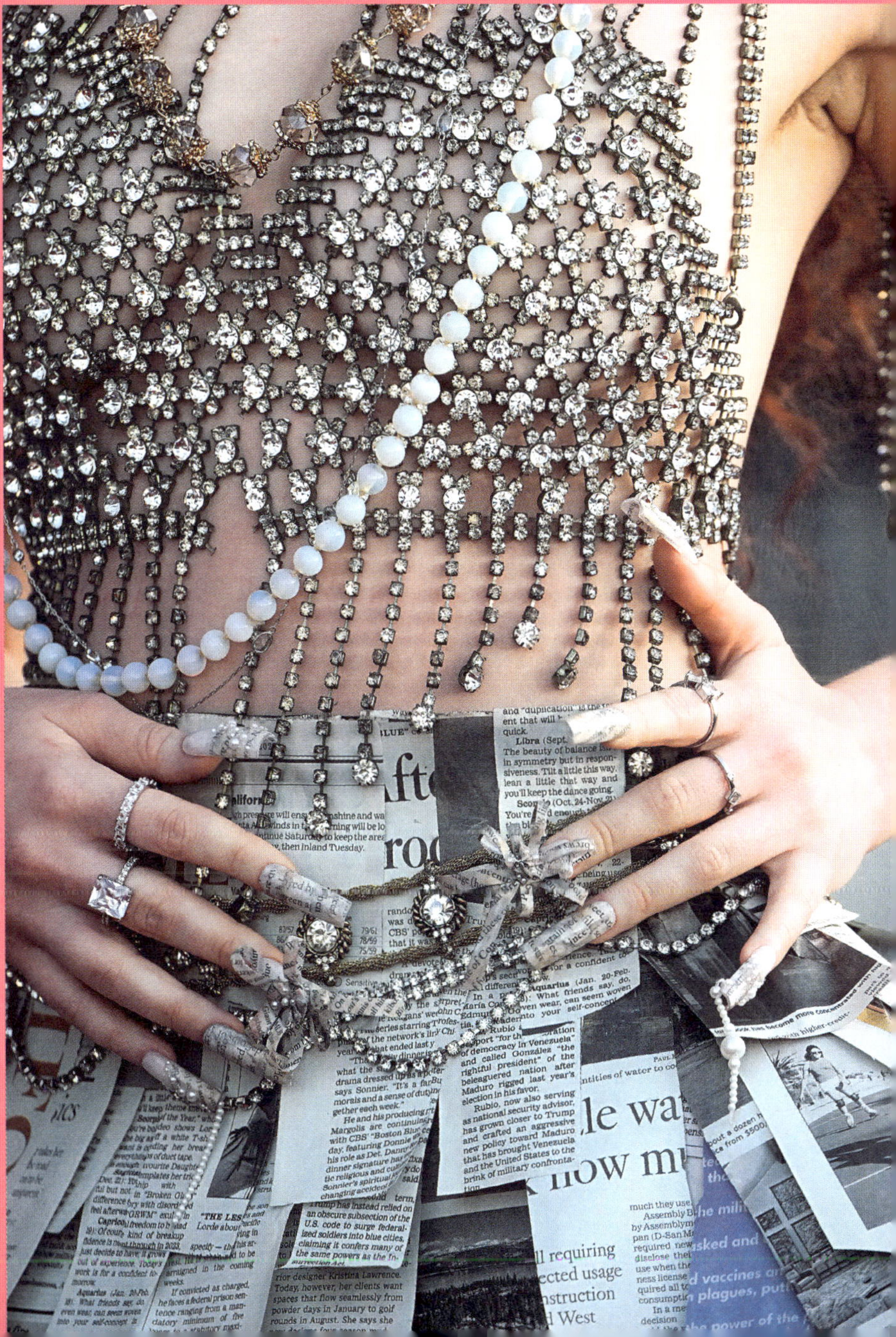
Libra (Sept.
The beauty of balance lies in symmetry but in responsiveness. Tilt a little this way, lean a little that way and you'll keep the dance going.
Aquarius (Jan. 20-Feb.
What friends say, do, even wear, can seem woven into your self-concept
Rubio, now also serving as national security advisor, has grown closer to Trump and crafted an aggressive new policy toward Maduro that has brought Venezuela and the United States to the brink of military confrontation.
an obscure subsection of the U.S. code to surge federalized soldiers into blue cities, claiming it confers many of the same powers as the
Today, however, her clients want spaces that flow seamlessly from powder days in January to golf rounds in August. She says she
ll requiring
ected usage
nstruction
d West

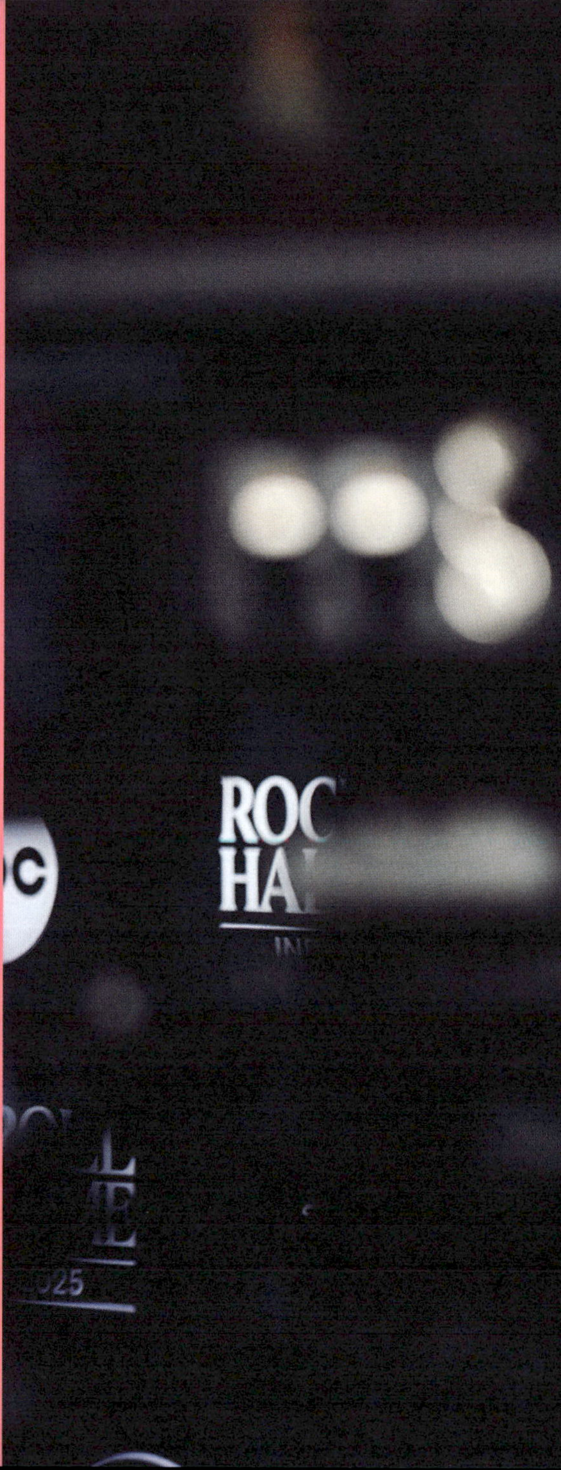

Roan wears a look comprised of a 1940s diamanté rhinestone top, newspaper skirt crafted by Efrain Nava and statement headpiece by artist Manny Robertson, inspired by a design Cyndi Lauper wore in her 1986 video for the single "True Colors".

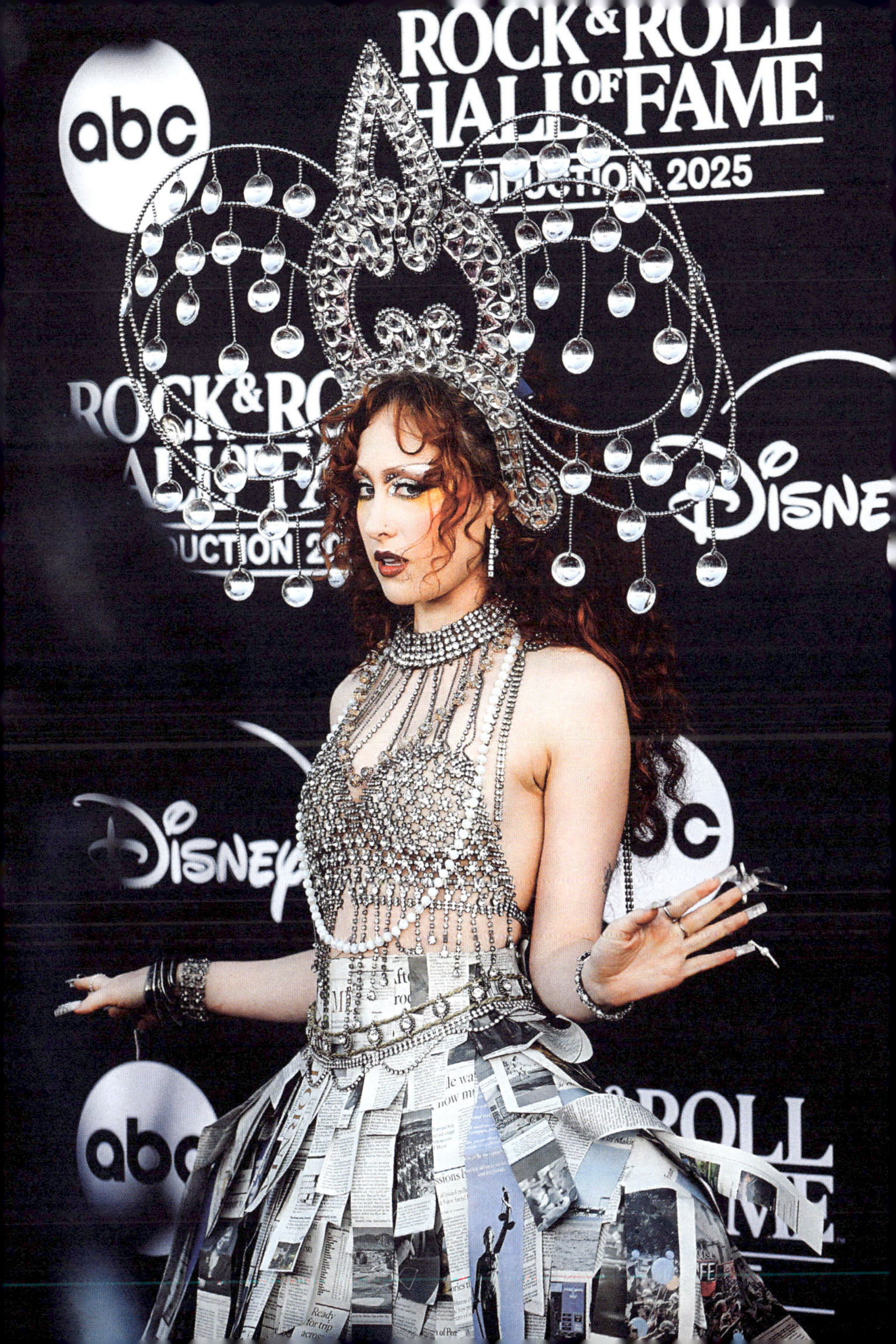
ROCK & ROLL
HALL OF FAME
2025

To further understand Roan's journey to sitting in the front row at Paris Fashion Week, it is helpful to understand the story behind her stylist and close collaborator, Genesis Webb. Growing up in Oklahoma City, she spent much of her youth in the local punk scene as she struggled to find her calling. Eventually Webb relocated to LA, where she would find herself assisting for Nicola Formichetti, the mastermind behind many of Lady Gaga's hit looks as well as top roles at labels like Diesel and Mugler. Working for Formichetti eventually led her to work with Roan on a shoot, and the two quickly connected over their Midwestern roots and being something of an outlier in an industry rife with inflated egos and nepotism. Webb's background of both subcultural youth and high-fashion escapades were key in creating Roan's trademark looks and offer opportunities to further explore the world of couture.

Roan's stylist Genesis Webb carved her career working for the likes of fashion designer Nicola Formichetti, pictured here with Lady Gaga and Sebastien Peigné following the Thierry Mugler Autumn/Winter 2011–12 ready-to-wear collection show in Paris, in March 2011.

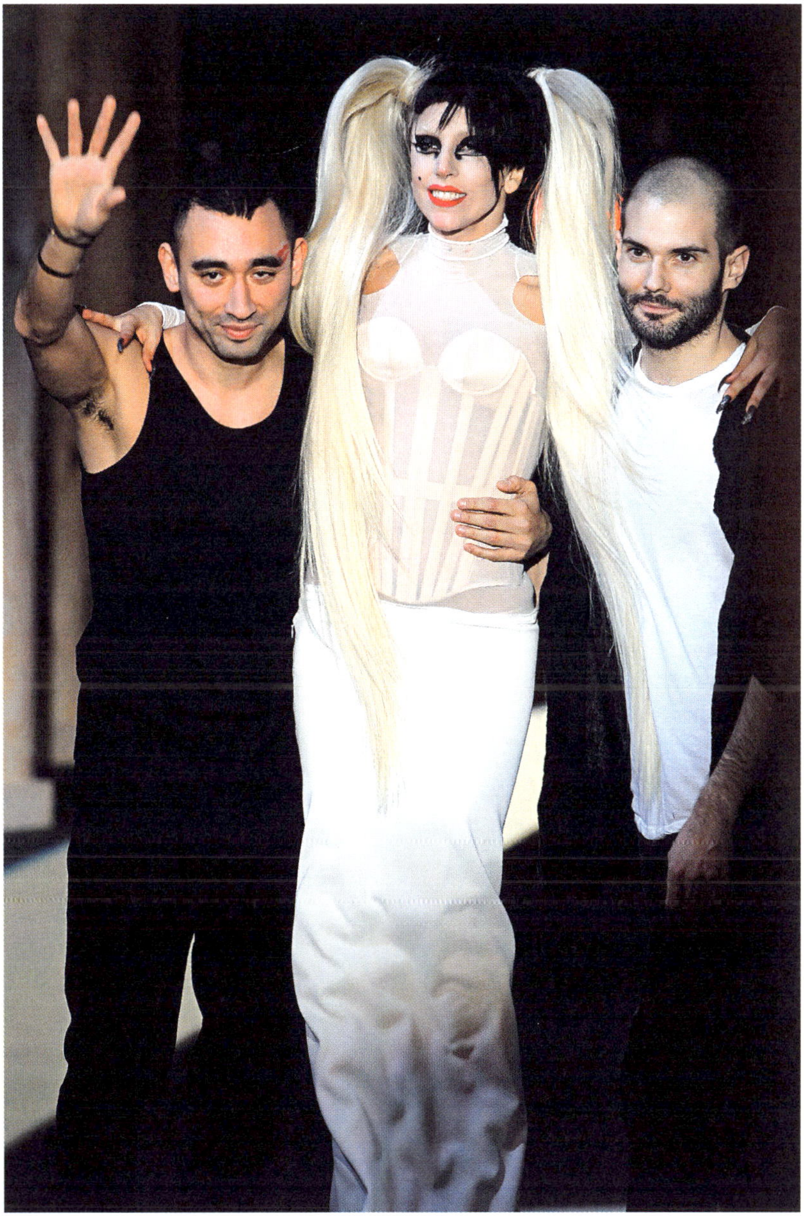

"The more thought she continues to put into her makeup, hair and outfits, it's only going to make her audience go wilder for her."

MAKE-UP ARTIST DONNI DAVY, *FASHIONIST*, JUNE 2025

A model poses on the runway in a latex look as part of the Thierry Mugler Autumn/Winter 1995 collection.

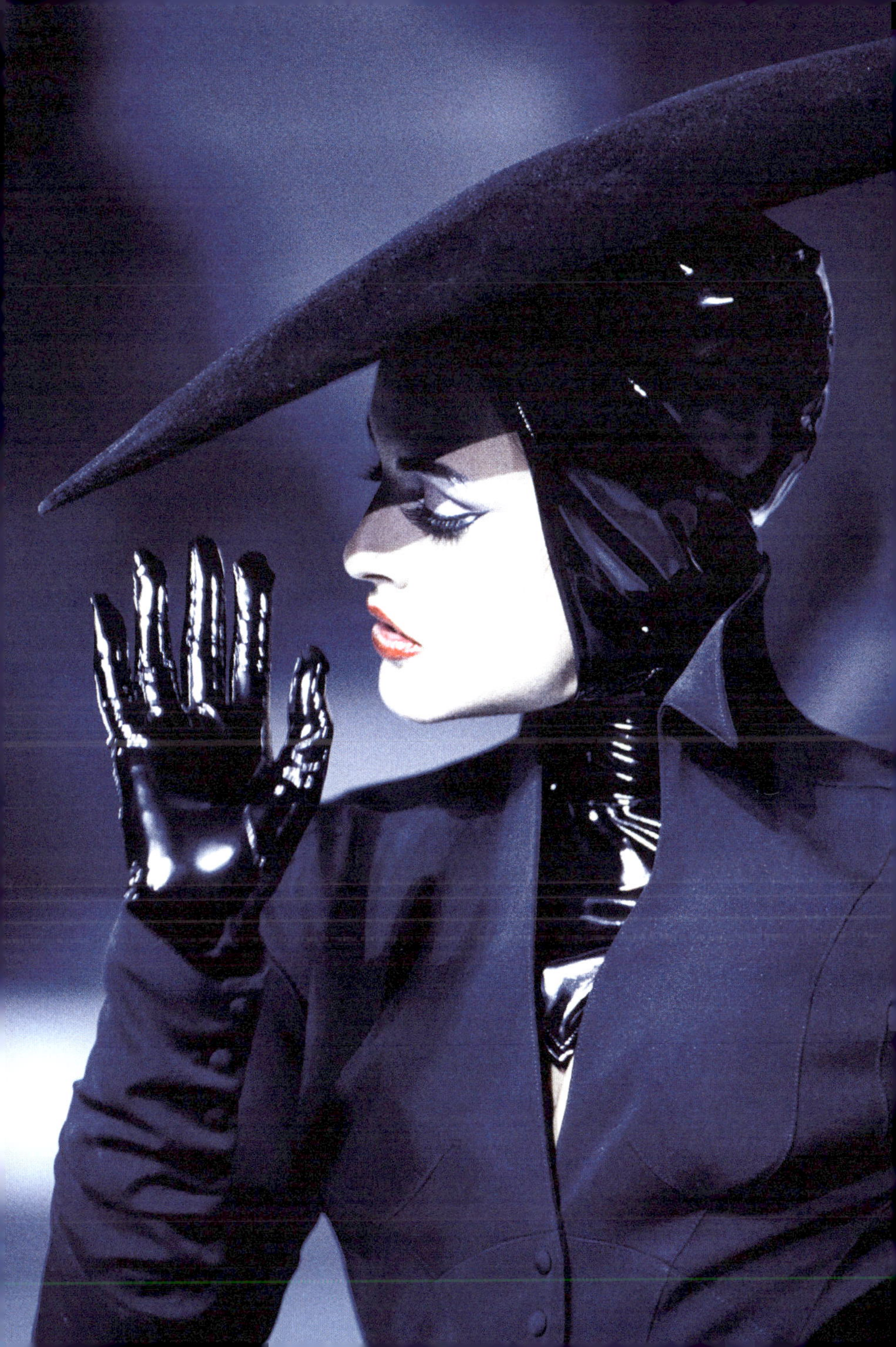

Roan's first Paris Fashion Week appearance was on 6 March 2025, when she sat in the front row at the Rabanne Fall 2025 show, sporting a metallic, backless cut Rabanne dress. Her signature red curls were swapped for soft waves and though the white face remained, the dramatic eyes appeared to be kept monochrome as if to nod to a more mature aesthetic than her onstage looks. A mere few hours later, Roan arrived at the Palais de Tokyo for the Rick Owens show, this time wearing the strapless Prong dress from the fashion house, originally released as a part of its Spring/Summer 2022 collection. Since then, the Prong dress has become somewhat of an icon itself with names such as Kim Kardashian, Cardi B and Katy Perry all sporting variations of the style since its runway debut. Genesis Webb has often spoke about her love for Rick Owens, noting him as one of her main fashion icons in an early 2025 interview with *Metal* magazine. She stated, "He's more than just a style icon. His entire philosophy for his life is amazing. He's created this entire world to be able to live in." Roan paired the Prong dress with what Joel Calfee, assistant editor of *Harper's Bazaar* would go on to lovingly refer to as "scary" and "slightly unsettling", probably because of the pale lips, black dots spread across the middle of the face and, of course, the white contact lenses. Roan shared, in a clip with *Dazed*, "I always feel the coolest wearing Rick ... I like to look like, weird and scary. And I think that Rick is the best for that."

Rabanne's Fall 2025 show in Paris marked Roan's first ever fashion show. She is pictured here wearing a metallic dress from the label along with dangling crystal earrings.

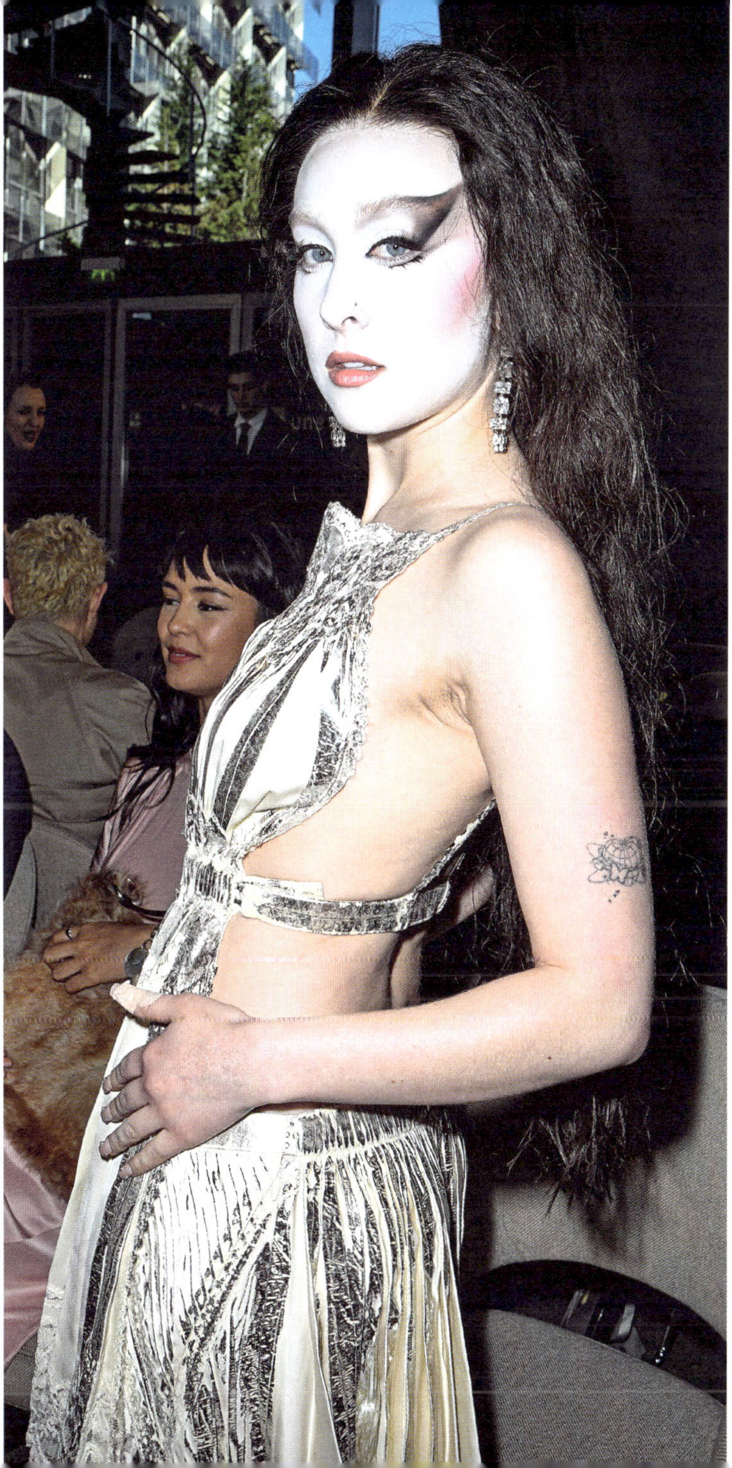

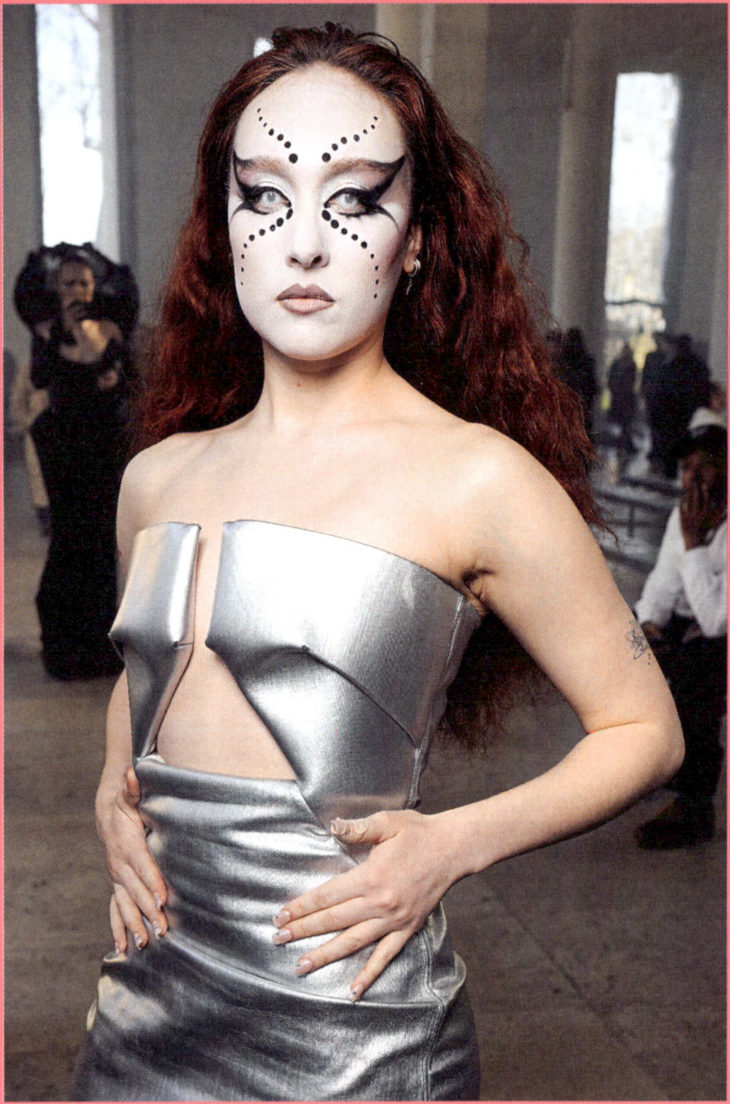

Roan attends the Rick Owens Fall 2025 show in Paris, wearing the Prong dress from the American fashion house.

On the Saturday evening, Roan popped by the Alexander McQueen show in a look that had some fans drawing comparisons to Riff Raff from *The Rocky Horror Picture Show*, due to the pantyhose cap and the red locks streaming out the sides. The undoubtedly avant-garde look was also comprised of a structured double-breasted blazer from McQueen and an exaggerated collar shirt from the same designer. It seems Roan enjoyed the show as she appeared to pluck one look straight from the runway to wear to the 9th annual Fashion Los Angeles Awards just a few weeks later. This ensemble inspired headlines such as "Chappell Roan Is a Giver of High Glamour in a Harlequin-Inspired McQueen Dress" from *Harper's Bazaar*. The dramatic collared dress, created by Irish designer Seán McGirr at the helm, featured a gothic-inspired floral jacquard, dramatic ruffle sleeves and a thigh-grazing hemline. Roan honoured McGirr's runway pairing, wearing the piece with its matching embroidered lace tights, but swapped the metallic boots worn on the runway for Christian Louboutin Bilougiela patent leather heels. While her hair may have been hidden away for the McQueen show in Paris, this time Roan's locks were very much on show, freeing the frizz for the occasion. This event would also play an important role in Roan and Webb being acknowledged as key players in the fashion world, with Webb receiving the award for Breakthrough Music Stylist of the Year. Roan gave a heartfelt speech at the event, stating, "There's no one who makes me feel cooler, or more cunt, or more powerful, or more Chappell Roan than Genesis." Past recipients of the award include Brett Alan Nelson, the stylist behind many of Doja Cat's looks, including the viral feline-inspired Met Gala look in Oscar de la Renta or the 2023 Paris Fashion Week look, which saw the American rapper covered in red paint and 30,000 crystals.

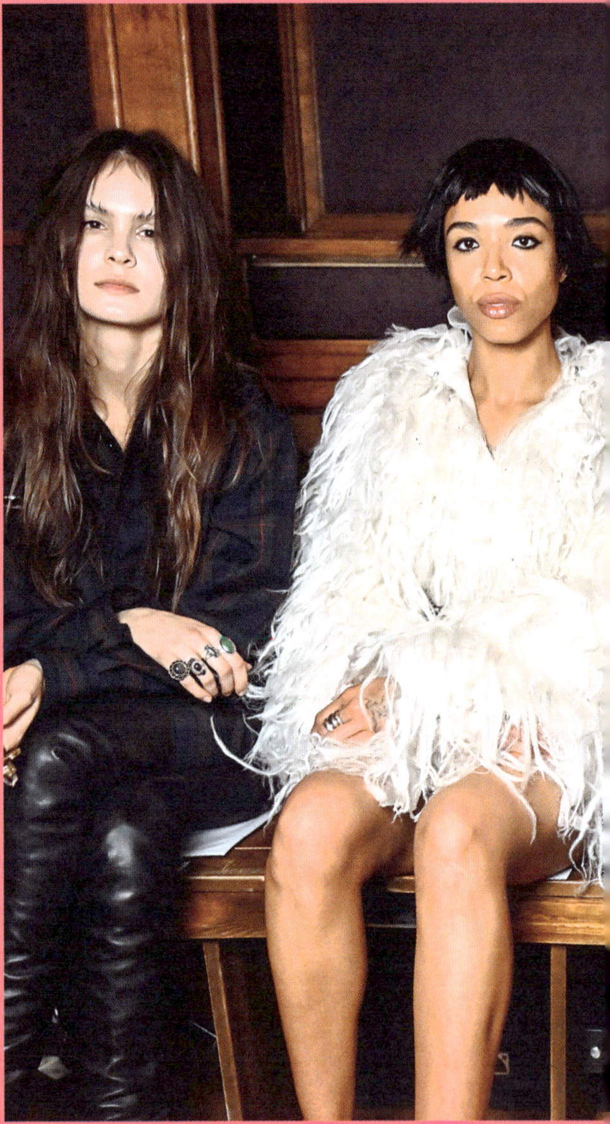

Sofia Isella, Zsela, Chappell Roan, Georgia Davies and Abigail Morris of The Last Dinner Party attend the McQueen Autumn/Winter 2025 show in Paris, on 8 March 2025.

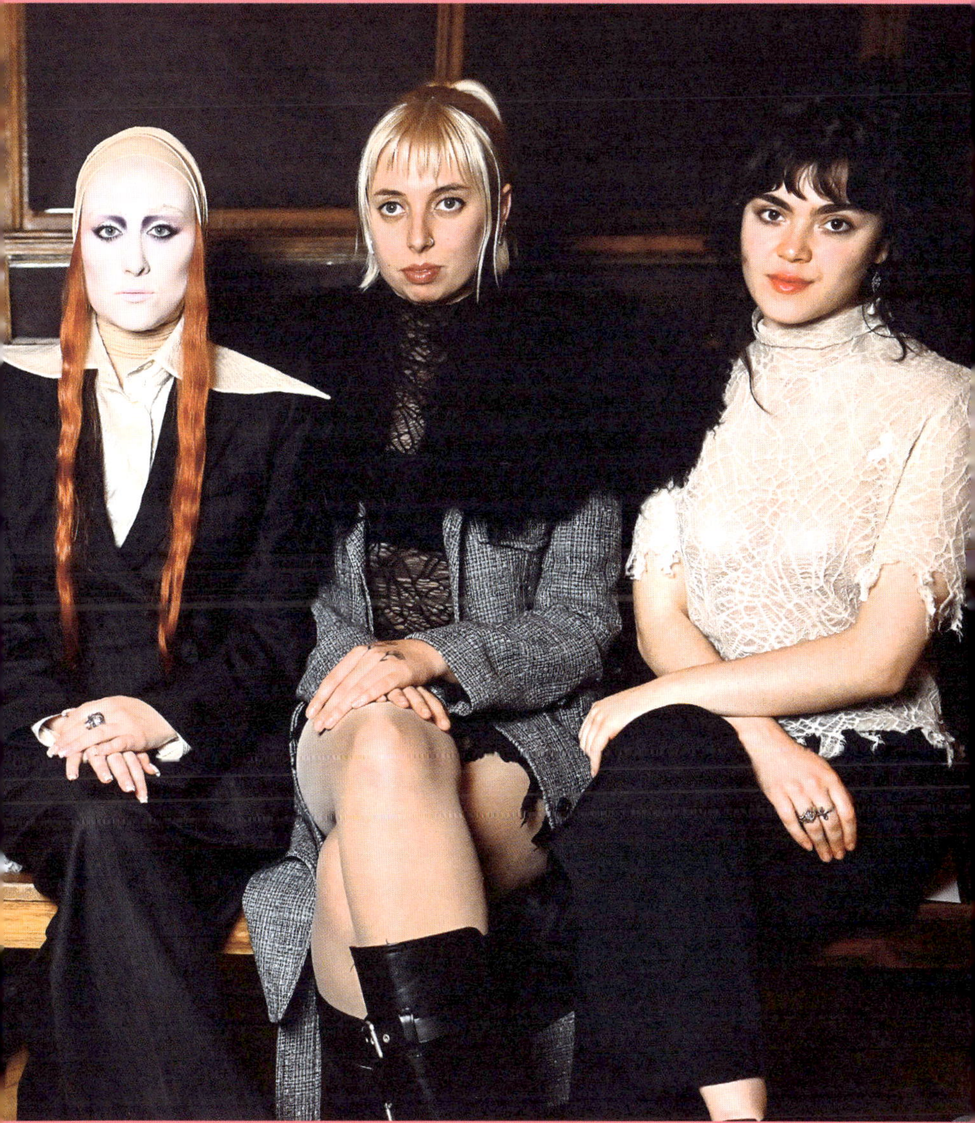

"I feel very special wearing couture! [...] It took a thousand hours to make this gown. [...] I feel so incredibly special to be wearing it."

CHAPPELL ROAN, @MAISONVALENTINO, MARCH 2025

Roan's final look for what *W Magazine*'s Kyle Munzenrieder appropriately referred to as a "high fashion baptism" fashion week came in the form of a dramatic gown by Valentino as she attended the Italian fashion house's Fall/Winter 2025 collection showcase. The black velvet bodice connected to a layered tulle skirt was covered in rows of embroidered pink flowers and golden leaves. The dress also featured disconnected puff sleeves in the same floral tulle design and a bright red bow tied around Roan's waist to complete the look. Perhaps a stark difference from her Rick Owens alien-esque make-up look that she donned a few days earlier, Roan's Valentino make-up was one of her softer looks, defined by its pencil-thin eyebrows, fluttery lashes and soft, berry-toned lips. Andrew Dahling, one of Roan's key collaborators, was credited with creating the look and reportedly used MAC's Maximal Sleek Satin Lipstick in the Lovers Only shade to create the sweet look.

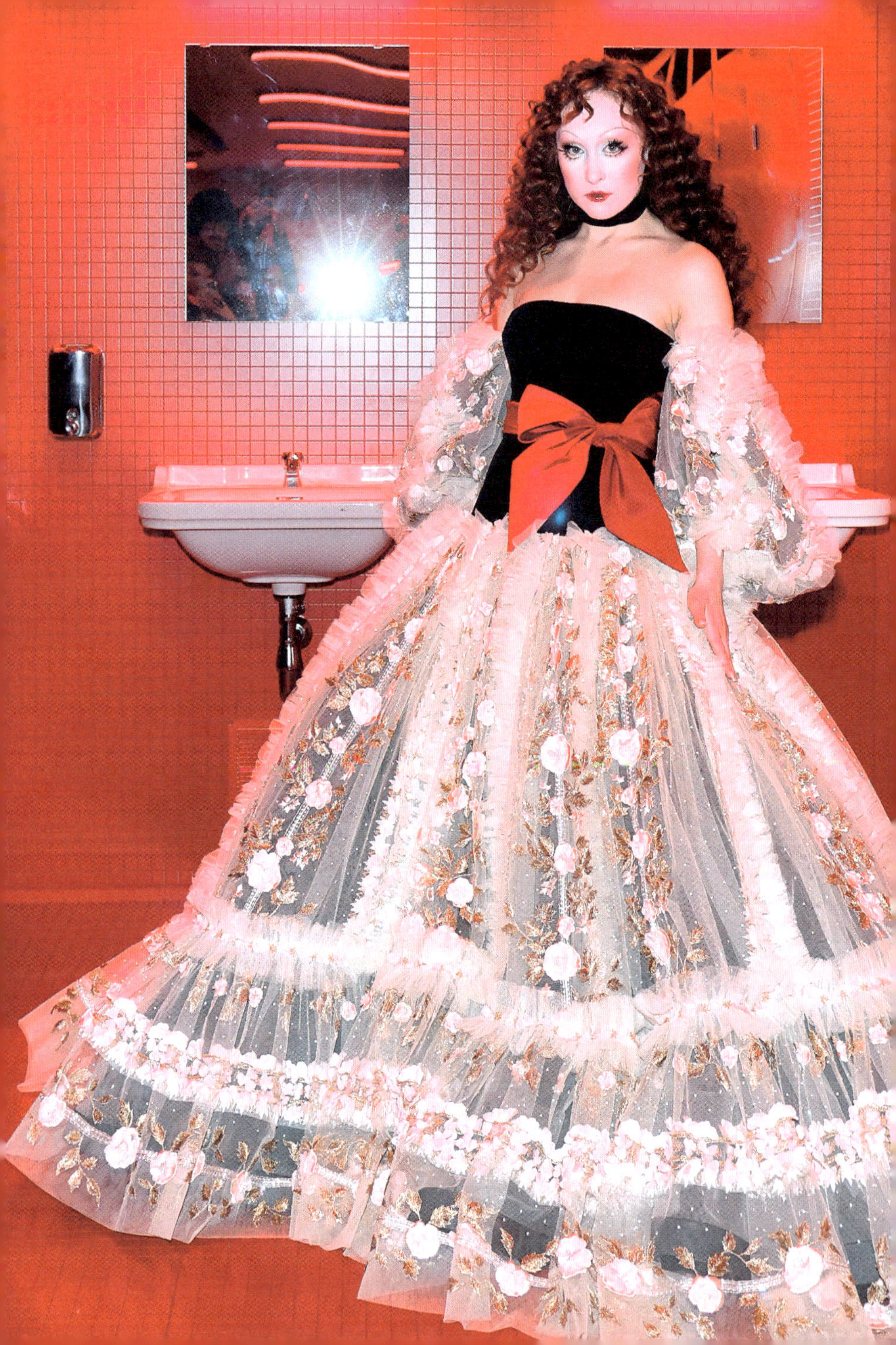

Roan attends Valentino's "Le méta-théâtre des intimités" show as part of Paris Fashion Week, on 9 March 2025.

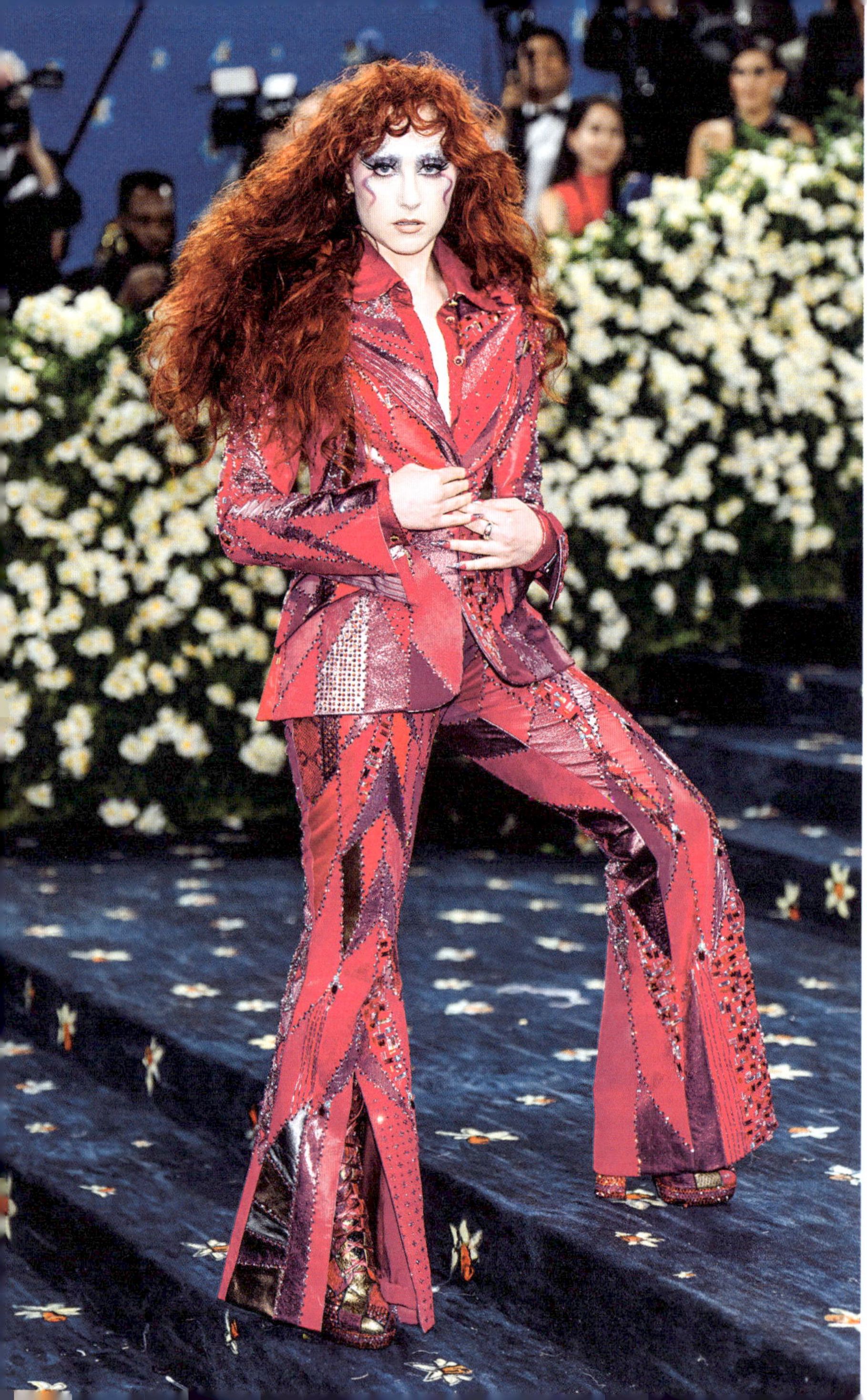

A few months later, in May 2025, Roan attended fashion's biggest night – the one and only Met Gala. Long revered for being the birthplace of some of fashion's most iconic looks, including Princess Diana's Dior slip dress look in 1996 and fellow chain mail-appreciator Zendaya in Jean Paul Gaultier in 2018. The theme behind the evening for Roan's first appearance at the event was "Tailored for You", inspired by the Met's exhibition *Superfine: Tailoring Black Style*. Roan worked with the acclaimed Paul Tazewell (costume designer of *Wicked*) to put together a look for the evening that fitted the brief while still tapping into Roan's distinct style. The team took inspiration from two iconic figures from the disco scene, Sylvester and Sly Stone. Webb shared on TikTok after the event: "We wanted to honor the theme of Black Dandyism through the lens of unapologetic self-expression. This leather patchwork is a nod to Sly Stone's radical silhouettes, while the tinsel, rhinestones, beading and the flamboyance celebrate Sylvester's defiant glamour." Roan herself also shared some insight into the inspiration for the look in a behind-the-scenes video, sharing, "We referenced Sylvester, really leaning into a queer kind of 1980s, 1970s disco drag music. Paul really taught me how to channel that love of larger-than-life fashion and larger-

Paul Tazewell worked with Roan and her team to create her first Met Gala look, upcycling pieces of leather from eBay to create the shimmer design for the 2025 event.

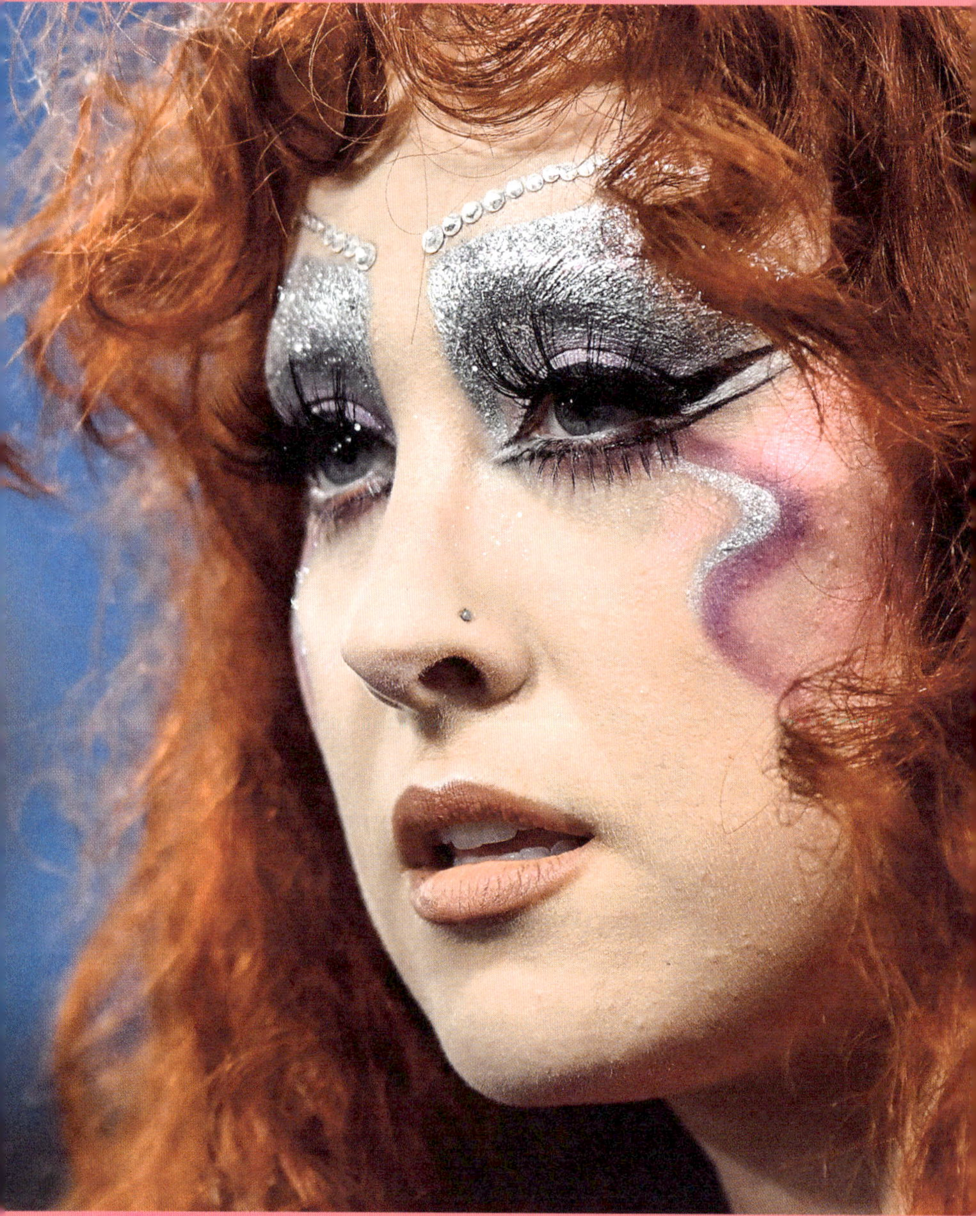

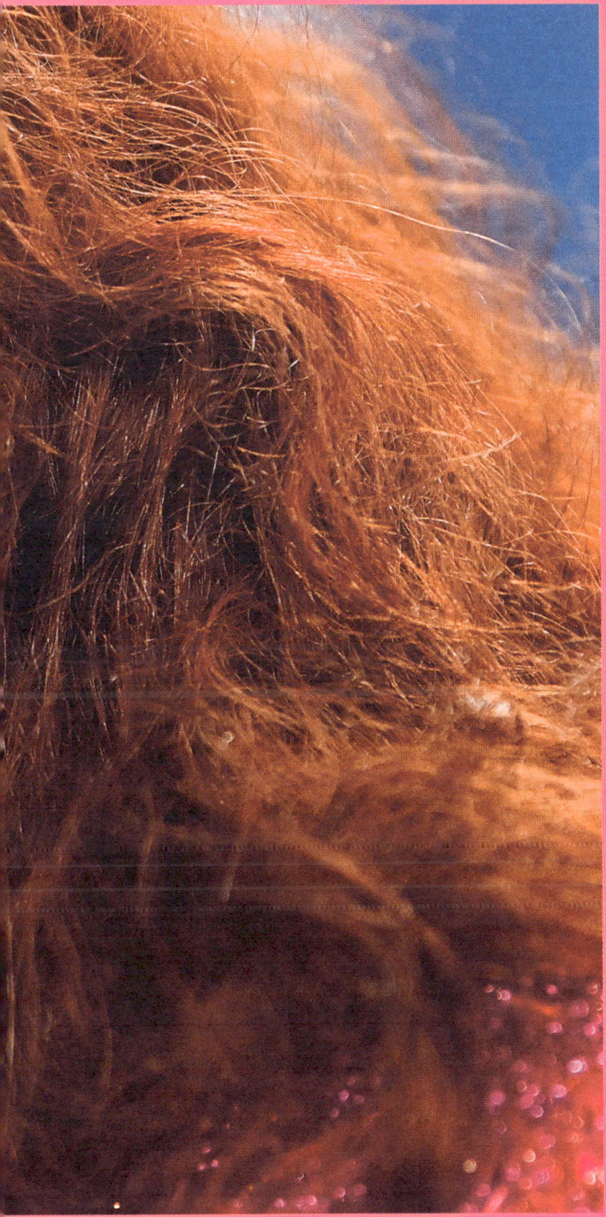

Roan took to Instagram after the 2025 Met Gala to thank everyone involved in making the look happen, including hair stylist Lucy Redway, stating: “you are an absolute angel and you made one of my favorite hair looks EVER !!!”

than-life fearlessness." Make-up artist extraordinaire Pat McGrath also shared her inspiration behind Roan's make-up for the evening, stating that they "channelled the glamour and freedom of the disco era – think Sylvester, Superfly, superfine tailoring, and unapologetic shine ... We layered shimmering metallics with illustrated wings, chrome lashes and rhinestone accents. It's maximalist, metallic and made to move." Roan's nails were brought to life by Dawn Sterling.

Though Roan and her team may take great inspiration from fashion designers, it is important to note that it is not always a one-way street. The legendary American fashion designer Betsey Johnson has notably been a huge admirer of Roan and her looks for years, using her label's official Instagram account to gush about her love for Roan in a reel in October 2024. In the clip, she shares her admiration for Roan and her deep understanding of clothing and its power. She also shares that Roan and her team borrowed the fuchsia Betsey Johnson dress for the NPR Tiny Desk Concert and that she even has a selection of other old designs that she'd love Roan to have – a gift that Roan's fans would likely very much support.

Sly Stone of Sly and The Family Stone poses here in 1973 in one of his trademark looks, which inspired Roan and her team for her 2025 Met Gala outfit.

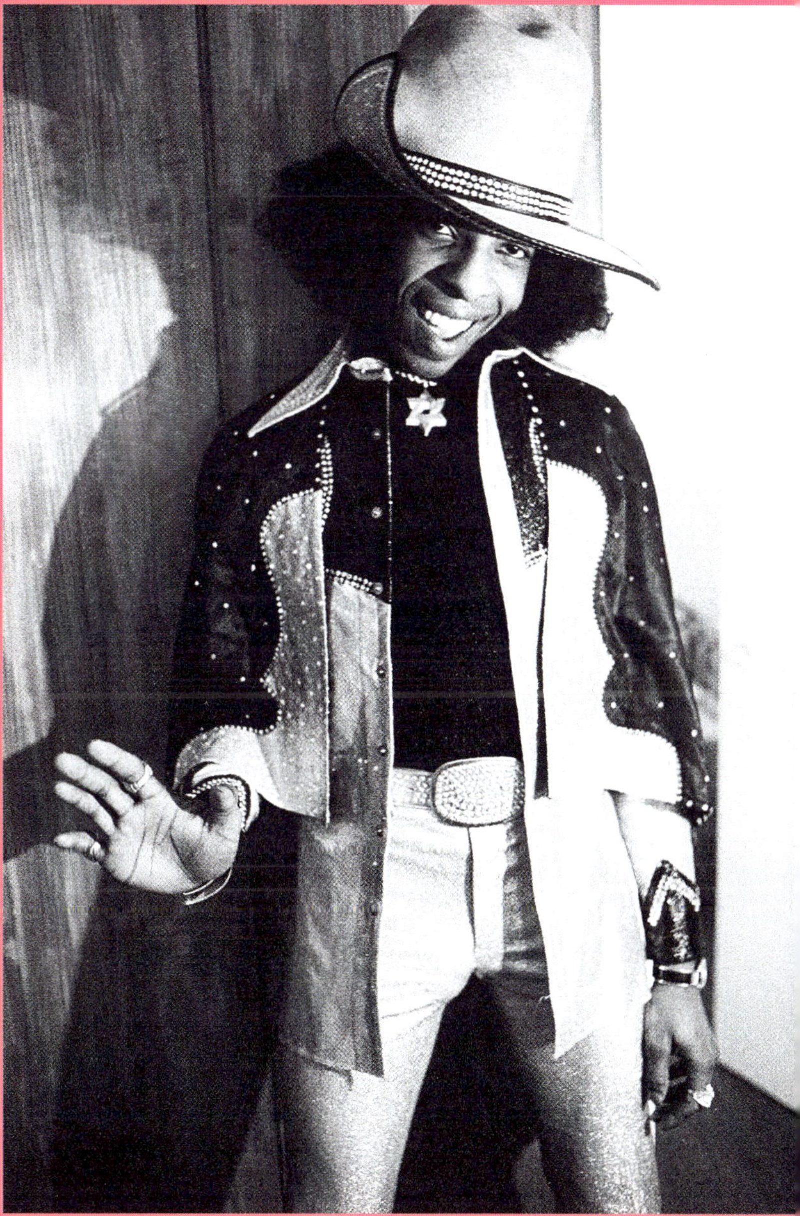

"We referenced Sylvester, really leaning into a queer kind of 1980s, 1970s disco drag music."

CHAPPELL ROAN

Disco star Sylvester, pictured here, was another inspiration behind Roan's first Met Gala look.

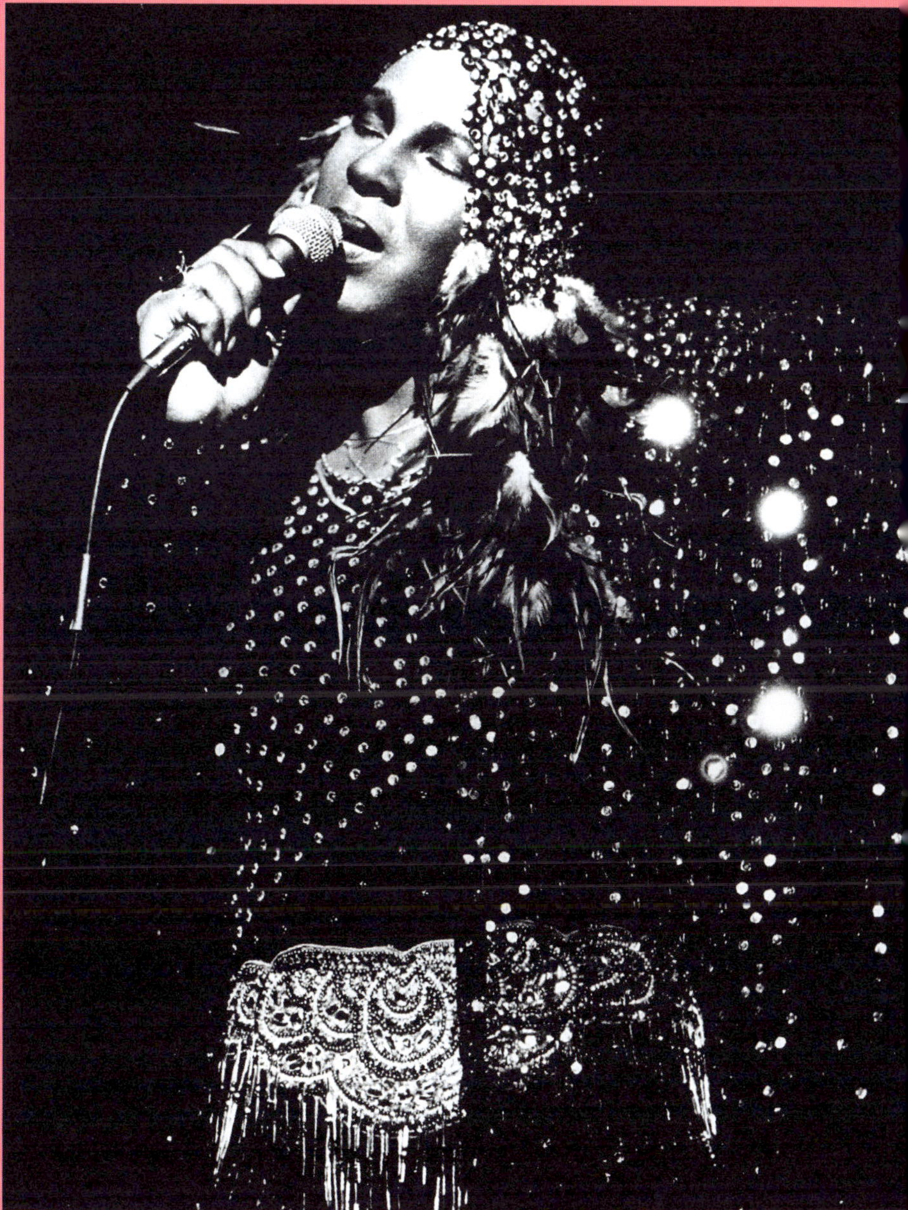

CHAPTER 4

Impact

There are plenty of pop stars who can belt out hits like there's no tomorrow while sporting shimmering looks that fans spend hours trying to emulate. Chappell Roan may be one of those pop stars – but she's also so much more. Roan's looks have played a critical part in her success, not only due to their transgressive references but also their role in communicating key messages that inspire not only fashion theorists but also sociologists from varying disciplines. For a girl who often speaks of her desire to simply create inclusive and fun environments for her audience, Roan does spark a ton of conversations that (to rework one of Gen Z's favourite catchphrases), really *are* that deep. In this chapter we explore the wider impact of Roan's fashion choices and the lasting impact of her looks, that will likely long outlive her tracks on the charts.

"There are so many places in the country where the only day [LGBTQ+] people get to wear rainbows is Pride ... I encourage people to wear what makes them feel hot, what makes them feel sexy ... The themes are an opportunity for everyone to dress up ... It just builds such community. I love it so much."

CHAPPELL ROAN, *KINDA COOL* 2023

Concert fashion

When it comes to the most intricate and extravagant outfits worn by the audience, Chappell Roan's shows are truly a sight to behold. Her distinct aesthetics combined with her messages of celebrating your authentic self and dedication to simply having fun, often result in a sea of fans sporting brightly coloured cowboy hats, dramatic make-up looks and recreations of some of the Missouri native's most memorable ensembles.

Perhaps also because she herself has felt the power that putting on a costume can have, Roan has been known to actively encourage her fans to dress up for her shows, communicating clear themes through her social media accounts. Journalist Jem Aswad shared his observations on this as he attended one of Roan's 2023 NYC shows, stating, "The theme for the show, as pronounced on Instagram, was 'So you wanna be a POP STAR', and the densely packed crowd more than obliged, with glitter and boa feathers and rouge and sparkly boots and jackets and more." Some of Roan's other themes for fans to follow include "Mermaid", "Midwest Princess" and "Goth, Grunge and Glitter". Each theme came with a collage of examples of influence pics to further cement the style. Pink Von Dutch hats appeared among a sea of camo for her Midwest Princess theme dates, a still from the 2006 teen film favourite *Aquamarine* is set among ocean-inspired make-up looks for the mermaid-themed dates, and then there's the "Pink Pony Club" dates where Roan displays inspiration pics such as Dolly Parton in a shimmering pink dress and baby pink boots from Jeremy Scott's Fall/Winter 2016 collection.

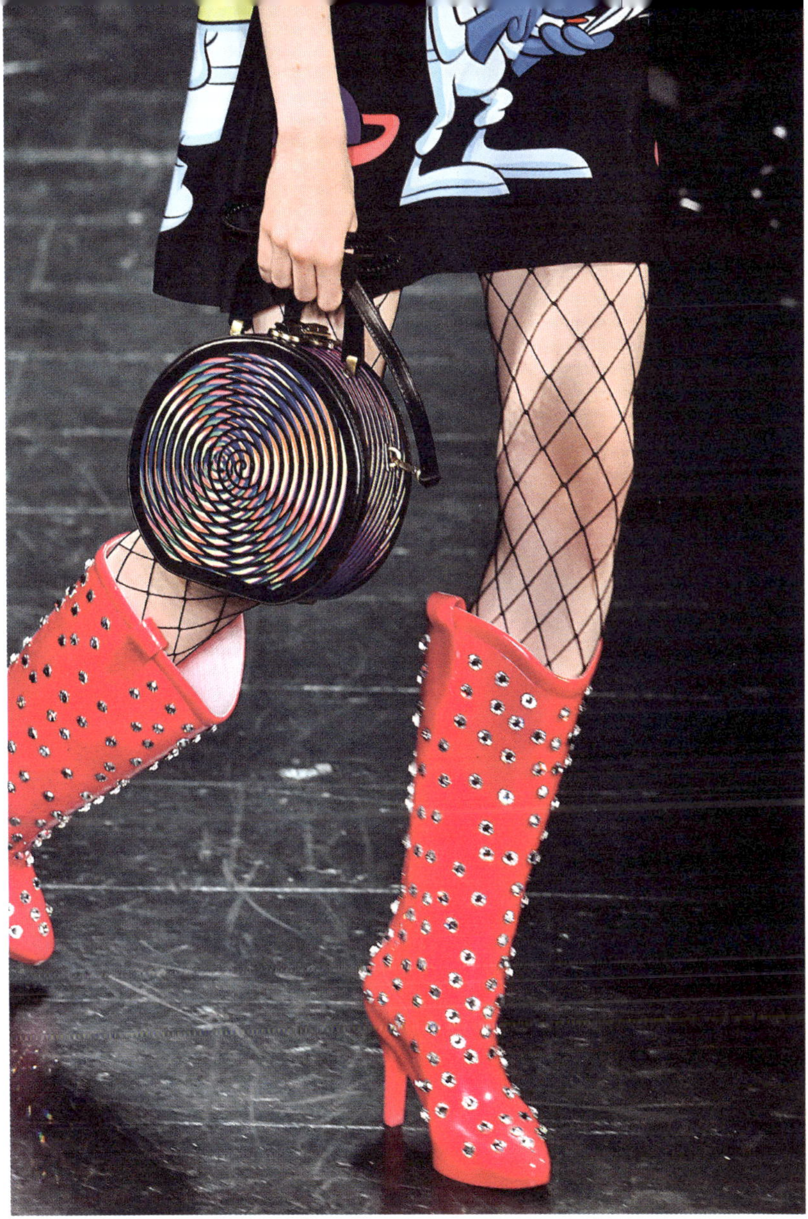

This Jeremy Scott look from the designer's Fall/Winter 2016 collection appeared on Roan's mood board for her "Pink Pony Club"-themed shows on her 2023 tour.

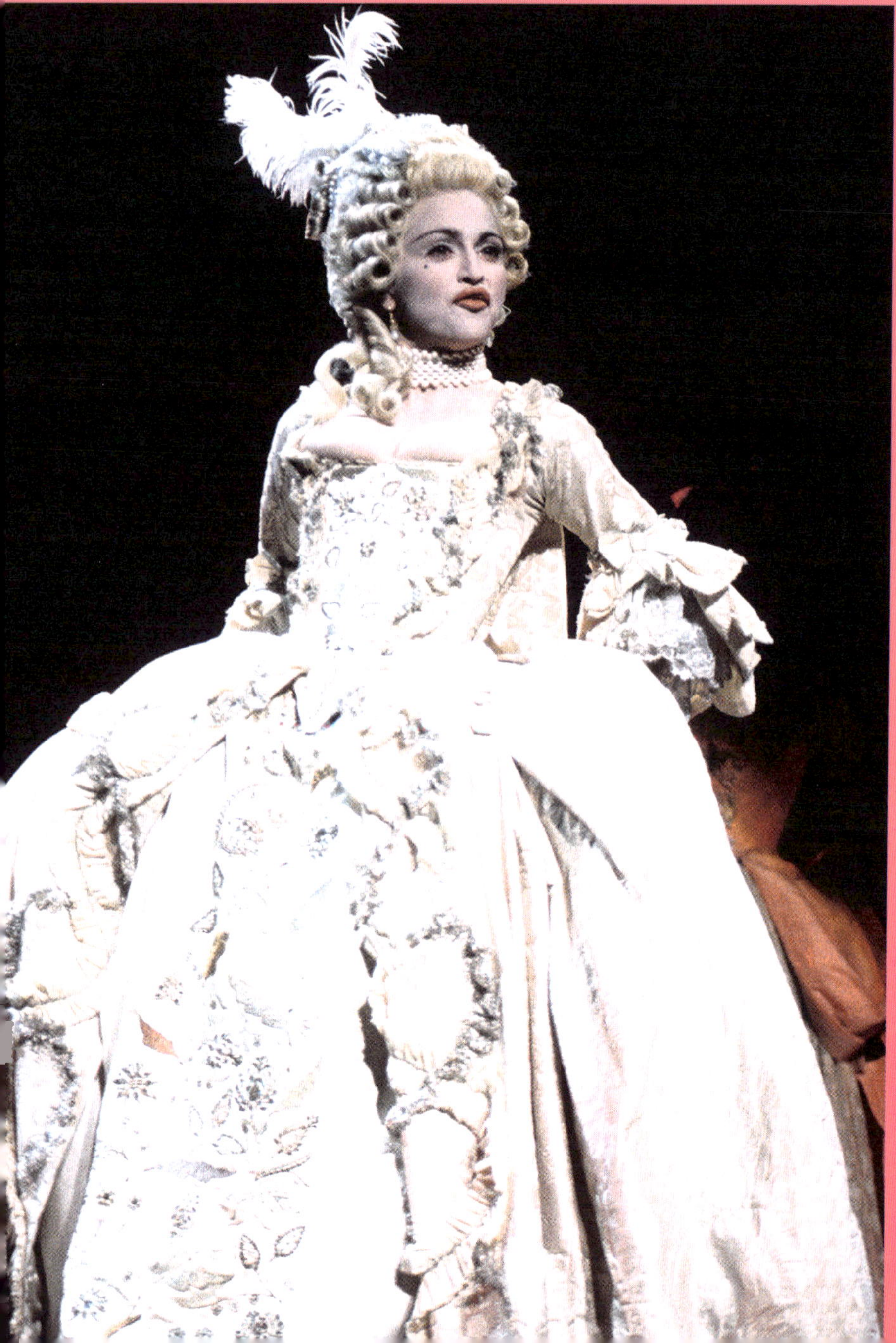

Though Roan offers plenty of branded merch at her shows, her promotion of DIY looks and rejection of fast fashion collaborations ("No, H&M does not fit in this world," Roan told *Rolling Stone* magazine in 2024, continuing, "Also, fuck H&M."), she encourages fans to experience the power of customized looks and creative expression in a way that many pop stars don't. Guy Trebay of *The New York Times* remarked on this in his January 2025 piece, stating, "Unlike, say, Madonna – another trendsetter whose stage costumes grew increasingly elaborate as she scaled pop heights and that were created in collaboration with couturiers like Jean Paul Gaultier – Ms. Roan's looks remain accessible to fans, DIY and relatively affordable."

Madonna performed at the 1990 MTV Video Music Awards dressed as Marie Antoinette, wearing a gown by costume designer James Acheson.

Hyper-femme visibility

Clothing has long been used as a tool for queer individuals to signal to their respective partners or peers of their sexual orientation or, likewise, as a way to protect themselves from homophobic attacks. Fashion theorists such as Shaun Cole and Vicki Karaminas have dedicated much of their careers to studying this and other aspects of "queer style", explaining, in materials that coincide with the 2024 rerelease of their 2013 publication simply titled *Queer Style*, "The impulse underpinning queer style is undeniably creative, which means that it is impelled by invention and delights in aesthetics. Performance and posing and its centrality to queer style does in no way imply a superficial masquerade that conceals an inner and altogether different essence". The text goes on to state, "Rather it implies the primacy of presentness and shows that as an expression of not being conscripted into preordained and essentialized roles within a stable social model". It signs off by stating that queer style is "an attitude to life and being that is not only transgressive, it is celebratory, suggesting that life need not be a consignment but a creation." Though she may have only become a household name a few years ago, Chappell Roan has clearly demonstrated the power that clothing can have, not only on creating a strong persona and creative expression but on building community and queer visibility.

During an October 2023 show in Fort Lauderdale, Florida, Roan pays homage to pop icon Cher with this look, an almost identical replica from one of the "Love Hurts" singer's 1992 tour styles.

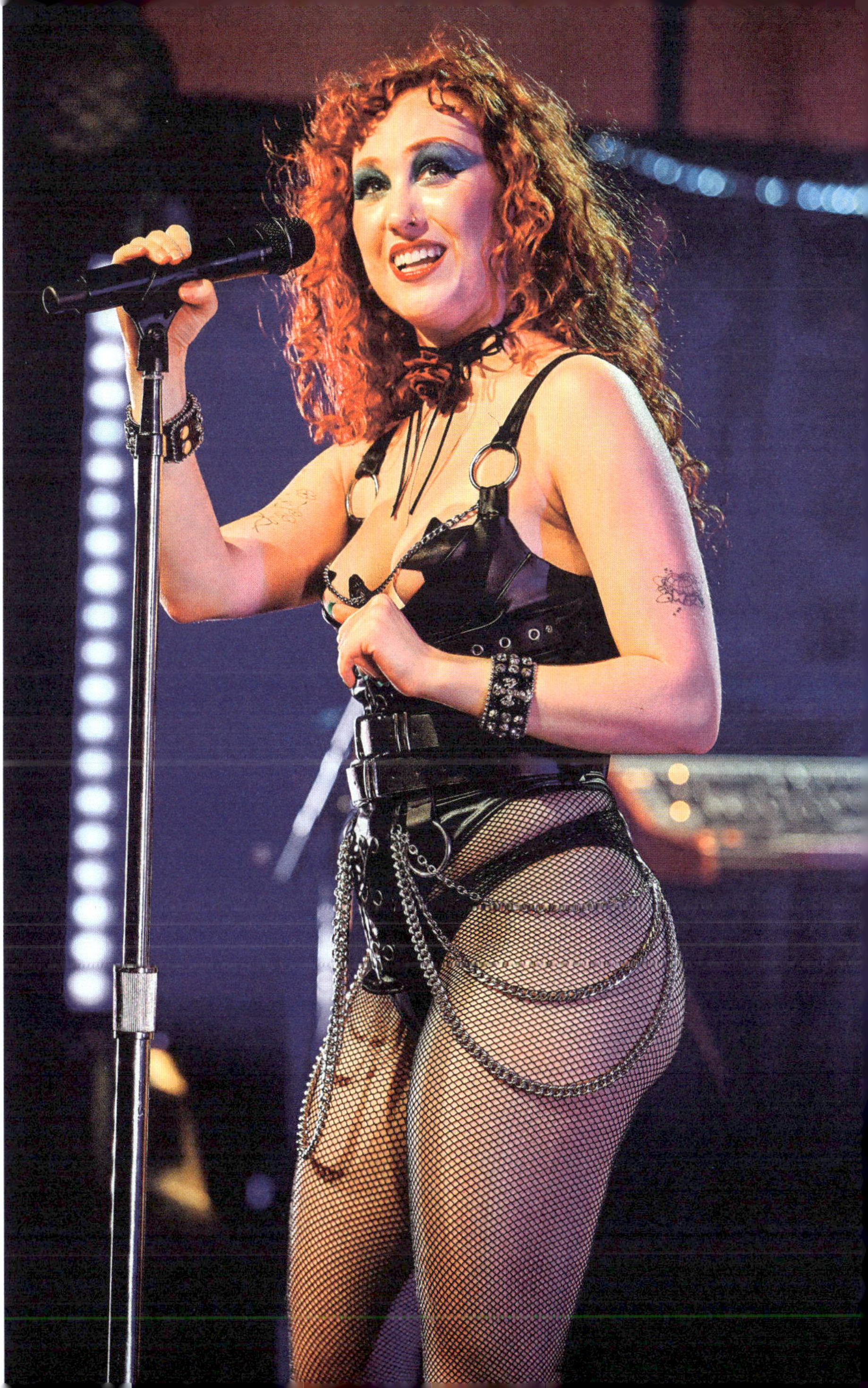

"The theatrical femme is a sapphic presenting their gender and sexuality in a theatrical way e.g. through costume ... Femme theatricality does not pander to patriarchal notions of beauty. Central to femme theatricality is reinvention; how explorations in our costume and presentation can lead to explorations in our gender and sexualities."

AMBER WILKINSON
***BOSHEMIA* MAGAZINE**

Though much of the study of queer dress has been focused on past generations, Roan's fashion represents a younger generation of queer women who reject much of the existing framework that dress scholars have often focused on. One way that Roan's approach to queer dress can be analysed is through her "high femme" (sometimes referred to as "hyper femme") persona. A "high femme" is often described as a queer woman who exudes stereotypically feminine traits and traditionally feminine attire. Though high femmes have always existed, Roan has done wonders for visibility with her global platform and candid discussions of the reality of being a queer woman today. In a September 2024 piece for *Gay Times*, writer Deia Penn shared, "For a generation of young queer women, it's a reminder that camp is ours, and that drag is ours, and that we deserve to take up space in our own community. It's also a reminder that being a queer woman, especially a feminine queer woman, is a sparkly, joyful thing."

And the significance of Roan's aesthetic approach doesn't stop with her clothing either, as Ellen Atlanta wrote in a piece for *Dazed Beauty* in July 2024: "Roan's aesthetic choices are not just about personal style – they carry political weight. By championing drag-inspired looks and queer culture references, she's unapologetically projecting her identity and making a bold statement in a time when LGBTQ+ rights are under attack. The homage to drag goes beyond mere aesthetics – Roan actively collaborates with and uplifts drag artists, creating a symbiotic relationship that feels authentic and respectful. Her visuals serve as a form of resistance, celebrating the power of personal expression in the face of oppression."

Queer joy

In 2023, Roan shared in an interview with Ilana Kaplan of *People* magazine: "I think people like to party and I think my project feels like a party". She continued, "I think that people just want to be happy and reflect, sing, dance and dress up, and feel free. The project gives people an opportunity to express themselves without judgment and freedom to discover themselves in the same way that I feel like the project allows me to discover myself."

"Queer joy" is a term that comes up again and again when analysing the dress aspect of Roan and her fan base. Not only can dress be a critical tool for queer individuals due to its ability to communicate aspects of identity, allowing us to build community, but it can also be incredibly effective in acting as a catalyst for joy. Madison Moore, scholar and author of *Fabulous: The Rise of the Beautiful Eccentric*, shared their view on this in a 2018 interview with *The New York Times*: "Fabulousness doesn't take a lot of money," Dr Moore said, "It requires high levels of creativity, imagination and originality; it's dangerous, political, risky and largely practiced by queer, trans, transfeminine people of color or other marginalized groups; it's about making a spectacle of oneself in a world that seeks to suppress and undervalue fabulous people." Jonathan Graffam-O'Meara of Monash University in Melbourne, Australia, also weighs in on this in relation to Roan specifically, stating in 2024 in *The Conversation*, "Conjuring and enacting such utopias is a

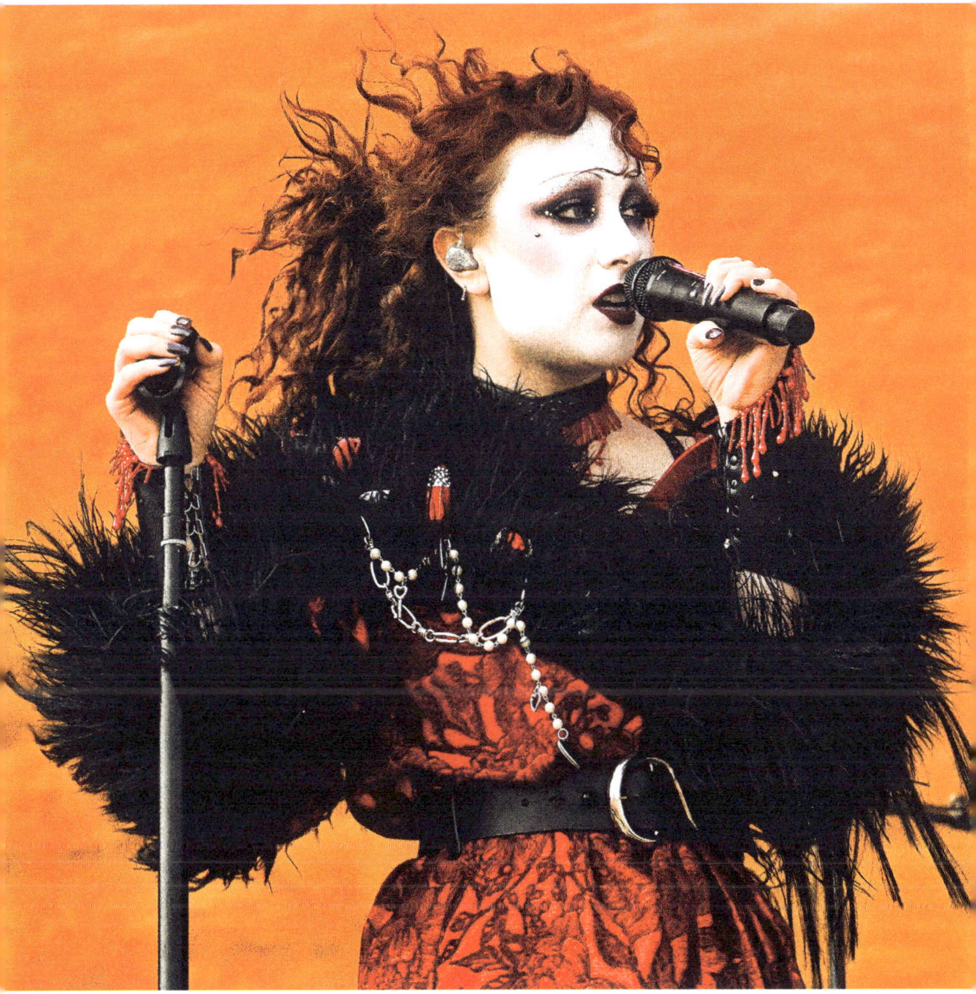

ABOVE Roan in a custom robe featuring ostrich feathers created by LA-based designer Lacey Dalimonte, onstage in Boston, on 26 March 2024.

OVERLEAF A laid-back Chappell poses for the *Los Angeles Times* on 14 August 2023.

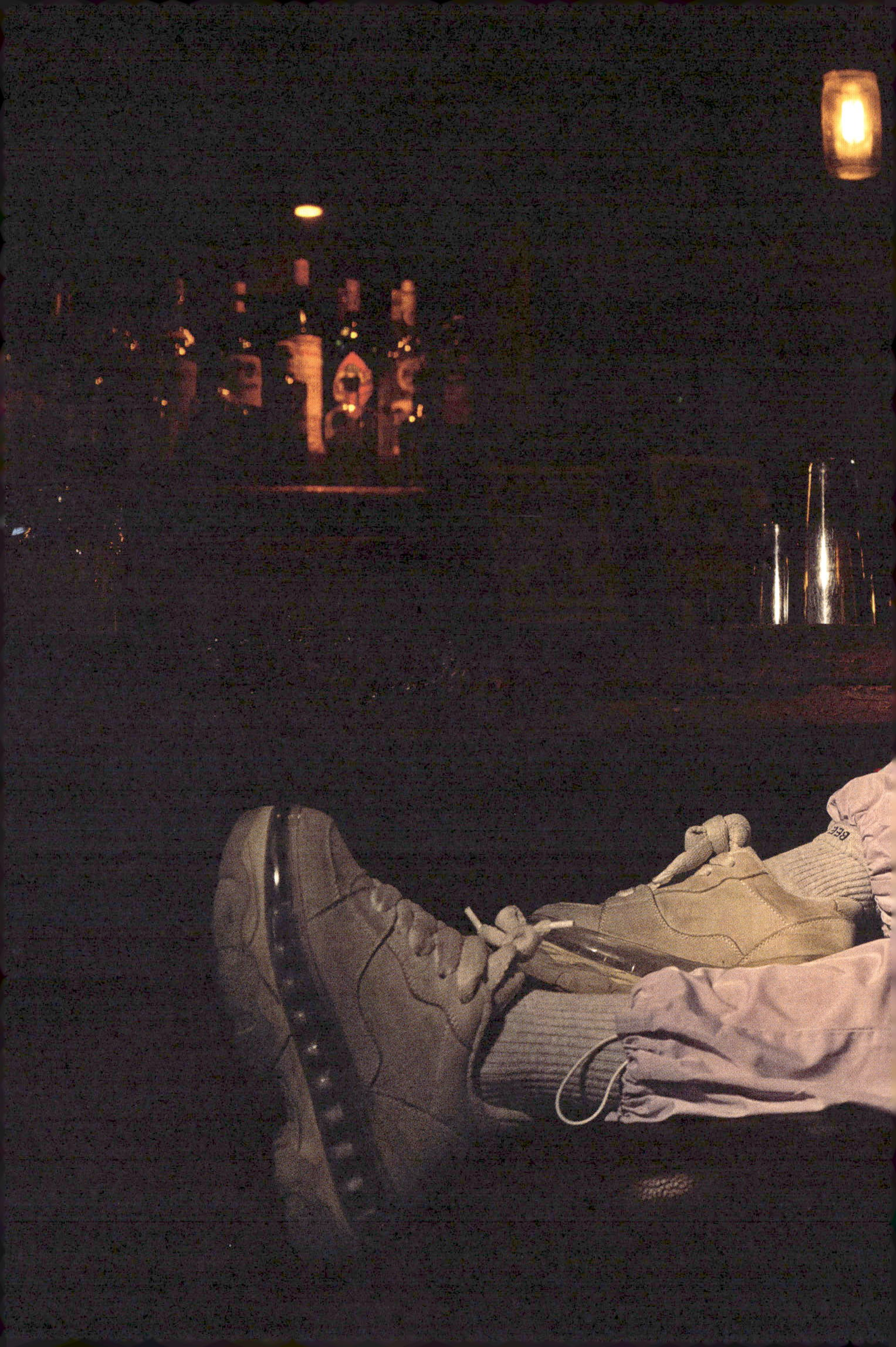

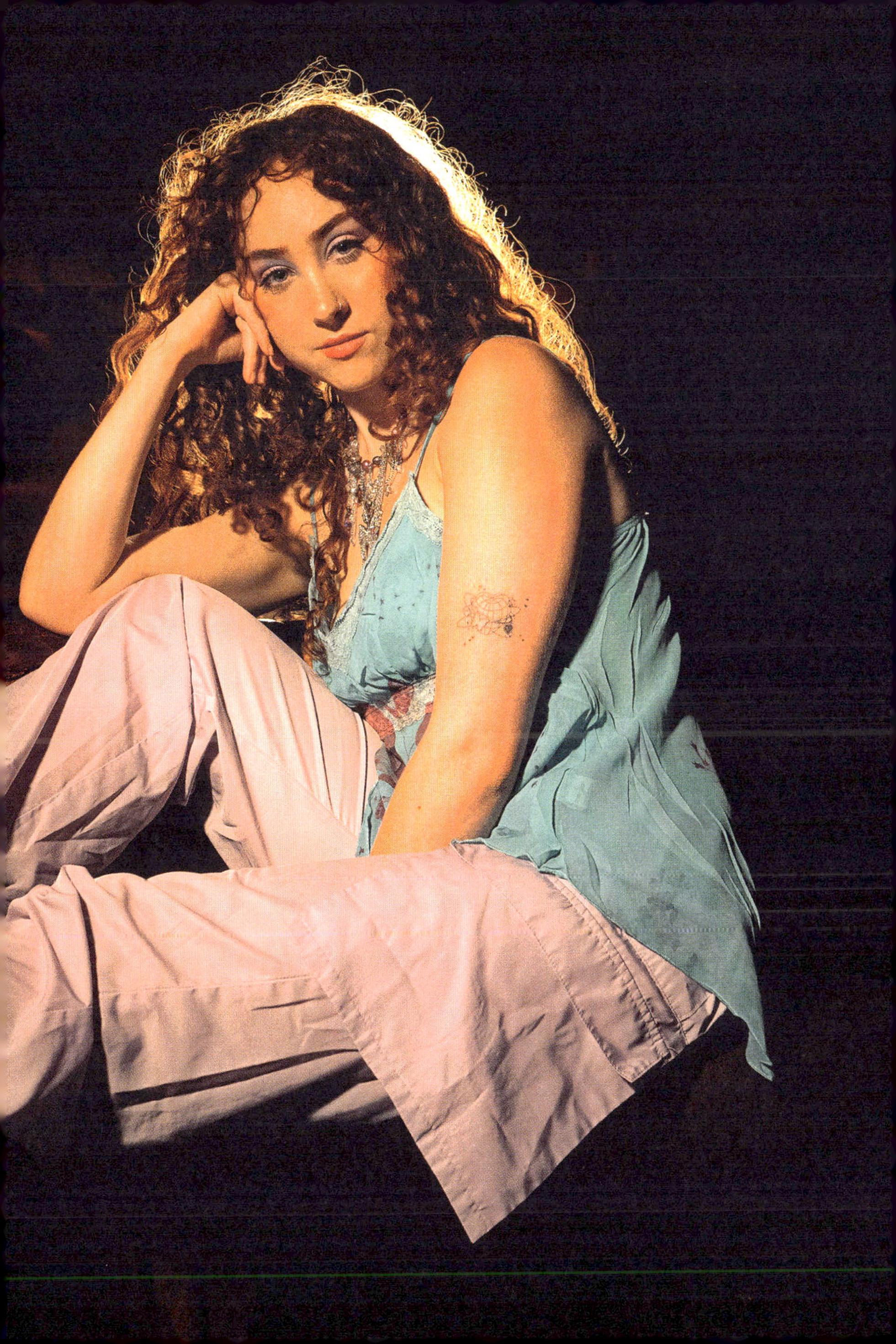

"When she performs live, the songs become something completely new, transformed by an audience which sees itself in Roan's own journey, connecting with lyrics about 'forbidden' slumber party crushes, self-discovery, queer chaos – and queer joy."

CAT CARDENAS,
W MAGAZINE

survival strategy for queer people and other marginalised individuals, especially those craving the relief of alternative worlds and improved possible futures that deny the homophobic and transphobic everyday realities that surround us."

Fans spending countless hours crafting outfits to mimic their favourite artists ahead of their live shows isn't anything new, though it has undoubtedly increased in popularity since 2020. Rosanna Elettra, a stylist and photographer who has photographed some of the biggest tours of the last few years, told the BBC in a 2023 article examining the phenomenon, "After extended periods of social isolation and the rising cost of living, fans are looking to maximise their experience, and dressing up in homage to their favourite artists is part of this experience. They want to feel part of the tour and then share it online with other fans." And with many of Roan's fans being keen admirers of drag artists or even drag artists themselves, the DIY element is turned up full blast. Though next to impossible to provide exact numbers of how many people have recreated Roan's iconic looks online, a quick TikTok or Instagram search will offer seas of fans putting their own twist on the glittery outfits and dramatic make-up, and the true diehards will even invest in weaves and wigs to get Roan's signature scarlet locks.

"I think that people *just want to be* happy *and reflect, sing, dance and dress up, and* feel free."

CHAPPELL ROAN

Sparkles and a strong cut crease eye are essential parts of any make-up look from Roan, demonstrated here in an image from September 2023.

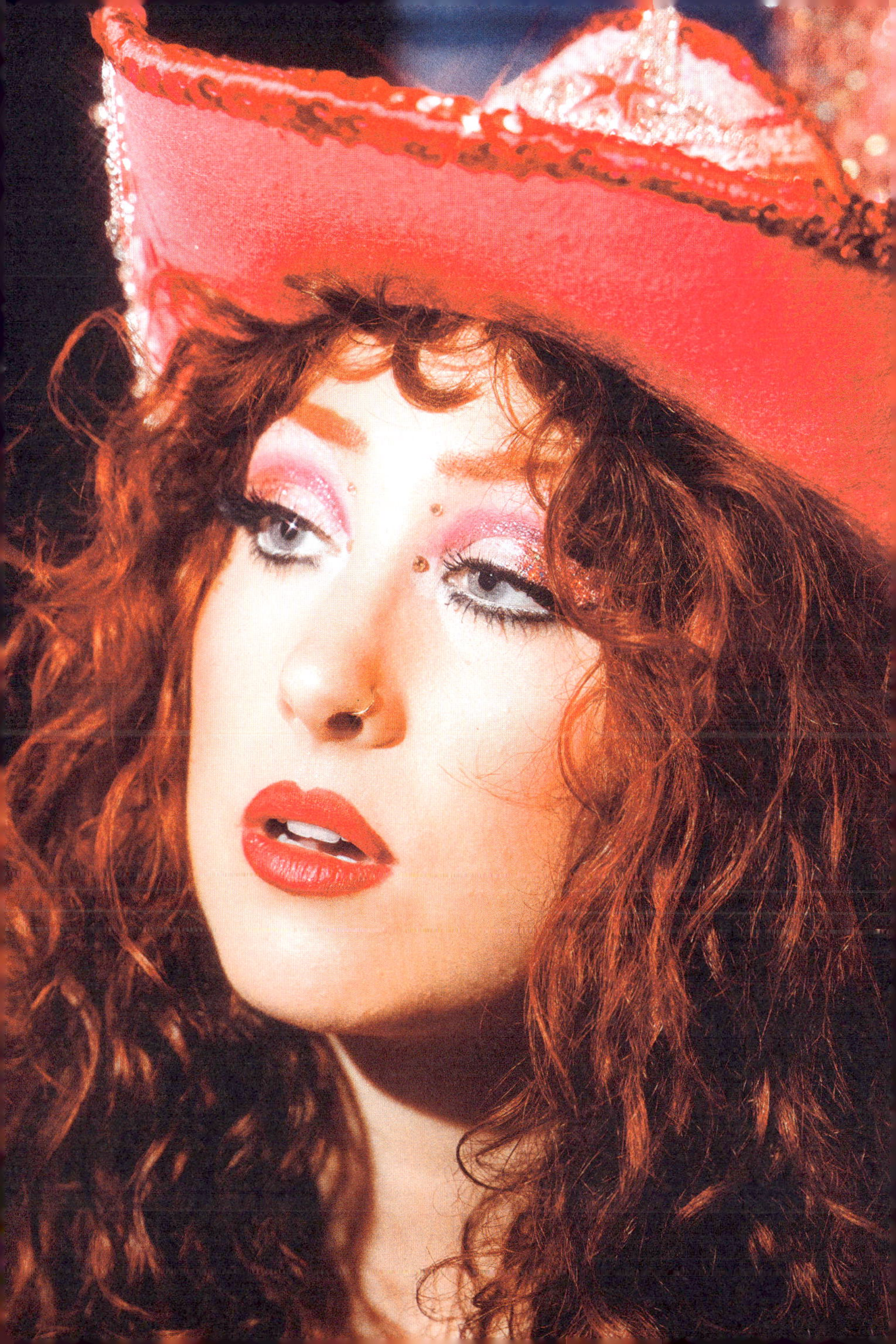

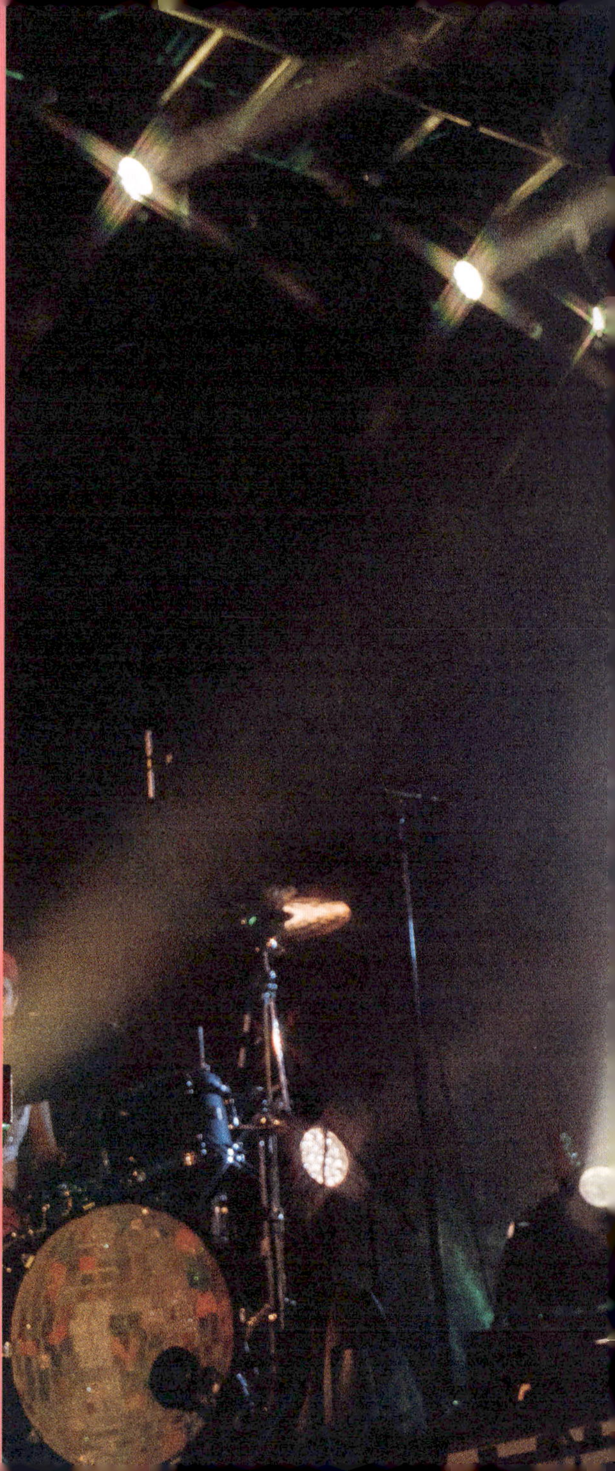

Roan performs her debut album, *The Rise and Fall of a Midwest Princess*, at the House of Blues in Chicago, on 5 October 2023.

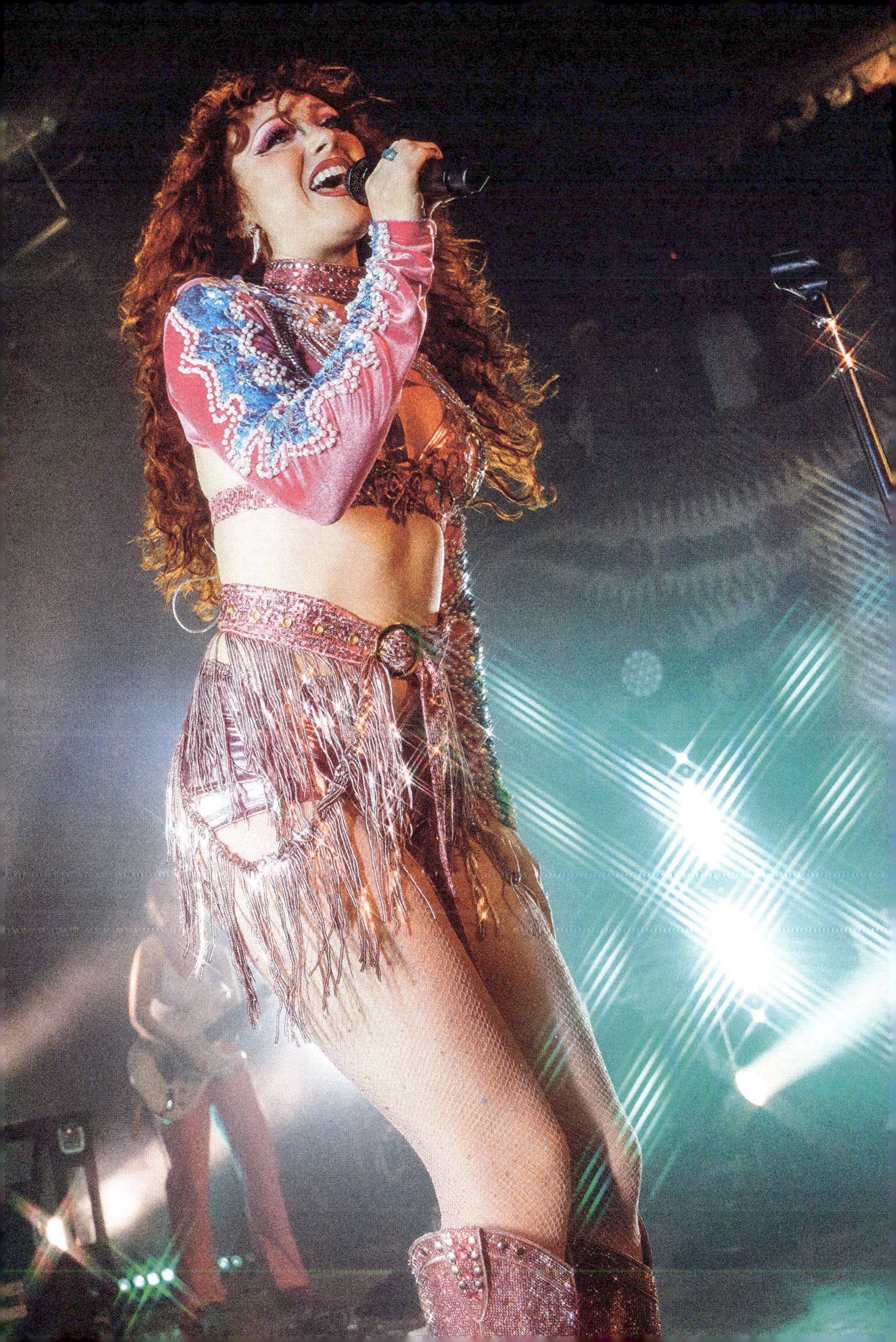

The rodeo goes rainbow

Though the pop music scene has been somewhat of a haven for LGBTQI+ folks for some time, country music hasn't always been such a welcoming environment. It would be fair to say that while much of Roan's musical output does align itself more with the playful pop sound, her singles "Pink Pony Club" and "The Giver" tap into the country scene which Roan was raised on. Roan reportedly was influenced by country hits such as 2004's "Save a Horse (Ride a Cowboy)" by Big & Rich and 1993's "Chattahoochee" by Alan Jackson. And as we learned in the earlier section outlining her Americana looks, the world of the Wild West has also been a big influence on her wardrobe. Despite (or perhaps as a result of) its ultra-conservative roots, country music has seen a marked shift in the mainstream since the late 2010s. In 2019, openly gay rapper Lil Nas X released his cover of Billy Ray Cyrus' "Old Town Road" and it sat at the top of the *Billboard* Hot 100 for 19 weeks. In the same year, Orville Peck released his debut album *Pony*, which garnered international acclaim before he quickly went on to collaborate with artists such as Shania Twain in 2020 and Lady Gaga in 2021. Roan even credits Peck with influencing her approach as an artist.

Two rodeo clowns in the ring at a small-town rodeo in New Mexico.

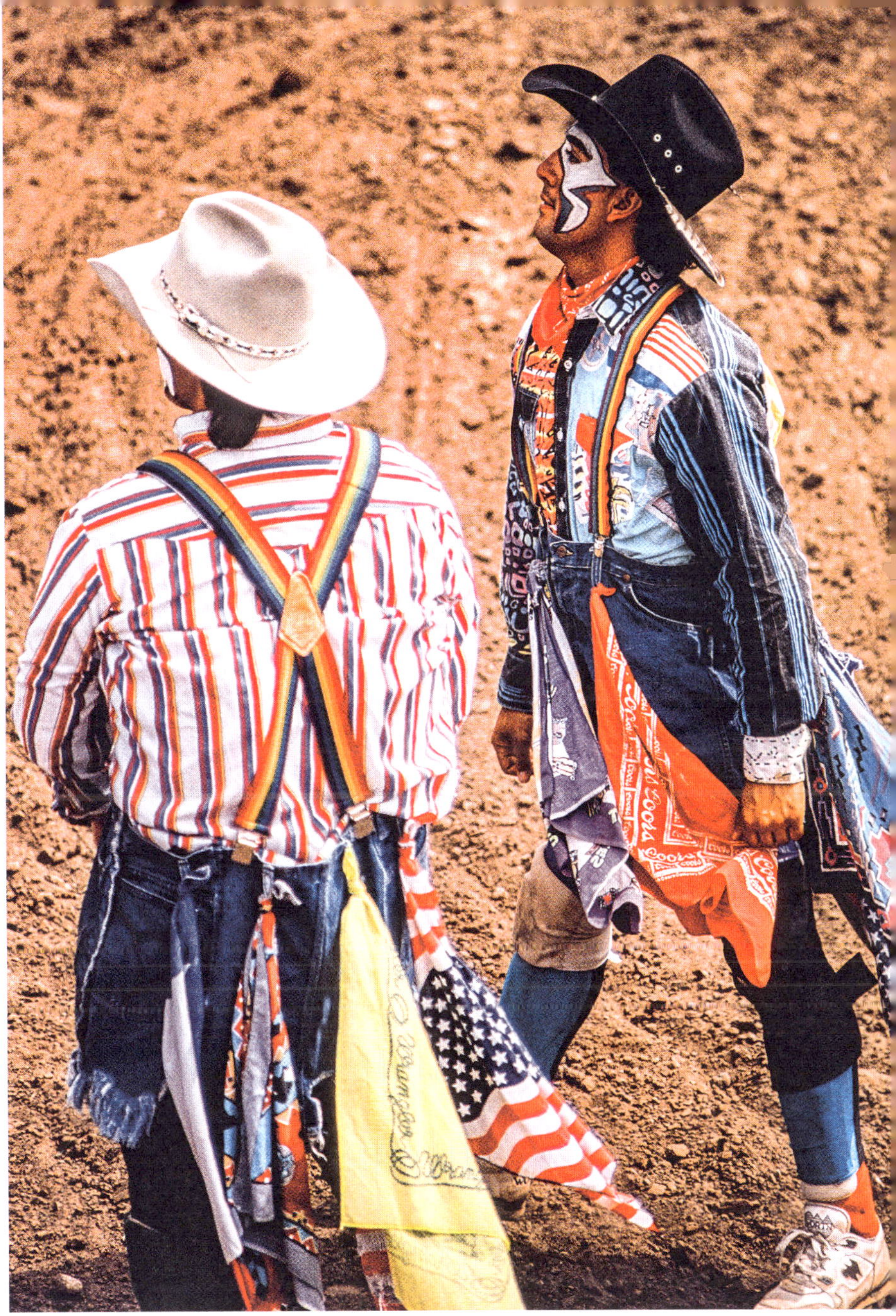

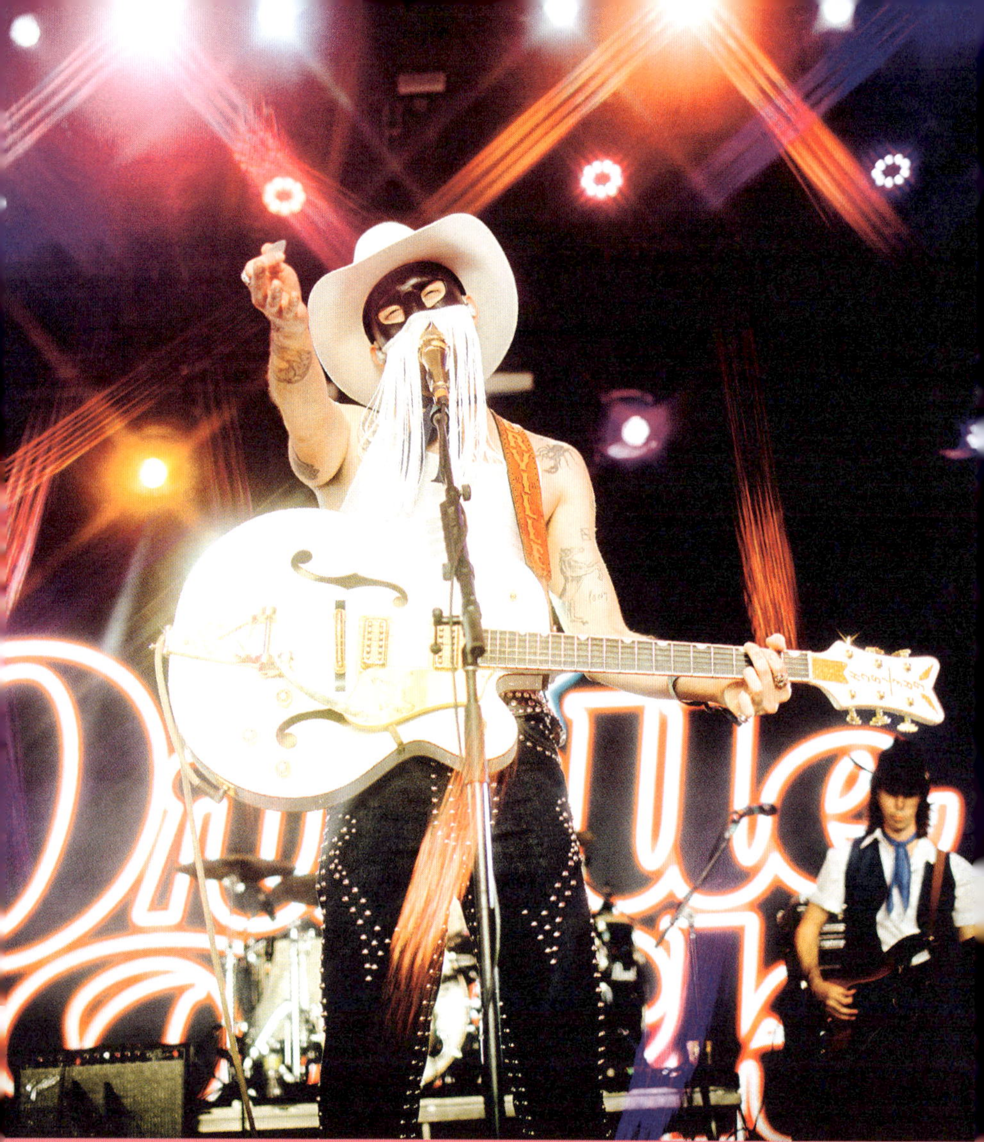

ABOVE Modern queer country icon Orville Peck performs at Coachella, on 24 April 2022.

OPPOSITE Roan entertains at Zilker Metropolitan Park in Austin, Texas in October 2024, leather chaps and all.

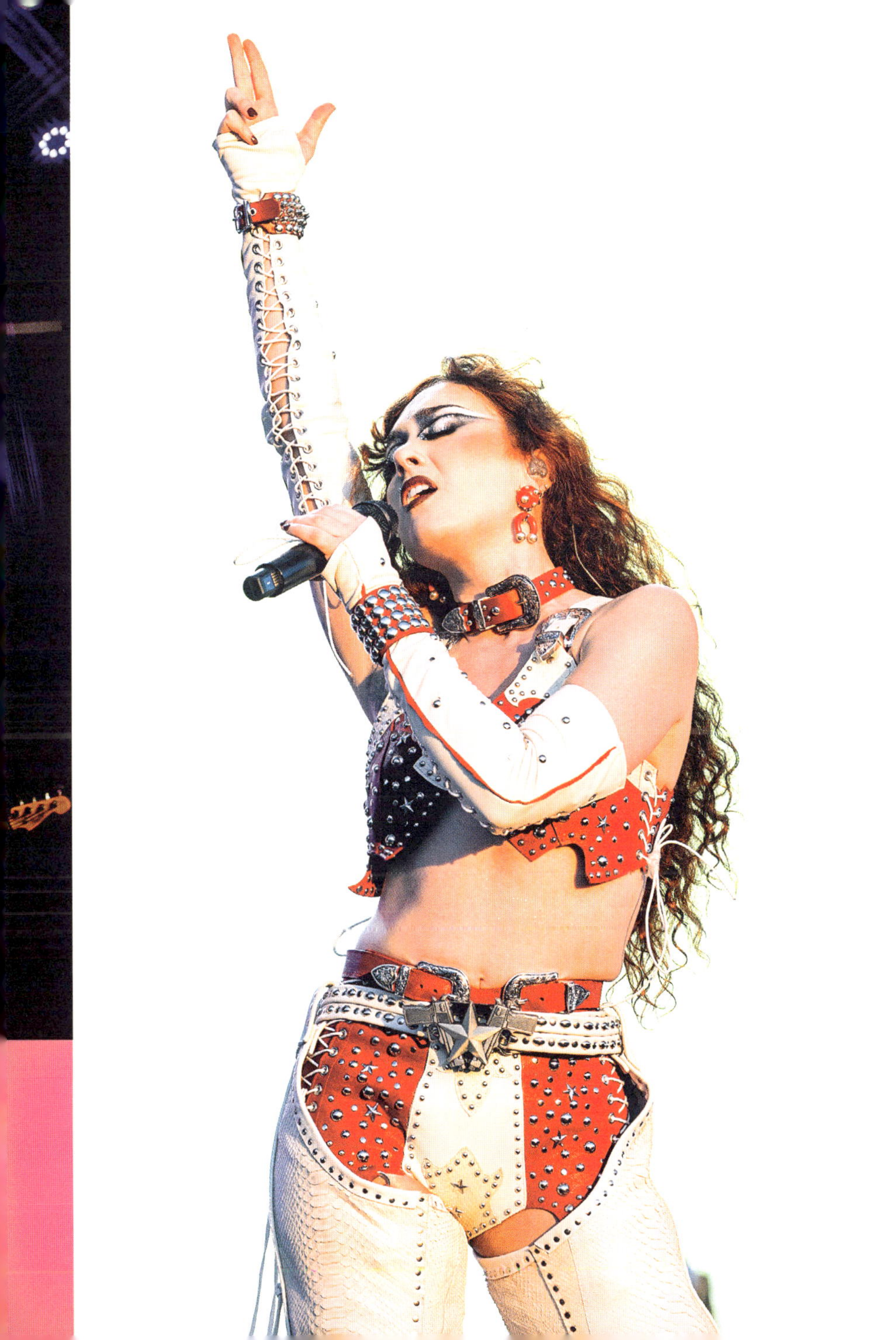

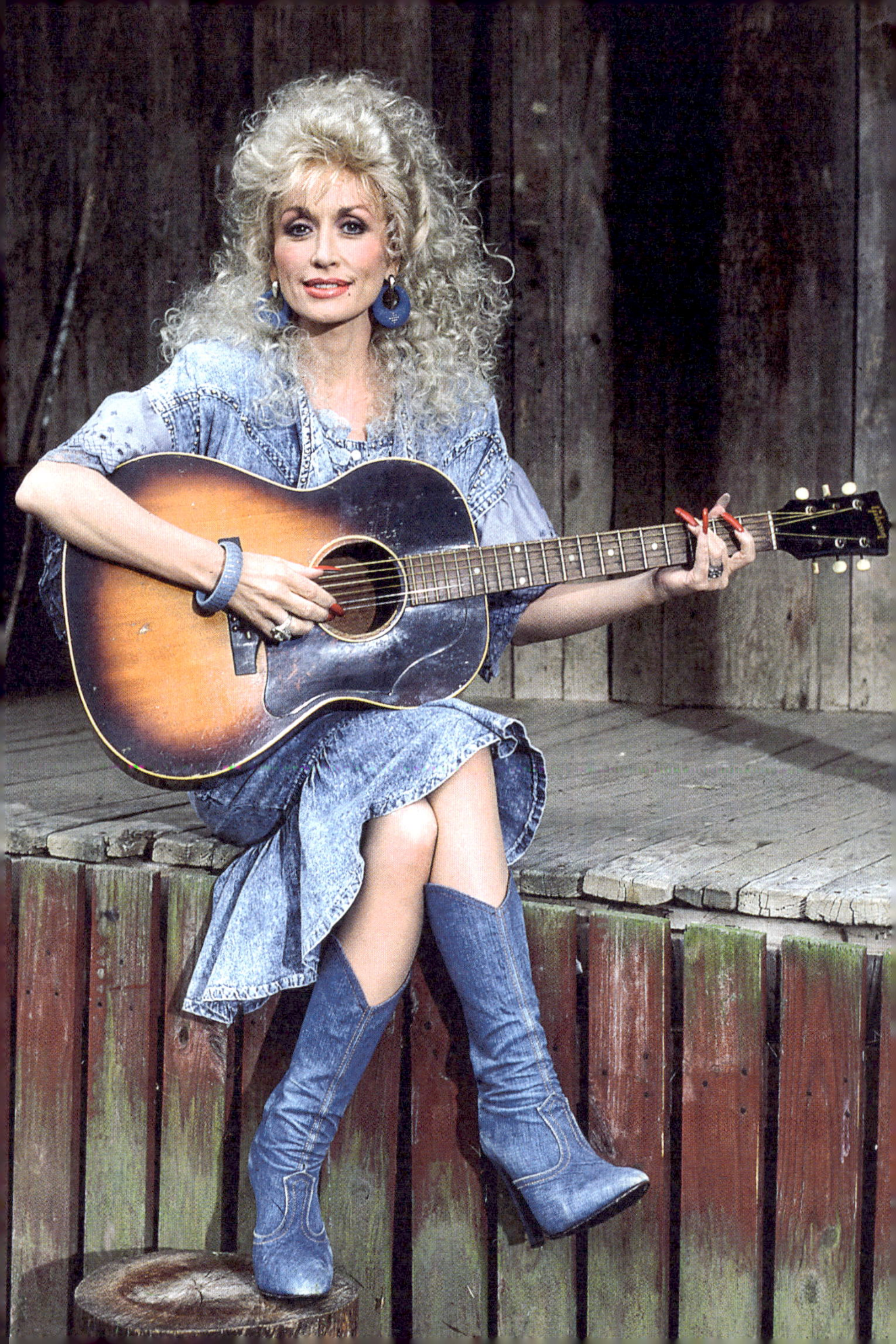

"I went to see him, and his show changed my whole life. It changed how I do shows ... I told myself from that show, 'If I ever perform my own headline shows, I'm going to have local drag queens open up for me, too.' So he changed my life, and now we're friends", she shared with Canadian music journalist Nardwuar the Human Serviette in a 2024 interview. Drag queen and recording artist Trixie Mattel (famously a fan of Roan's, remarking in *Paper Magazine* that Roan is the "missing link" between drag queens and pop stars) has also been at the forefront of Queer Country's acceptance into the mainstream, and they often dress up as country icons such as Dolly Parton and Loretta Lynn alongside releasing their own country tunes. Roan told Kelleigh Bannen on Apple Music's *The Kelleigh Bannen Show*, "I think I have a special relationship with where I'm from because of country music. So to kind of honor that part of myself by making a country song where it's like 'You know what? Yes, I'm gay, yes I'm ultra-pop, yes I am a drag queen.' That is also someone who can perform a Country song."

OPPOSITE Country music icon – and strong female role model – Dolly Parton, pictured here in 1978.

OVERLEAF Promotional posters for Chappell Roan's "The Giver" single in LA, March 2025.

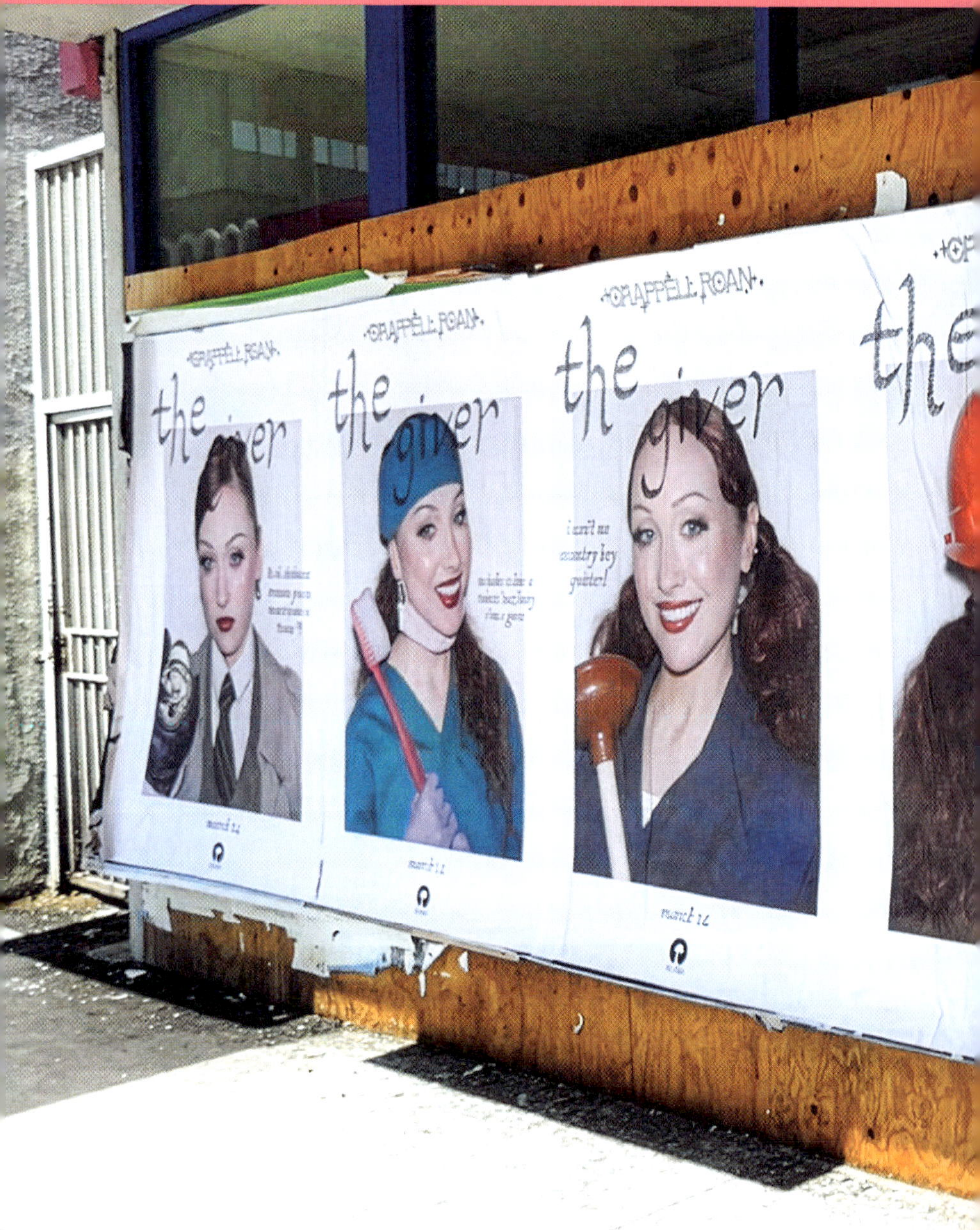
CHAPPELL ROAN
the giver
march 14

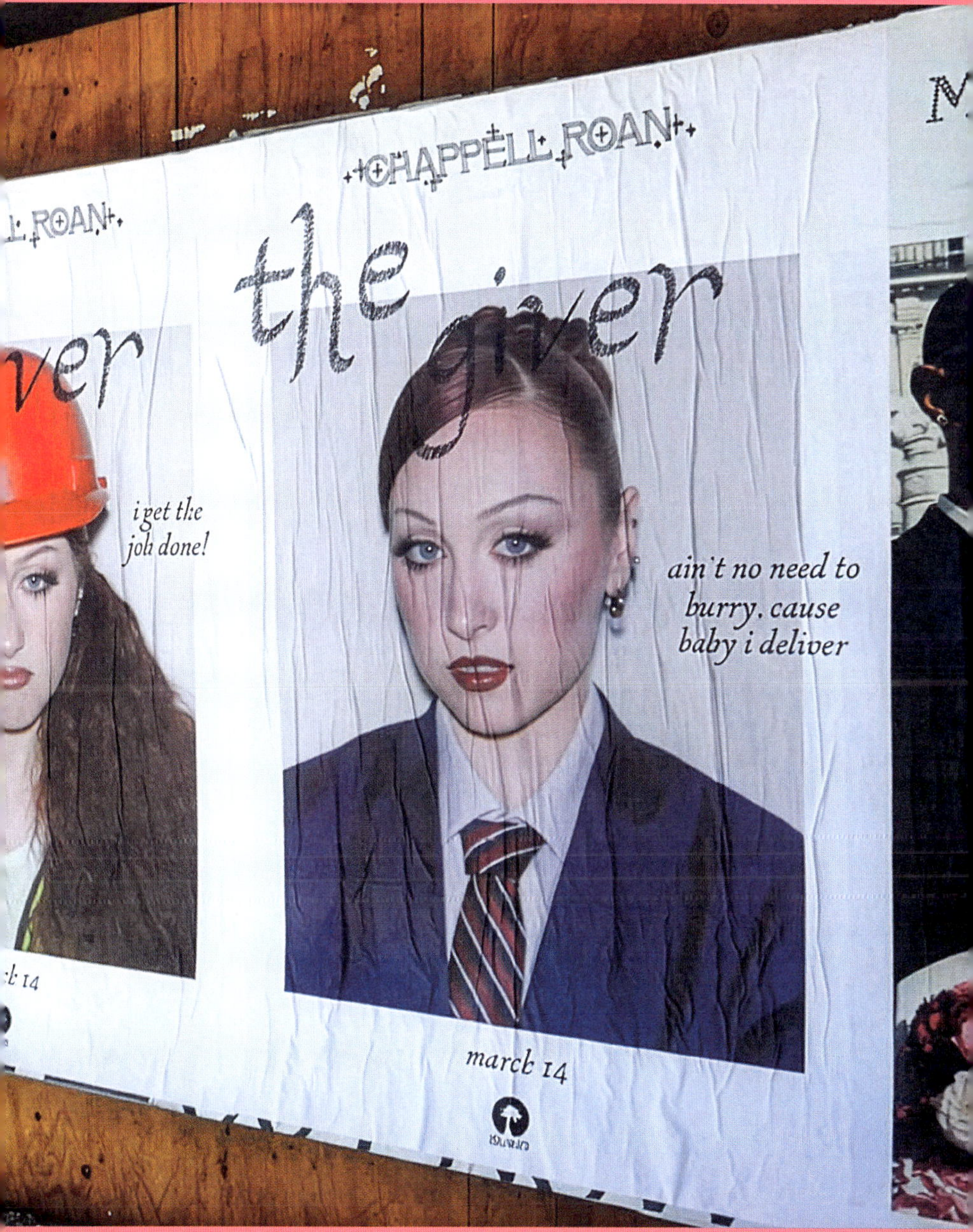

CHAPPELL ROAN
the giver
ain't no need to
hurry. cause
baby i deliver
march 14
i get the
job done!

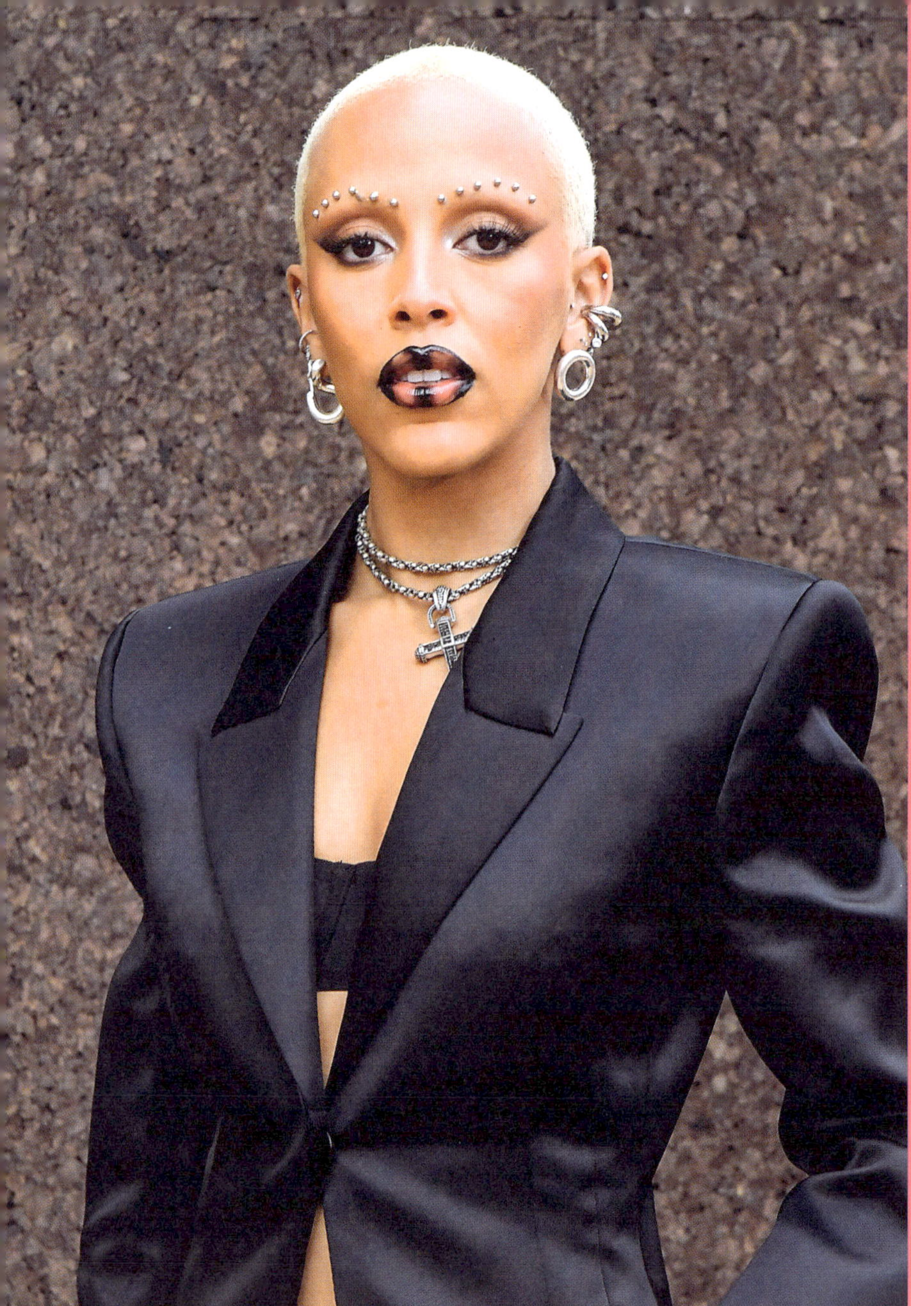

Moving beyond the male gaze

In 1975, film theorist Laura Mulvey used the term "male gaze" to discuss how much of female portrayals in film and television was dictated by being appealing to male heterosexual audiences. In her seminal essay *Visual Pleasure and Narrative Cinema*, Mulvey stated, "In a world ordered by sexual imbalance, pleasure in looking has been split between active/male and passive/female." In other words, many portrayals of women in film are dictated by their aesthetic value to men. Though the term was commonly used in academic circles, especially those based in gender, performance or film studies, the term found new popularity in the late 2010s and early 2020s with the rise of gender analysis on social media. With its new-found spot in the lexicon of young women online, stars such as Billie Eilish, Doja Cat, Julia Fox and, of course, Chappell Roan became front and centre figures for conversations around how decentring men's approval can change the course of fashion and style expression.

Doja Cat attends the Givenchy Womenswear Spring/ Summer 2023 show in Paris, on 2 October 2022.

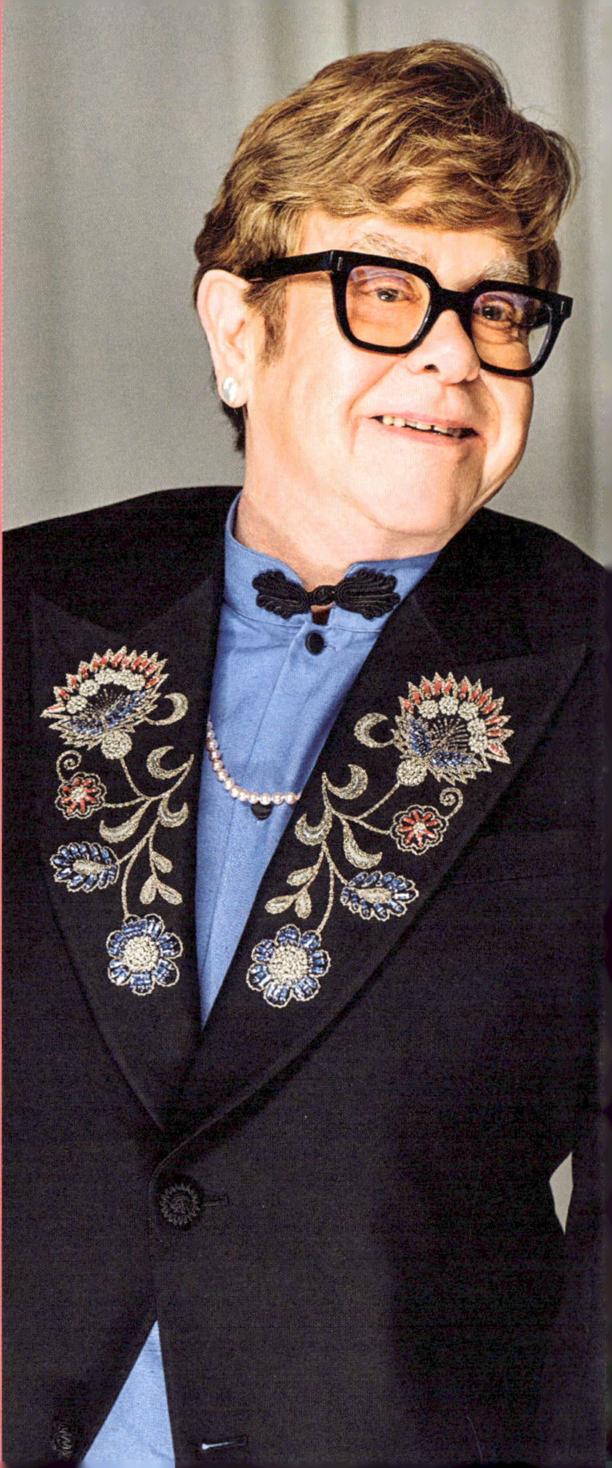

Roan wears Valentino to the Elton John AIDS Foundation's 33rd Annual Academy Awards Viewing Party in West Hollywood, California, on 2 March 2025.

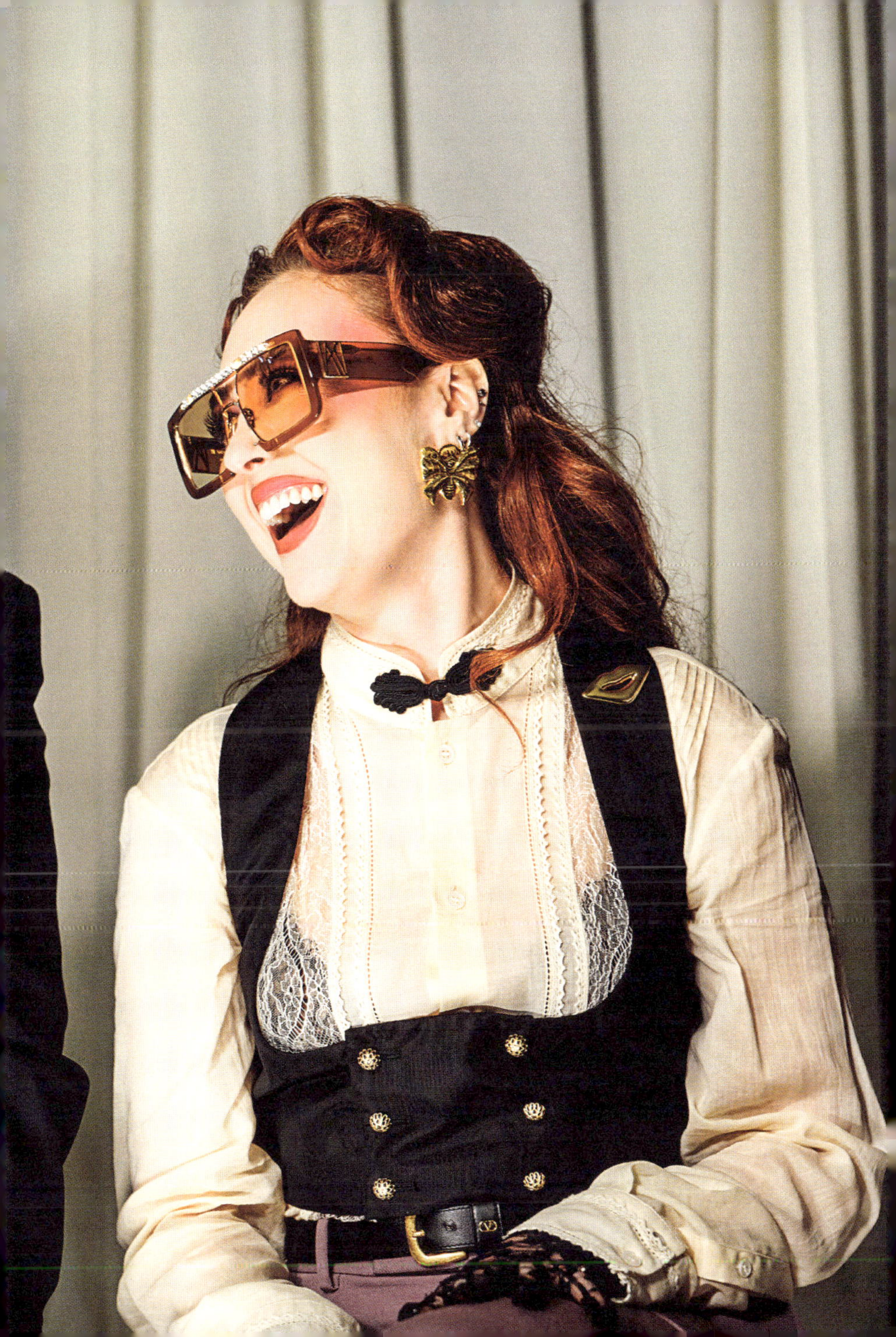

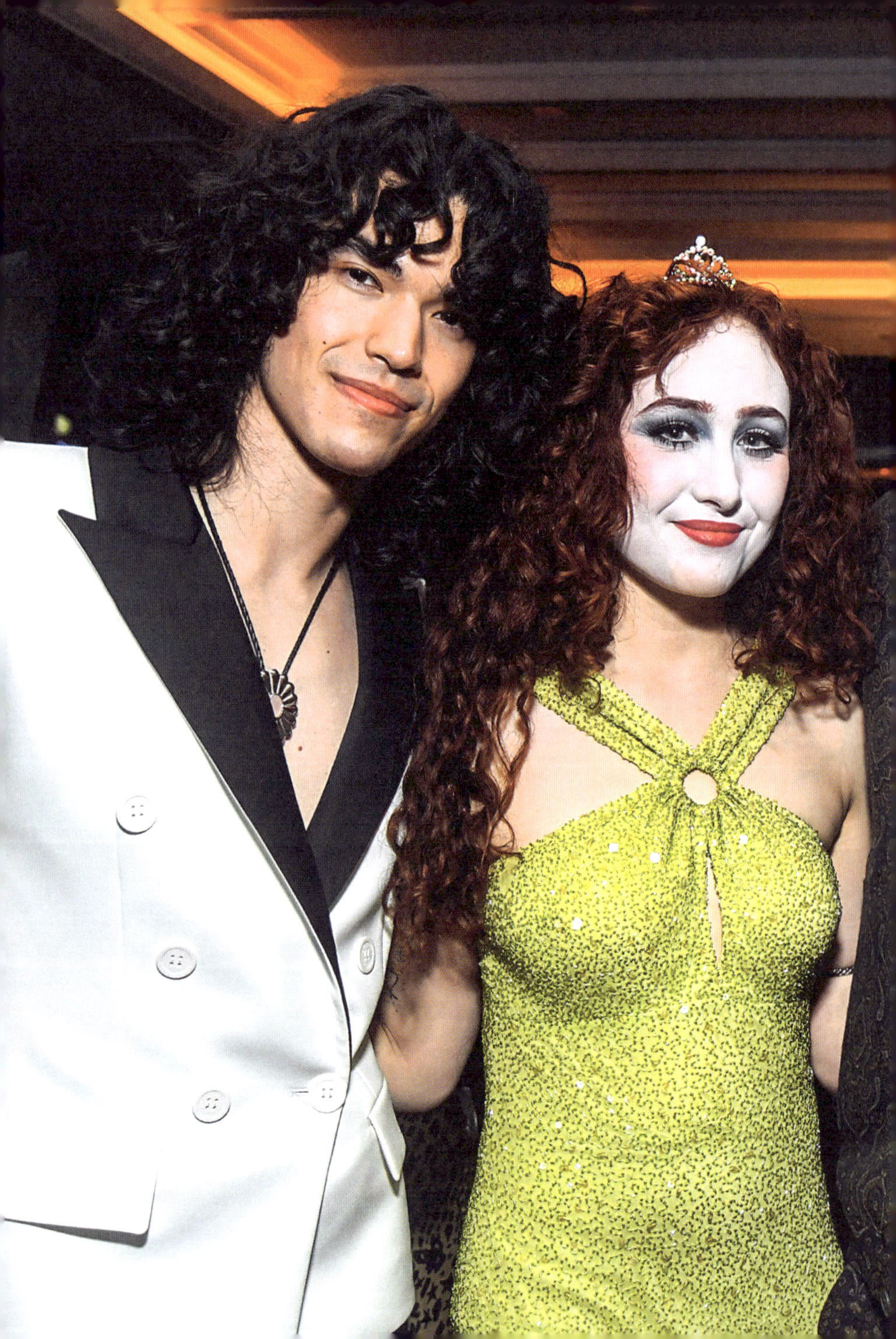

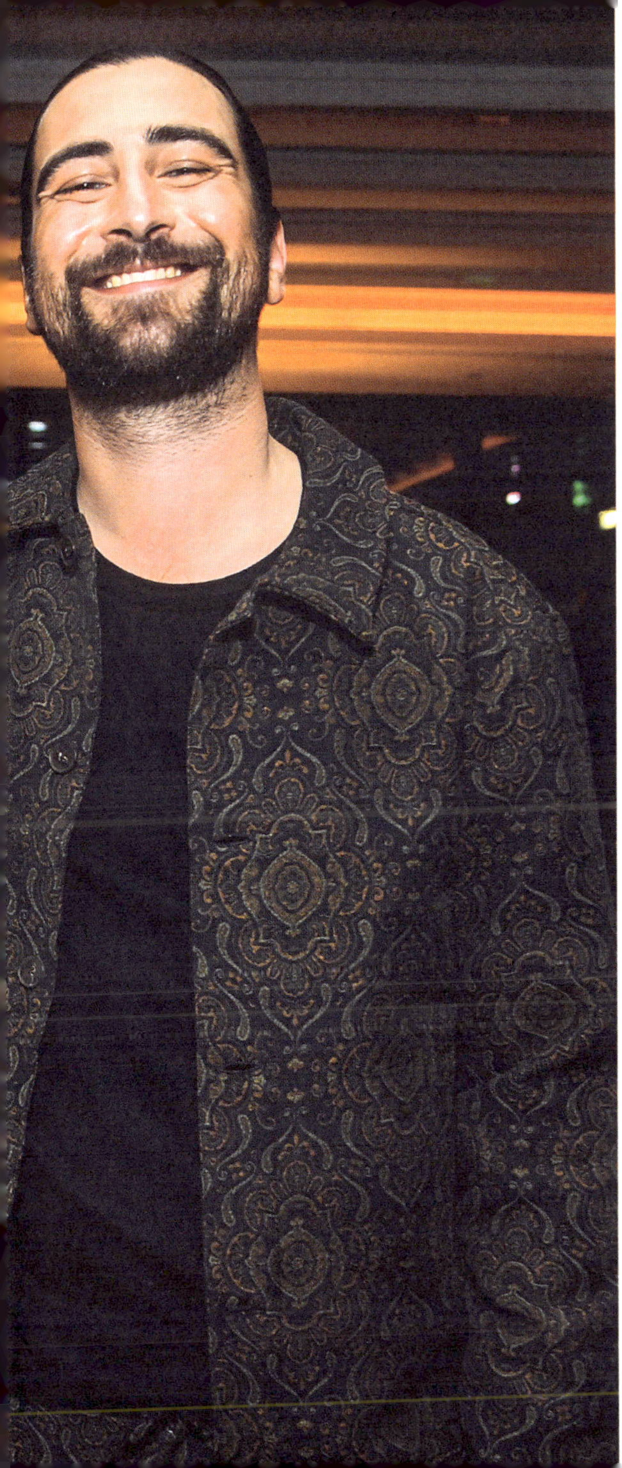

Conan Gray, Chappell Roan and Noah Kahan attend Republic Records Celebrates Artist Community at Bar Lis in Los Angeles, on 31 January 2024.

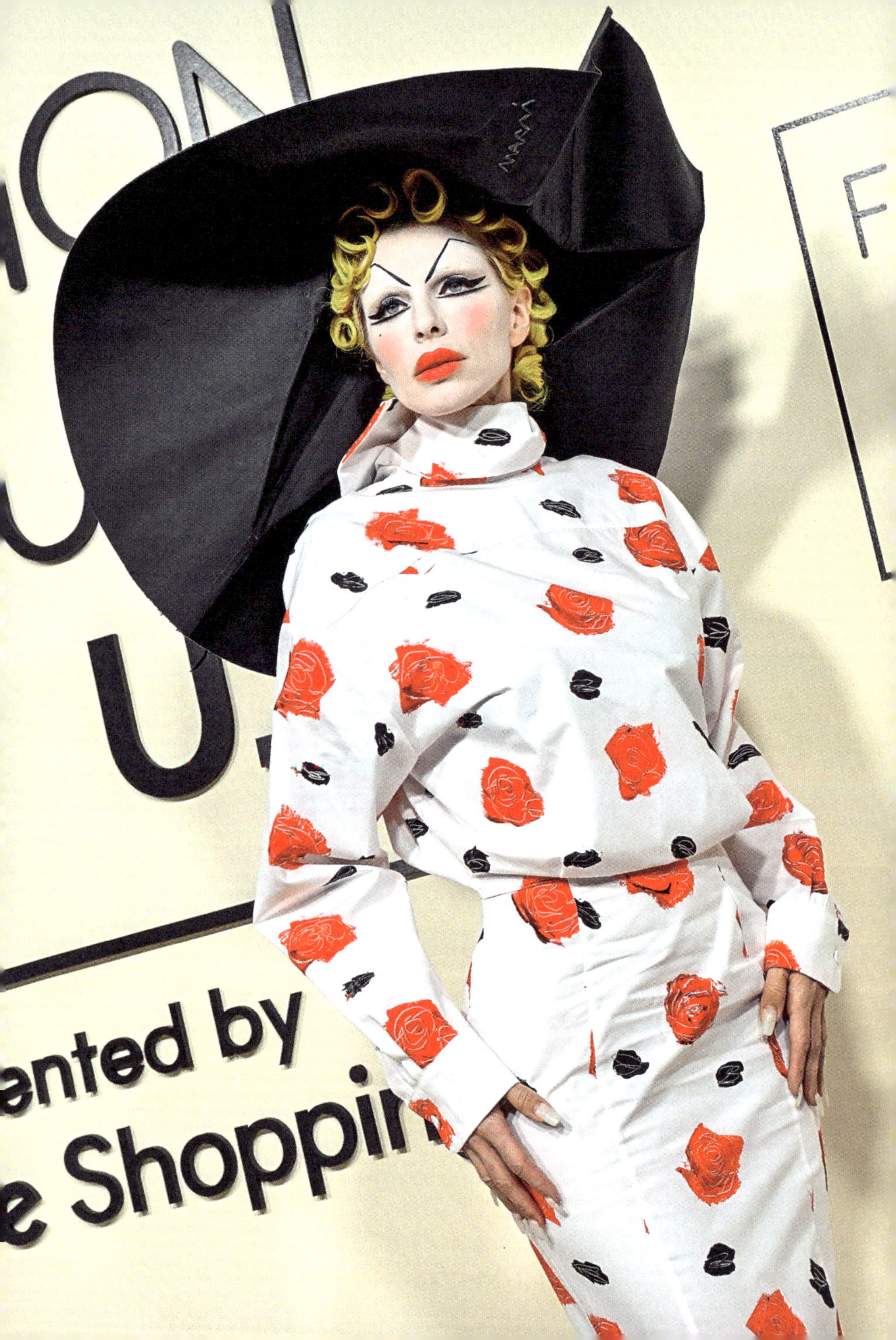
ented by
e Shoppin

Roan herself has openly stated that she doesn't always want to look attractive, sharing with Jimmy Fallon on *The Tonight Show Starring Jimmy Fallon*, "I love looking pretty and scary. Or, like, pretty and tacky. Or just not pretty. I love that, too." In her famous *Call Her Daddy* podcast interview in 2025, she remarked, "I love looking like kind of crazy and scary." Though these comments may not be a deep dive into the philosophical aspect of Mulvey's theory of the male gaze discussed above, it does give us insight into how Roan's priorities when working with her team to compile her costumes can result in a refreshing take on fashion for fans across the world.

In their frankly titled article "Why Men Hate Chappell Roan", one writer, identifying simply as Sumeyya, theorized on how this may have an impact on many men's reaction to Roan, stating, "Her style is specific – she pulls from stars and icons who came before her, and everything is big, colourful, bright, hyper-feminine and bordering gaudy in the best ways possible. Her visuals are ugly to many men. They're not meant to attract them and she doesn't want to attract them – when someone who doesn't care about men, doesn't speak on them all too much (unless they're humorous jabs), dresses for the 'girls', and dances to the beat of her own drum, men lose their minds." The article continues, "She's grabbed the mic in her manicured nails, and she's making her time count. She's building her world, and it bars the patriarchy out, it gives other women the power to do the same. She emboldens."

OPPOSITE Julia Fox attends the Fashion Trust U.S. Awards 2025 in Hollywood, California, on 8 April 2025.

OVERLEAF Roan is spotted filming in New York City in July 2025 for the music video for her single "The Subway".

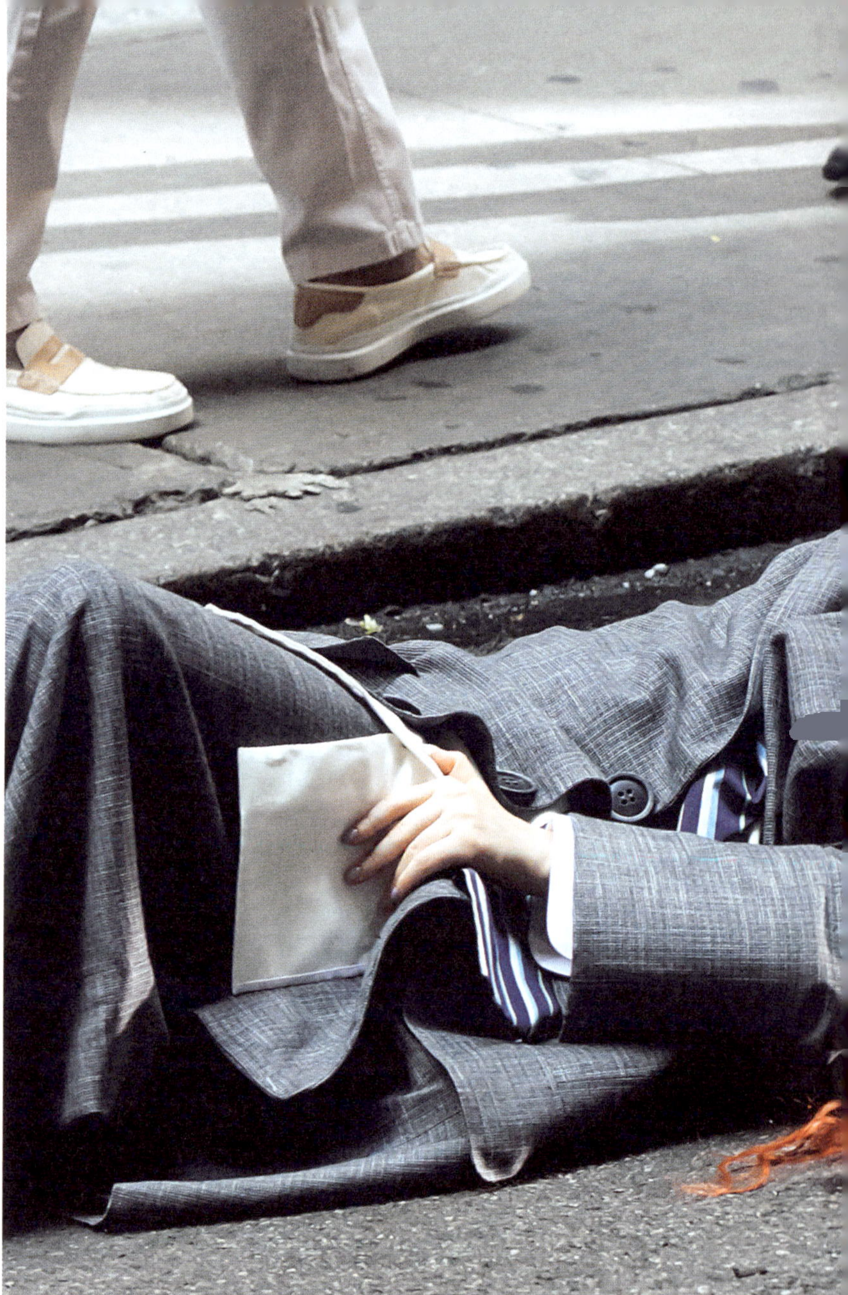

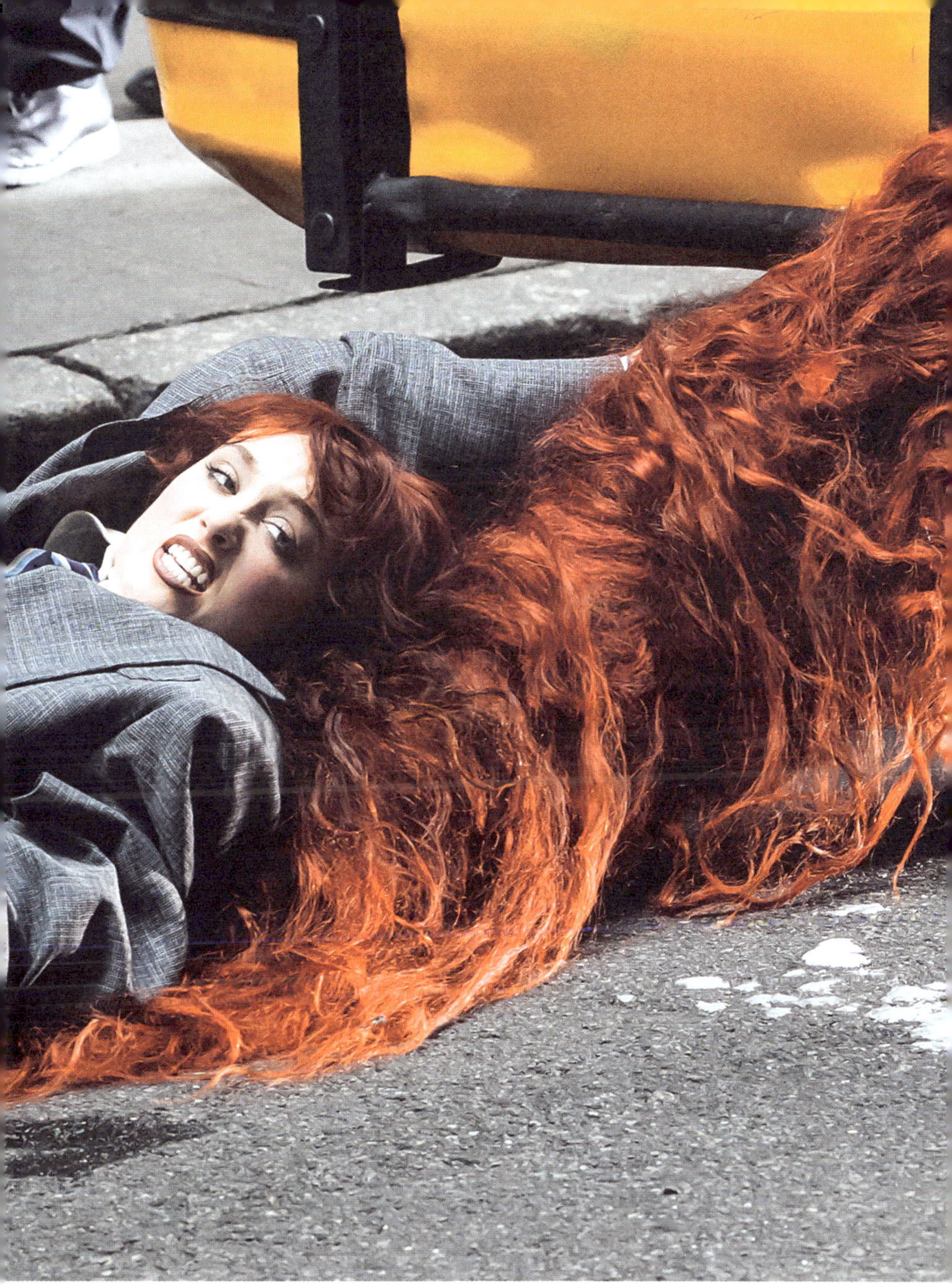

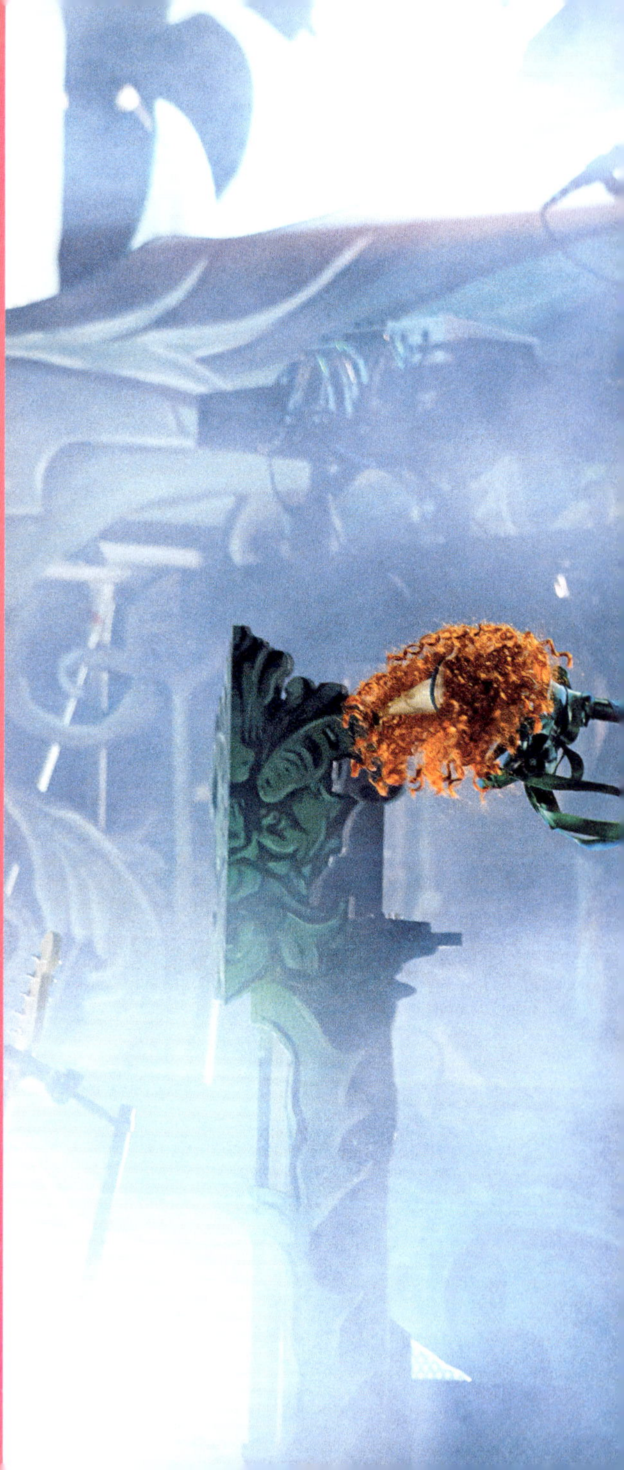

Roan puts on an electric performance in a custom Gunnar Deatherage design onstage at Budapest's Sziget Festival in 2025.

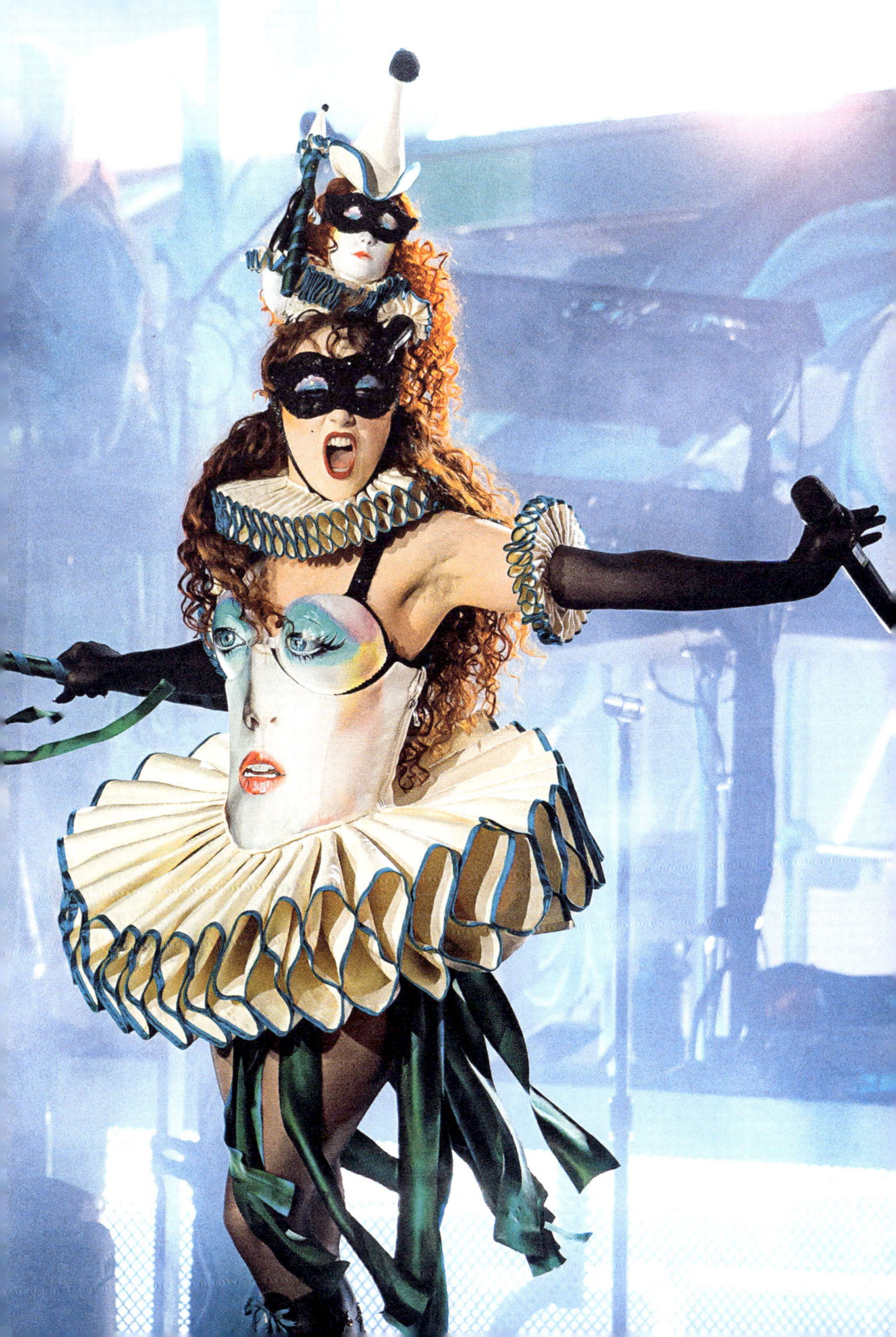

Index

Credits

The publishers would like to thank the following sources for their kind permission to reproduce the pictures in this book.

Alamy: Ovidiu Hrubaru 113; /Barry King 206-207; /MediaPunch Inc 187; /Patti McConville 87; /Kamilla Patera 16-17; /Pictorial Press Ltd 177; / TT News Agency 76-77; /ZUMA Press, Inc 111

Getty Images: adoc-photos/Corbis via Getty Images 65; /Axelle/Bauer-Griffin/FilmMagic 130-131, 214; /Jorgen Angel/Redferns 97; /Axelle/ Bauer-Griffin/FilmMagic 78-79; /Robyn Beck/ AFP via Getty Images 104; /Jim Bennett 26; / Daniel Berehulak 66; /BG048/Bauer-Griffin/ GC Images 216-217; /Gareth Cattermole 75; / Dominique Charriau/WireImage 208; /Stephen J. Cohen 89; /Mike Coppola/Getty Images for MTV 135; /Yuri Cortez/AFP via Getty Images 31; /Jed Cullen/Dave Benett/Getty Images for McQueen 164-165; /Maarten de Boer/Getty Images for the Elton John AIDS Foundation 210-211; /Jim Dyson 6-7, 15, 49; /Rodin Eckenroth/Getty Images for ONE/SIZE Full Beat 80-81; /Steve Eichner 108-109; /Fairchild Archive/WWD/Penske Media via Getty Images 84; /Santiago Felipe/FilmMagic 117; /Gina Ferazzi/Los Angeles Times via Contour RA by Getty Images 192-193; /Florilegius/Universal Images Group via Getty Images 121, 138; / Proust Frederic/Sygma via Getty Images 136; / Jon G. Fuller/VWPics/Universal Images Group via Getty Images 201; /Swan Gallet/WWD via Getty Images 162; /Bruce Glikas/WireImage 105; /Erika Goldring/WireImage 67, 68-69, 20; / Steve Granitz/FilmMagic 74; /Francois Guillot/ AFP via Getty Images 157; /Frazer Harrison 151; /Heritage Art/Heritage Images via Getty Images 125; /Shirley Markham Collection/ Heritage Images via Getty Images 133; /Katja Ogrin/Redferns 12; /Steve Jennings/FilmMagic 47; /Jason Kempin 50; /Vivien Killilea/Getty Images for GLAAD 23; /Scott Kowalchyk/CBS via Getty Images 11; /Jeff Kravitz/FilmMagic 153; /Pascal Le Segretain 62; /LMPC via Getty Images 127; /Terry Lott/Sony Music Archive via Getty Images 99; /Dominique Maitre/ WWD via Getty Images 161; /Mary Mathis for The Washington Post via Getty Images 38, 52, 72, 197, 198-199; /Dania Maxwell /Los Angeles Times via Getty Images 115, 116; /Kevin Mazur/ Getty Images for MTV 128; /Kevin Mazur/Getty Images for The Recording Academy 103; /Kevin Mazur/WireImage 25, 184; /Emma McIntyre 149; /Catherine McGann 107; /Michael Ochs Archives 42, 94; /Gary Miller/FilmMagic 54; / Joseph Okpako 24; /Joseph Okpako/WireImage 218-219; /Pictorial Parade/Archive Photos 96; / Christopher Polk/Billboard via Getty Images 61; /Ki Price 90-91; /Michael Putland 175; /Kerstin Rodgers/Redferns 98; /Alberto E. Rodriguez/ Getty Images for Republic Records 212-213; / Christian Rose/Roger Viollet via Getty Images 93; /Saliva Films 88; /Rebecca Sapp/Getty Images for The Recording Academy 148; /Ilya S. Savenok 118; /John Shearer/Getty Images for MTV 137; /John Shearer/Getty Images for The Recording Academy 58-59; /Arthur Sidey/Mirrorpix 41; /Daniel Simon/Gamma-Rapho via Getty Images 159; /John Seakwood/ Disney General Entertainment Content via Getty Images 204; /John Springer Collection/ CORBIS/Corbis via Getty Images 83; /Pierre Suu 147; /Eric Thayer/Los Angeles Times via Getty Images 154-155; /TheStewartofNY 170; / Ben Trivett/Contour by Getty Images 122-123; /Astrida Valigorsky 44-45, 191; /Jack Vartoogia 63; /Andrew H Walker/WWD/Penske Media via Getty Images 183; /VCG Wilson/Corbis via Getty Images 102; /Angela Weiss/AFP via Getty Images 172-173; /Matt Winkelmeyer 71, 202; / Kevin Winter/Getty Images for The Recording Academy 140-141; /Vittorio Zunino Celotto/ Getty Images for Valentino 168-169

James Higuchi/@jus1oh: 19

Jason Martin: 28-29

Shutterstock: Ralph Arvesen 142-143; /David Fisher 100; /Michael Hurcomb 35; /Chad Salvador 152